The State Economic Handbook
2010 Edition

Anderson Economic Group, LLC
Scott D. Watkins, Editor
Patrick L. Anderson, Editor

palgrave
macmillan

THE STATE ECONOMIC HANDBOOK 2010

This book contains data obtained from original public and private sources. All material from copyrighted sources has been reprinted with approval. Business climate rankings from Forbes Magazine are reprinted by permission of Forbes Magazine © 2008 Forbes Inc. Tax climate rankings from the Tax Foundation are reprinted by permission of The Tax Foundation © 2009. Voter participation and presidential election results are reprinted by permission of Dave Leip's Atlas of U.S. Presidential Elections, http://www.uselectionatlas.org (February 2009). All other data presented are from works created by the U.S. Government, other sources in the public domain, or Anderson Economic Group, LLC.

First published in 2009 by
PALGRAVE MACMILLAN™
in the United States—a division of St. Martin's Press LLC,
175 Fifth Avenue, New York, NY 10010.

Where this book is distributed in the UK, Europe and the rest of the world, this is by Palgrave Macmillan, a division of Macmillan Publishers Limited, registered in England, company number 785998, of Houndmills, Basingstoke, Hampshire RG21 6XS.

Palgrave Macmillan is the global academic imprint of the above companies and has companies and representatives throughout the world.

Palgrave® and Macmillan® are registered trademarks in the United States, the United Kingdom, Europe and other countries.

ISBN: 978–0–230–62116–9
ISSN: 1938–4939

A catalog record for this book is available from the Library of Congress.

A catalogue record for this book is available from the British Library.

Design by Newgen Imaging Systems (P) Ltd., Chennai, India.

First edition: December 2009

10 9 8 7 6 5 4 3 2 1

Printed in the United States of America.

Table of Contents

Acknowledgments viii

Introduction 1

Alabama.. 5

Alaska 10

Arizona 15

Arkansas 20

California.. 25

Colorado 30

Connecticut... 35

Delaware.. 40

Florida 45

Georgia 50

Hawaii 55

Idaho 60

Illinois.. 65

Indiana 70

Iowa 75

Kansas 80

Kentucky 85

Louisiana 90

Maine... 95

Maryland 100

Massachusetts 105

Michigan 110

Minnesota.. 115

Mississippi 120

Missouri 125

Montana 130

Nebraska 135

Nevada 140

New Hampshire 145

New Jersey.. 150

New Mexico.. 155

New York 160

North Carolina 165

North Dakota.. 170

Ohio... 175

Oklahoma.. 180

Oregon... 185

Pennsylvania 190

Rhode Island 195

South Carolina 200

South Dakota.. 205

Tennessee 210

Texas 215

Utah... 220

Vermont... 225

Virginia 230

Washington 235

West Virginia 240

Wisconsin 245

Wyoming 250

About the Data 255

Glossary of Terms 257

Ranking the States 265
    Population Growth, 2007–25 Projected Compound Average
    Annual Rate 265
    Youth Population (Percent under 18 Years of Age), 2007 266
    Percent of Individuals below Poverty Level, 2007 267
    Change in Per Capita Income, 2006–7 268
    Change in Civilian Labor Force Size, 2000–7 269
    Population Age 25+ with Masters Degree of Higher, 2007 270
    Net Change in Establishments (Births Less Deaths), 2005–6 271
    Change in State and Local Taxes Per Capita, 2004–5–2005–6 272
    Participation of Population Age 18+, 2008 Presidential Election 273

Index 275

Acknowledgments

This book could not have been completed if not for the assistance of the staff at Anderson Economic Group, LLC who spent time collecting and organizing data, maintaining databases, analyzing and checking figures, and researching each of the 50 states.

The editors wish to particularly thank Tyler Marie Theile for her assistance in the collection and organization of the data, as well as in writing the state profiles. Also deserving of recognition are Lauren Branneman and Katie Hayes for assisting in data collection and analysis. Theodore Bolema, Jason Eli, Ilhan Geckil, and Alex Rosean also receive our thanks for their assistance in checking the data for accuracy. Becky Scott of PSPublications in Lansing, Michigan, is thanked for her assistance in developing the XML scripts used to automate much of the data formatting and publishing.

Introduction

Many of our most important decisions center on "where?" Where is the best market for my services? Where should my family move? Where will my target customers be located 20 years from now? And the list goes on.

The experts at Anderson Economic Group, LLC have assembled this 2010 edition of *The State Economic Handbook* to help navigate the troves of data available for use in making informed location decisions. This handbook is intended to serve both as a quick reference for top-level decisions, and as a starting point for more in-depth research. It includes carefully selected variables that give a broad picture of the economic, demographic, and political environments in each state. It also carefully documents the sources of the information, allowing you to access the original source if necessary.

Just as in the 2008 and 2009 editions, we present important information on each state about population, workforce and industry, voter behavior, taxation, and more. This newest edition includes state-by-state election results from the November 2008 gubenatorial, congressional, and presidential elections, all presented for the first time alongside industry, demographic, tax, and other important state-level data.

These data, which come from various federal agencies, Forbes Magazine, Anderson Economic Group, the Tax Foundation, and other such sources, are not assembled in any other single volume. We selected the data in this book based on what our business, government, and non-profit clients actually use to make decisions in real-world situations.

Organization of the Book

This book provides a concise look at key economic, demographic, and political information for each of America's 50 states. Data is presented on a state-by-state basis, and the states are ordered alphabetically, from Alabama to Wyoming. There is also a State Ranking section near the end of the book to present a clear look at how the states compare. Following the ranking section is a brief discussion on the data sources used in the book, as well as a glossary of terms that provides a clear understanding of what each variable presented really means.

Each state's section begins with a map of the state showing its major population centers, the main road network, the capital city, and where the state is located relative to others. A narrative is provided to highlight key demographic and economic trends, and to assess the state's economy and demography relative to the nation as a whole.

In addition to the maps and the narrative there are five data sections for each state. First is demographic and socioeconomic data from 2000, 2006, and 2007, including population and income figures. This is followed by a section on workforce and industry, which covers the labor force, education attainment, and employment and payroll information. It also includes a listing of the state's top 10 industries in terms of 2006 employment, with comparison information for 1998.

The third data section for each state presents tax and business climate information. Tax revenues, by type of tax, are presented for the 2004–5 and the 2005–6 fiscal years. Business climate rankings, as reported by Anderson Economic Group, LLC; Forbes Magazine; and the Tax Foundation; are also provided. The number of firm births and terminations in 2004–5, as reported by the Census Bureau, is also included in this section.

Voting behavior and elected officials is the next data section for each state. Included is voter turnout, popular vote, and electoral vote data for the past four presidential elections. Information on Gubernatorial and Congressional office holders is also provided.

The last data section for each state presents the names and web sites for four business and economic agencies in the state. The agencies selected for listing were the state-level chamber of commerce, the state's economic development agency, the state office or agency for small business development and assistance, and the state office for business and corporate registrations.

About Anderson Economic Group, LLC

This book was prepared by Anderson Economic Group, LLC, a consulting firm specializing in economics, finance, business valuation, public policy, and land use economics. The firm assists businesses, state and local governments, and nonprofits with location analyses, market strategies, economic development, and policy analyses, often relying on the data presented in this book.

Scott D. Watkins, a senior consultant with Anderson Economic Group, is the editor of this publication. His work focuses on market and industry analyses, economics, and public policy. Recent reports by Mr. Watkins include "Automation Alley's Annual Technology Industry Report" 2009 edition, "Benchmarking for Success: Education Performance among the American States," and "Economic Impact of Big Ten Football Games in Michigan." Mr. Watkins holds an M.B.A. from the Eli Broad College of

Business at Michigan State University. He also has a bachelor's degree in international relations from the James Madison College at Michigan State University.

Patrick L. Anderson, Principal and CEO at Anderson Economic Group, is this book's executive editor. Mr. Anderson is the author of more than 100 published works on economics, finance, and public policy, and his views are often cited in news reports throughout the United States. His first book, *Business Economics and Finance*, was published in 2004, and his paper on "Pocketbook Issues and the Presidency" was awarded the Edmund Mennis Award for the best contributed paper in 2004 by the National Association for Business Economics.

Prior to founding Anderson Economic Group, Mr. Anderson served as the Chief of Staff of the Michigan Department of State, and as Deputy Budget Director for the State of Michigan. He is a graduate of the University of Michigan, where he earned a master's degree in public policy and a bachelor's degree in political science. The Michigan Chamber of Commerce awarded Mr. Anderson its 2006 *Leadership Michigan Distinguished Alumni* award for his civic and professional accomplishments.

Contacting Anderson Economic Group

For more information on Anderson Economic Group please visit the company's web site at www.AndersonEconomicGroup.com.

To offer suggestions for future editions of *The State Economic Handbook,* or to notify us of a typographical or data error, please e-mail statehandbook@AndersonEconomicGroup.com. Any errata or significant data notes will be available on the State Economic Handbook page at www.AndersonEconomicGroup.com. Please note that minor data revisions, especially of demographic data, occur regularly and may be the cause of small differences in data reported at a later date.

Alabama

Alabama, located in the East South Central region of the United States, has a population of 4.6 million people, making it the twenty-third most populous state in 2007. The state's population increased by 180,751 people from 2000 to 2007, and is projected to increase to 4.8 million by 2025. This 0.2% projected annual growth rate compares to the projected national average of 0.8%. From 2006 to 2007 the state's population grew by 0.6%. Per capita personal income in Alabama was $32,401 in 2007, up from $30,841 in 2006. For 2007, this was ninth lowest in the country and $6,163 below the national average. From 2000 to 2007 the per capita income in Alabama grew at a compound annual rate of 4.5%, compared to 3.7% nationally.

In 2006, the state's largest industry in terms of employment was manufacturing, followed by retail trade. The fastest growing industry was professional, scientific, and technical services, with 5.2% annual growth from 1998 to 2006. The state's workforce is generally less educated than other states—80.1% of the state's adult population

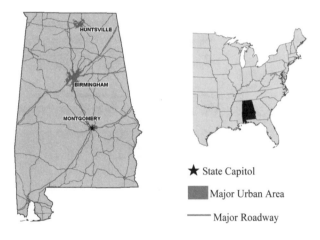

★ State Capitol

▬ Major Urban Area

——— Major Roadway

Demographic and Socioeconomic Profile

Demographics and Socioeconomic Figures			
Population and Households	**2000**	**2006**	**2007**
Total Population	4,447,100	4,599,030	4,627,851
Number of Households	1,737,080	1,796,058	1,816,313
Average Household Size	2.5	2.5	2.5
Age and Ethnicity			
Median Age	35.8	37.2	37.3
Population 18 Years of Age and Older	3,324,488	3,483,362	3,503,201
Population 65 Years of Age and Older	580,028	610,371	624,747
Caucasian Population	3,161,671	3,237,958	3,254,107
African-American Population	1,153,044	1,209,321	1,212,118
Hispanic Population	72,627	111,432	119,415
Asian Population	29,908	45,882	44,561
Foreign-Born Population (%)	2.0	2.8	3.0
Income			
Per Capita Personal Income (USD)	$23,764	$30,841	$32,401
Median Household Income (USD)	$34,135	$38,783	$40,554
Individuals below Poverty Level	16.1%	16.6%	16.9%

Data: U.S. Census, American Community Survey; U.S. Department of Commerce, Bureau of Economic Analysis

has graduated from high school, compared to an 80.4% national average. Nationally, an average of 27.0% hold a bachelor degree or higher compared to 21.4% in Alabama; and 8.0% hold professional or graduate degrees (national average is 10.1%).

In fiscal year 2005–6, Alabama had total tax revenues of $12.8 billion. The largest share was generated from sales and gross receipts taxes, followed by individual income taxes. The per capita tax burden in Alabama was $2,776 for 2005–6, some $1,216 below the national average. In terms of business taxes, the state ranked seventh in a 2008 analysis by Anderson Economic Group. Forbes Magazine and the Tax Foundation ranked the state's business climate twenty-eighth and twenty-first, respectively.

Population Projections

Year	2010	2015	2020	2025
Total Population	4,596,330	4,663,111	4,728,915	4,800,092
Median Age	38.5	39.4	40.3	40.9
Population 18 Years of Age and Older	3,504,146	3,574,114	3,642,576	3,706,831
Population 65 Years of Age and Older	648,889	739,580	842,607	953,727

Data: U.S. Census Bureau

Workforce and Industry Profile

Workforce

	2000	2006	2007
Civilian Labor Force	2,154,545	2,199,562	2,175,716
Labor Force Participation Rate	63.8%	61.5%	61.1%
Unemployment Rate	4.1%	3.6%	3.5%
Average Wage per Job (USD)	$29,041	$33,440	$34,950
Education Attainment (Population 25 Years and Older)	(%)	(%)	(%)
High School Graduate or Higher	75.3	80.1	80.4
Bachelors Degree or Higher	19.0	21.1	21.4
Graduate or Professional Degree	6.9	7.7	8.0

Data: U.S. Census Bureau, American Community Survey; U.S. Department of Commerce, Bureau of Economic Analysis; U.S. Department of Labor, Bureau of Labor Statistics

Industry Overview

	1998	2005	2006
Total Employees	1,604,110	1,667,526	1,713,399
Total Payroll ($1,000)	40,330,597	53,365,320	55,941,677
Total Establishments	100,316	101,976	103,460
Establishments with 1–19 Employees	86,193	86,944	87,926
Establishments with 20–49 Employees	8,791	9,420	9,745
Establishments with 50–249 Employees	4,558	4,836	4,997
Establishments with 250–999 Employees	674	667	683
Establishments with 1,000+ Employees	100	109	109

Data: U.S. Census Bureau, County Business Patterns

Major Industries (Ranked by 2006 Employment; Payroll in $1,000s)

Industry	1998 Employment	2006 Employment	1998 Payroll	2006 Payroll
Manufacturing	352,422	291,239	10,341,656	11,028,280
Retail Trade	226,485	247,237	3,651,939	5,182,321
Health Care and Social Assistance	201,111	233,220	5,738,000	8,411,145
Accommodation and Food Services	127,254	152,471	1,175,671	1,705,818
Admin., Support, Waste Mngt., Remediation Services	100,378	128,781	1,706,594	2,790,379
Construction	101,007	111,115	2,635,107	3,961,866
Professional, Scientific, Technical Services	65,195	97,540	2,519,999	5,071,233
Other Services (except Public Admin.)	80,060	85,151	1,219,639	1,694,908
Wholesale Trade	79,147	79,498	2,540,100	3,470,329
Finance and Insurance	67,933	70,709	2,554,861	3,964,801

Data: U.S. Census Bureau, County Business Patterns

Taxes and Business Climate

State and Local Taxes

Combined Revenues ($1,000)	2004–5	2005–6
Revenue from Property Taxes	1,792,320	1,926,854
Revenue from Sales and Gross Receipts Taxes	5,732,583	6,130,104
Revenue from Individual Income Taxes	2,644,726	2,876,442
Revenue from Corporate Income Taxes	397,308	558,768
Revenue from Other Taxes	1,119,738	1,276,186
Total Tax Revenue	11,686,675	12,768,354
Per Capita Taxes		
Property Tax Per Capita	395	419
Sales and Gross Receipts Tax Per Capita	1,263	1,333
Individual Income Tax Per Capita	583	625
Corporate Income Tax Per Capita	88	122
Other Taxes Per Capita	247	277
Total Taxes Per Capita	2,574	2,776

Data: U.S. Census Bureau; Anderson Economic Group, LLC

Business Climate Measures

Anderson Economic Group: 2008 Business Tax Ranking (1 is Best)	7
Forbes Magazine: 2008 Best States for Business Ranking (1 is Best)	28
Tax Foundation: 2009 Business Tax Climate Ranking (1 is Best)	21
2004–5 Employer Firm Births	9,674
2004–5 Employer Firm Terminations	8,759

Data: Anderson Economic Group; Tax Foundation; Forbes Magazine; U.S. Census, Statistics of U.S. Businesses

Voting Behavior and Elected Officials

Voter Registration and Turnout (%)

	1996	2000	2004	2008
Registered Voters Who Voted	62.1	66.1	72.5	73.9
Population Age 18+ Who Voted	47.7	50.3	55.5	59.9

Data: Dave Leip's Atlas of U.S. Presidential Elections

Presidential Election Results (Nationwide Winner Listed First)

2008	Popular Vote (%)	Electoral Votes
Barack Obama (Democrat)	38.7	0
John McCain (Republican)	60.3	9
Other	0.9	0
2004		
George W. Bush (Republican, Incumbent)	62.5	9
John Kerry (Democrat)	36.8	0
Other	0.7	0
2000		
George W. Bush (Republican)	56.5	9
Albert Gore (Democrat)	41.6	0
Ralph Nader (Green)	1.1	0
Other	0.8	0
1996		
William Clinton (Democrat, Incumbent)	43.2	0
Robert Dole (Republican)	50.1	9
H. Ross Perot (Reformist)	6.0	0
Other	0.7	0

Data: Dave Leip's Atlas of U.S. Presidential Elections

Governor and U.S. Congressional Seats

Governor	Party	Year Term Began	Term	Max. Consecutive Terms
Bob Riley	R	2007	Second	2

U.S. Senators	Party	Year Elected	Term Expires	
Jeff Sessions	R	1996	2015	
Richard C. Shelby	R	1986	2011	

U.S. Representatives	Republican	Democrat	Other
	4	3	0

Data: National Governors Association; U.S. Senate, Office of the Clerk; U.S. House of Representatives

Business and Economic Agencies

Agency	Website Address
Business Council of Alabama	www.bcatoday.org
Alabama Development Office	www.ado.state.al.us
Alabama Small Business Dev. Consortium	www.asbdc.org
Alabama Secretary of State	www.sos.state.al.us

Data: Various agency websites

Alaska

With a population of 683, 478 people, Alaska was the fourth least populous state in the United States in 2007. From 2000 to 2007 the state's population increased by 56,546 people, and is projected to increase to 820,881 people by 2025. This 1.0% projected annual growth rate is higher than the projected national average of 0.8%. From 2006 to 2007 the state's population grew by 2.0%. The state's 2007 per capita personal income of $39,934 was higher compared to $38,622 in 2006 and the fifteenth highest in the United States, some $1,370 above the national average. Per capita income in Alaska grew at a compound annual rate of 4.2% from 2000 to 2007, compared to 3.7% nationally.

Alaska's largest industry in terms of 2006 employment was health care and social assistance. The fastest growing industry was administrative, support, waste management, and remediation services, with 8.4% annual growth from 1998 to 2006. The second fastest growing industry was management of companies and enterprises. The state's workforce is generally less

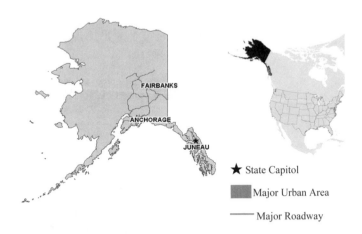

★ State Capitol

▨ Major Urban Area

── Major Roadway

Demographic and Socioeconomic Profile

Demographics and Socioeconomic Figures			
Population and Households	**2000**	**2006**	**2007**
Total Population	626,932	670,053	683,478
Number of Households	221,600	229,878	236,421
Average Household Size	2.7	2.8	2.8
Age and Ethnicity			
Median Age	32.4	33.5	33.3
Population 18 Years of Age and Older	436,425	490,366	502,359
Population 65 Years of Age and Older	35,093	44,035	47,081
Caucasian Population	434,225	460,170	465,234
African-American Population	21,968	21,476	25,821
Hispanic Population	25,765	37,498	38,440
Asian Population	25,496	30,151	32,936
Foreign-Born Population (%)	5.9	7.0	7.2
Income			
Per Capita Personal Income (USD)	$29,867	$38,622	$39,934
Median Household Income (USD)	$51,571	$59,393	$64,333
Individuals below Poverty Level	9.4%	10.9%	8.9%

Data: U.S. Census, American Community Survey; U.S. Department of Commerce, Bureau of Economic Analysis

educated than other states—26.0% hold a bachelor degree or higher (national average is 27.0%); and 9.9% hold professional or graduate degrees compared to the national average of 10.1%; however, 90.5% of the state's adult population has graduated from high school, compared to an 84.1% national average.

Alaska's total tax revenue was $3.7 billion for fiscal year 2005–6, up from the 2004–5 total revenue of $2.9 billion. The largest share of tax revenue in 2005–6 was generated from motor and other taxes, followed by property taxes. On a per capita basis, residents of Alaska paid taxes of $5,469, compared to the national average of $3,992 for 2005–6. In terms of business taxes, the state ranked forty-eighth in a 2008 analysis by Anderson Economic Group. Forbes Magazine and the Tax Foundation ranked the state's business climate forty-eighth and fourth, respectively.

Population Projections

Year	2010	2015	2020	2025
Total Population	694,109	732,544	774,421	820,881
Median Age	32.5	32.3	32.9	33.3
Population 18 Years of Age and Older	510,126	533,371	555,795	584,703
Population 65 Years of Age and Older	56,548	75,023	96,388	115,135

Data: U.S. Census Bureau

Workforce and Industry Profile

Workforce

	2000	2006	2007
Civilian Labor Force	319,002	346,769	351,701
Labor Force Participation Rate	73.1%	71.3%	70.8%
Unemployment Rate	6.2%	6.7%	6.2%
Average Wage Per Job (USD)	$35,142	$43,920	$45,770
Education Attainment (Population 25 Years and Older)	(%)	(%)	(%)
High School Graduate or Higher	88.3	89.7	90.5
Bachelors Degree or Higher	24.7	26.9	26.0
Graduate or Professional Degree	8.6	9.5	9.9

Data: U.S. Census Bureau, American Community Survey; U.S. Department of Commerce, Bureau of Economic Analysis; U.S. Department of Labor, Bureau of Labor Statistics

Industry Overview

	1998	2005	2006
Total Employees	196,135	231,088	241,621
Total Payroll ($1,000)	6,883,920	9,774,285	10,780,246
Total Establishments	18,212	19,808	19,892
Establishments with 1–19 Employees	16,424	17,723	17,768
Establishments with 20–49 Employees	1,212	1,393	1,399
Establishments with 50–249 Employees	486	588	609
Establishments with 250–999 Employees	85	90	101
Establishments with 1,000+ Employees	5	14	15

Data: U.S. Census Bureau, County Business Patterns

Major Industries (Ranked by 2006 Employment; Payroll in $1,000s)				
Industry	1998 Employment	2006 Employment	1998 Payroll	2006 Payroll
Health Care and Social Assistance	28,919	39,455	1,061,078	1,749,702
Retail Trade	32,186	35,344	743,092	939,722
Accommodation and Food Services	20,086	24,236	343,467	521,041
Construction	12,915	20,770	642,928	1,438,475
Transportation and Warehousing	17,005	18,999	745,246	1,023,936
Admin., Support, Waste Mngt., Remediation Services	9,881	18,828	289,675	762,145
Professional, Scientific, Technical Services	9,497	14,099	446,785	870,932
Other Services (except Public Admin.)	9,991	10,536	211,565	291,005
Manufacturing	12,117	10,221	352,818	423,241
Wholesale Trade	7,040	8,587	275,492	413,029

Data: U.S. Census Bureau, County Business Patterns

Taxes and Business Climate

State and Local Taxes		
Combined Revenues ($1,000)	2004–5	2005–6
Revenue from Property Taxes	892,307	969,186
Revenue from Sales and Gross Receipts Taxes	400,070	435,637
Revenue from Individual Income Taxes	0	0
Revenue from Corporate Income Taxes	588,694	821,664
Revenue from Other Taxes	1,065,963	1,438,241
Total Tax Revenue	2,947,034	3,664,728
Per Capita Taxes		
Property Tax Per Capita	1,333	1,446
Sales and Gross Receipts Tax Per Capita	598	650
Individual Income Tax Per Capita	0	0
Corporate Income Tax Per Capita	879	1,226
Other Taxes Per Capita	1,592	2,146
Total Taxes Per Capita	4,402	5,469

Data: U.S. Census Bureau; Anderson Economic Group, LLC

Business Climate Measures	
Anderson Economic Group: 2008 Business Tax Ranking (1 is Best)	48
Forbes Magazine: 2008 Best States for Business Ranking (1 is Best)	48
Tax Foundation: 2009 Business Tax Climate Ranking (1 is Best)	4
2004–5 Employer Firm Births	1,908
2004–5 Employer Firm Terminations	1,639

Data: Anderson Economic Group; Tax Foundation; Forbes Magazine; U.S. Census, Statistics of U.S. Businesses

Voting Behavior and Elected Officials

Voter Registration and Turnout (%)				
	1996	2000	2004	2008
Registered Voters Who Voted	58.2	60.3	66.2	65.8
Population Age 18+ Who Voted	56.9	65.4	68.0	64.9

Data: Dave Leip's Atlas of U.S. Presidential Elections

Presidential Election Results (Nationwide Winner Listed First)		
2008	Popular Vote (%)	Electoral Votes
Barack Obama (Democrat)	37.9	0
John McCain (Republican)	59.4	9
Other	2.7	0
2004		
George W. Bush (Republican, Incumbent)	61.1	3
John Kerry (Democrat)	35.5	0
Other	3.4	0
2000		
George W. Bush (Republican)	58.6	3
Albert Gore (Democrat)	27.7	0
Ralph Nader (Green)	10.1	0
Other	3.6	0
1996		
William Clinton (Democrat, Incumbent)	33.3	0
Robert Dole (Republican)	50.8	3
H. Ross Perot (Reformist)	10.9	0
Other	5.0	0

Data: Dave Leip's Atlas of U.S. Presidential Elections

Governor and U.S. Congressional Seats

Governor	Party	Year Term Began	Term	Max. Consecutive Terms
Sarah Palin	R	2007	First	2

U.S. Senators	Party	Year Elected	Term Expires	
Mark Begich	D	2009	2015	
Lisa Murkowski	R	2002	2011	

U.S. Representatives		Republican	Democrat	Other
		1	0	0

Data: National Governors Association; U.S. Senate, Office of the Clerk; U.S. House of Representatives

Business and Economic Agencies

Agency	Website Address
Alaska State Chamber	www.alaskachamber.com
Alaska Department of Commerce, Community & Economic Development	www.dced.state.ak.us
Alaska Small Business Dev. Center	www.aksbdc.org
Division of Corporations, Business, and Professional Licensing	www.dced.state.ak.us/occ

Data: Various agency websites

Arizona

Arizona is located in the Mountain region of the United States. Arizona has a population of 6.3 million people, making it the sixteenth most populous state in 2007. The state's population increased by 1.2 million people from 2000 to 2007, and is projected to increase to 9.5 million by 2025. This 2.3% projected annual growth rate is above the national average of 0.8%. From 2006 to 2007 the state's population grew by 2.8%. Per capita personal income in Arizona was $32,900 in 2007, up from $31,949 in 2006. For 2007, this was $5,664 below the national average and the tenth lowest in the country. The state's per capita income grew at a compound annual rate of 3.6% from 2000 to 2007, compared to 3.7% nationally.

The state's workforce generally has less education than other states—83.5% of the state's adult population has graduated from high school, compared to an 84.1% national average; 25.3% hold a bachelor degree or higher (national average is 27.0%); and 9.2% hold professional or graduate degrees

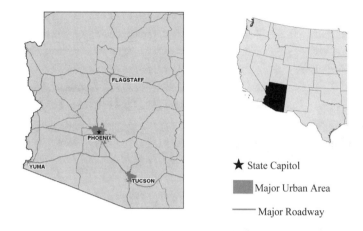

★ State Capitol

▮ Major Urban Area

— Major Roadway

Demographic and Socioeconomic Profile

Demographics and Socioeconomic Figures			
Population and Households	2000	2006	2007
Total Population	5,130,632	6,166,318	6,338,755
Number of Households	1,901,327	2,224,992	2,251,546
Average Household Size	2.6	2.7	2.8
Age and Ethnicity			
Median Age	34.2	34.6	34.9
Population 18 Years of Age and Older	3,767,931	4,539,463	4,668,200
Population 65 Years of Age and Older	667,607	789,751	819,176
Caucasian Population	3,871,715	4,741,310	4,841,990
African-American Population	154,316	207,837	224,991
Hispanic Population	1,295,317	1,803,377	1,881,719
Asian Population	91,223	144,858	151,414
Foreign-Born Population (%)	12.8	15.1	15.6
Income			
Per Capita Personal Income (USD)	$25,660	$31,949	$32,900
Median Household Income (USD)	$40,558	$47,265	$49,889
Individuals below Poverty Level	13.9%	14.2%	14.2%

Data: U.S. Census, American Community Survey; U.S. Department of Commerce, Bureau of Economic Analysis

(national average is 10.1%). In 2006, the state's largest industry in terms of employment was health care and social services, followed by accommodation and food services. The fastest growing industry was educational services, with 9.9% annual growth from 1998 to 2006.

In fiscal year 2005–6, Arizona had total tax revenues of $19.9 billion. The largest share was generated from sales and gross receipts taxes, followed by property taxes. The per capita tax burden in Arizona was $3,234 for 2005–6, some $758 below the national average, and a $154 increase from the 2004–5 per capita tax burden. In terms of business taxes, Arizona ranked thirty-fifth in a 2008 report by Anderson Economic Group. The state's business climate was ranked eighteenth by Forbes Magazine and twenty-second by the Tax Foundation.

Population Projections

Year	2010	2015	2020	2025
Total Population	6,637,381	7,495,238	8,456,448	9,531,537
Median Age	36.4	37.3	38.2	38.8
Population 18 Years of Age and Older	4,948,917	5,602,941	6,328,068	7,170,395
Population 65 Years of Age and Older	922,010	1,181,358	1,520,622	1,940,356

Data: U.S. Census Bureau

Workforce and Industry Profile

Workforce

	2000	2006	2007
Civilian Labor Force	2,505,306	2,977,094	3,036,011
Labor Force Participation Rate	65.1%	64.2%	63.8%
Unemployment Rate	4.0%	4.1%	3.8%
Average Wage Per Job (USD)	$32,610	$36,260	$37,560
Education Attainment (Population 25 Years and Older)	(%)	(%)	(%)
High School Graduate or Higher	81.0	83.8	83.5
Bachelors Degree or Higher	23.5	25.5	25.3
Graduate or Professional Degree	8.4	9.2	9.2

Data: U.S. Census Bureau, American Community Survey; U.S. Department of Commerce, Bureau of Economic Analysis; U.S. Department of Labor, Bureau of Labor Statistics

Industry Overview

	1998	2005	2006
Total Employees	1,763,508	2,159,823	2,335,098
Total Payroll ($1,000)	49,052,246	76,340,525	85,056,889
Total Establishments	110,245	131,651	137,845
Establishments with 1–19 Employees	94,264	111,990	116,543
Establishments with 20–49 Employees	9,997	12,060	12,873
Establishments with 50–249 Employees	5,221	6,613	7,322
Establishments with 250–999 Employees	656	872	987
Establishments with 1,000+ Employees	107	116	120

Data: U.S. Census Bureau, County Business Patterns

Major Industries (Ranked by 2006 Employment; Payroll in $1,000s)				
Industry	1998 Employment	2006 Employment	1998 Payroll	2006 Payroll
Retail Trade	241,092	331,427	4,734,716	8,088,478
Health Care and Social Assistance	190,110	265,751	5,572,775	11,062,771
Accommodation and Food Services	187,762	254,041	2,091,494	3,539,205
Construction	143,373	249,417	4,191,730	9,303,291
Admin., Support, Waste Mngt., Remediation Services	178,828	240,054	3,566,564	6,615,066
Manufacturing	199,616	179,122	7,565,451	8,511,898
Finance and Insurance	92,132	143,883	3,647,327	7,913,804
Professional, Scientific, Technical Services	98,547	134,051	3,636,335	6,892,194
Wholesale Trade	84,631	97,006	3,175,460	4,870,256
Other Services (except Public Admin.)	73,577	87,230	1,386,582	2,070,532

Data: U.S. Census Bureau, County Business Patterns

Taxes and Business Climate

State and Local Taxes		
Combined Revenues ($1,000)	2004–5	2005–6
Revenue from Property Taxes	5,126,076	5,524,045
Revenue from Sales and Gross Receipts Taxes	8,749,977	9,347,395
Revenue from Individual Income Taxes	2,848,450	3,253,279
Revenue from Corporate Income Taxes	701,859	890,004
Revenue from Other Taxes	904,755	925,631
Total Tax Revenue	18,331,117	19,940,354
Per Capita Taxes		
Property Tax Per Capita	861	896
Sales and Gross Receipts Tax Per Capita	1,470	1,516
Individual Income Tax Per Capita	479	528
Corporate Income Tax Per Capita	118	144
Other Taxes Per Capita	152	150
Total Taxes Per Capita	3,080	3,234

Data: U.S. Census Bureau; Anderson Economic Group, LLC

Business Climate Measures

Anderson Economic Group: 2008 Business Tax Ranking (1 is Best)	35
Forbes Magazine: 2008 Best States for Business Ranking (1 is Best)	18
Tax Foundation: 2009 Business Tax Climate Ranking (1 is Best)	22
2004–5 Employer Firm Births	16,054
2004–5 Employer Firm Terminations	12,030

Data: Anderson Economic Group; Tax Foundation; Forbes Magazine; U.S. Census, Statistics of U.S. Businesses

Voting Behavior and Elected Officials

Voter Registration and Turnout (%)

	1996	2000	2004	2008
Registered Voters Who Voted	62.6	70.6	76.1	77.1
Population Age 18+ Who Voted	44.7	40.7	49.6	49.4

Data: Dave Leip's Atlas of U.S. Presidential Elections

Presidential Election Results (Nationwide Winner Listed First)

2008	Popular Vote (%)	Electoral Votes
Barack Obama (Democrat)	44.9	0
John McCain (Republican)	53.9	10
Other	1.7	0
2004		
George W. Bush (Republican, Incumbent)	54.8	10
John Kerry (Democrat)	44.4	0
Other	0.8	0
2000		
George W. Bush (Republican)	51.0	8
Albert Gore (Democrat)	44.7	0
Ralph Nader (Green)	3.0	0
Other	1.2	0
1996		
William Clinton (Democrat, Incumbent)	46.5	8
Robert Dole (Republican)	44.3	0
H. Ross Perot (Reformist)	8.0	0
Other	1.2	0

Data: Dave Leip's Atlas of U.S. Presidential Elections

Governor and U.S. Congressional Seats

Governor	Party	Year Term Began	Term	Max. Consecutive Terms
Jan Brewer	R	2009	First	2

U.S. Senators	Party	Year Elected	Term Expires	
Jon Kyl	R	1994	2013	
John McCain	R	1986	2011	

U.S. Representatives	Republican	Democrat	Other
	3	5	0

Data: National Governors Association; U.S. Senate, Office of the Clerk; U.S. House of Representatives

Business and Economic Agencies

Agency	Website Address
Arizona Chamber of Commerce	www.azchamber.com
Arizona Department of Commerce	www.azcommerce.com
Arizona Small Business Dev. Center	www.maricopa.edu/sbdc
Arizona Secretary of State	www.azsos.gov/business_services

Data: Various agency websites

Arkansas

Arkansas, located in the West South Central region of the United States, has a population of 2.8 million people, making it the nineteenth least populous state in 2007. The state's population increased by 161,397 people from 2000 to 2007, and is projected to increase to 3.2 million by 2025. This 0.6% projected annual growth rate compares to the projected national average of 0.8%. From 2006 to 2007 the state's population grew by 0.9%. Per capita personal income in Arkansas was $30,100 in 2007, up from $28,444 in 2006. For 2007, this was fourth lowest in the country and $8,464 below the national average. From 2000 to 2007 the per capita income in Arkansas grew at a compound annual rate of 4.6%, compared to 3.7% nationally.

In 2006, the state's largest industry in terms of employment was health care and social assistance, followed by retail trade. The fastest growing industry was mining, with 6.4% annual growth from 1998 to 2006. The state's workforce is generally less educated than other states—81.1% of the state's adult population has graduated from high school, compared

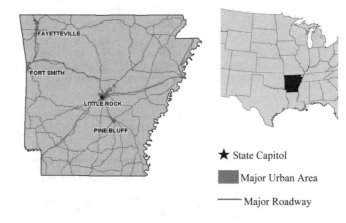

★ State Capitol

▉ Major Urban Area

── Major Roadway

Demographic and Socioeconomic Profile

Demographics and Socioeconomic Figures			
Population and Households	**2000**	**2006**	**2007**
Total Population	2,673,400	2,810,872	2,834,797
Number of Households	1,042,696	1,103,428	1,102,734
Average Household Size	2.5	2.5	2.5
Age and Ethnicity			
Median Age	36.0	37.1	37.0
Population 18 Years of Age and Older	1,993,342	2,117,836	2,133,305
Population 65 Years of Age and Older	374,729	388,860	397,936
Caucasian Population	2,137,166	2,208,224	2,226,758
African-American Population	417,881	437,680	442,279
Hispanic Population	85,576	138,283	146,542
Asian Population	19,081	28,168	33,933
Foreign-Born Population (%)	2.8	3.8	4.2
Income			
Per Capita Personal Income (USD)	$21,925	$28,444	$30,100
Median Household Income (USD)	$32,182	$36,599	$38,134
Individuals below Poverty Level	15.8%	17.3%	17.9%

Data: U.S. Census, American Community Survey; U.S. Department of Commerce, Bureau of Economic Analysis

to an 84.1% national average. Nationally, an average of 27.0% hold a bachelor degree or higher compared to 19.3% in Arkansas; and 6.5% hold professional or graduate degrees (national average is 10.1%).

In fiscal year 2005–6, Arkansas had total tax revenues of $8.7 billion. The largest share was generated from sales and gross receipts taxes, followed by individual income taxes. The per capita tax burden in Arkansas was $3,112 for 2005–6, some $880 below the national average. In terms of business taxes, the state ranked eleventh in a 2008 analysis by Anderson Economic Group. Forbes Magazine and the Tax Foundation ranked the state's business climate thirty-second and thirty-fifth, respectively.

Population Projections

Year	2010	2015	2020	2025
Total Population	2,875,039	2,968,913	3,060,219	3,151,005
Median Age	37.9	38.6	39.4	39.8
Population 18 Years of Age and Older	2,172,383	2,247,849	2,322,453	2,395,591
Population 65 Years of Age and Older	412,152	467,880	531,028	599,028

Data: U.S. Census Bureau

Workforce and Industry Profile

Workforce

	2000	2006	2007
Civilian Labor Force	1,260,256	1,364,646	1,361,176
Labor Force Participation Rate	62.2%	63.4%	63.0%
Unemployment Rate	4.2%	5.3%	5.1%
Average Wage Per Job (USD)	$26,317	$30,870	$32,450
Education Attainment (Population 25 Years and Older)	(%)	(%)	(%)
High School Graduate or Higher	75.3	80.5	81.1
Bachelors Degree or Higher	16.6	18.2	19.3
Graduate or Professional Degree	5.7	6.2	6.5

Data: U.S. Census Bureau, American Community Survey; U.S. Department of Commerce, Bureau of Economic Analysis; U.S. Department of Labor, Bureau of Labor Statistics

Industry Overview

	1998	2005	2006
Total Employees	944,935	1,017,424	1,041,998
Total Payroll ($1,000)	21,764,625	30,185,779	31,719,208
Total Establishments	62,353	66,039	66,795
Establishments with 1–19 Employees	54,335	57,236	57,733
Establishments with 20–49 Employees	4,974	5,594	5,717
Establishments with 50–249 Employees	2,547	2,712	2,841
Establishments with 250–999 Employees	435	432	439
Establishments with 1,000+ Employees	62	65	65

Data: U.S. Census Bureau, County Business Patterns

Major Industries (Ranked by 2006 Employment; Payroll in $1,000s)				
Industry	1998 Employment	2006 Employment	1998 Payroll	2006 Payroll
Manufacturing	232,671	200,622	6,121,981	6,657,113
Health Care and Social Assistance	130,129	159,017	3,187,490	5,274,305
Retail Trade	134,134	145,047	2,072,154	2,867,611
Accommodation and Food Services	73,562	90,235	657,263	959,676
Transportation and Warehousing	39,313	62,967	1,180,877	2,131,004
Construction	43,475	53,920	1,097,864	1,786,602
Admin., Support, Waste Mngt., Remediation Services	51,425	52,561	819,087	1,106,888
Wholesale Trade	42,470	48,821	1,231,247	1,987,152
Other Services (except Public Admin.)	39,816	45,151	579,680	904,497
Professional, Scientific, Technical Services	27,689	38,186	907,143	1,574,980

Data: U.S. Census Bureau, County Business Patterns

Taxes and Business Climate

State and Local Taxes		
Combined Revenues ($1,000)	2004–5	2005–6
Revenue from Property Taxes	1,172,261	1,320,137
Revenue from Sales and Gross Receipts Taxes	4,315,049	4,642,273
Revenue from Individual Income Taxes	1,875,065	2,012,835
Revenue from Corporate Income Taxes	277,315	368,529
Revenue from Other Taxes	414,236	403,244
Total Tax Revenue	8,053,926	8,747,018
Per Capita Taxes		
Property Tax Per Capita	423	470
Sales and Gross Receipts Tax Per Capita	1,557	1,652
Individual Income Tax per Capita	676	716
Corporate Income Tax per Capita	100	131
Other Taxes Per Capita	149	143
Total Taxes Per Capita	2,905	3,112

Data: U.S. Census Bureau; Anderson Economic Group, LLC

Business Climate Measures	
Anderson Economic Group: 2008 Business Tax Ranking (1 is Best)	11
Forbes Magazine: 2008 Best States for Business Ranking (1 is Best)	32
Tax Foundation: 2009 Business Tax Climate Ranking (1 is Best)	35
2004–5 Employer Firm Births	6,394
2004–5 Employer Firm Terminations	5,750

Data: Anderson Economic Group; Tax Foundation; Forbes Magazine; U.S. Census, Statistics of U.S. Businesses

Voting Behavior and Elected Officials

Voter Registration and Turnout (%)				
	1996	2000	2004	2008
Registered Voters Who Voted	64.6	59.2	62.6	64.5
Population Age 18+ Who Voted	47.2	46.2	51.6	50.9

Data: Dave Leip's Atlas of U.S. Presidential Elections

Presidential Election Results (Nationwide Winner Listed First)		
2008	Popular Vote (%)	Electoral Votes
Barack Obama (Democrat)	38.9	0
John McCain (Republican)	58.7	6
Other	2.4	0
2004		
George W. Bush (Republican, Incumbent)	54.3	6
John Kerry (Democrat)	44.6	0
Other	1.2	0
2000		
George W. Bush (Republican)	51.3	6
Albert Gore (Democrat)	45.9	0
Ralph Nader (Green)	1.5	0
Other	1.4	0
1996		
William Clinton (Democrat, Incumbent)	53.7	6
Robert Dole (Republican)	36.8	0
H. Ross Perot (Reformist)	7.9	0
Other	1.6	0

Data: Dave Leip's Atlas of U.S. Presidential Elections

Governor and U.S. Congressional Seats				
Governor	Party	Year Term Began	Term	Max. Consecutive Terms
Mike Beebe	D	2007	First	2
U.S. Senators	**Party**	**Year Elected**	**Term Expires**	
Mark Pryor	D	2002	2015	
Blanche Lincoln	D	1998	2011	
U.S. Representatives		**Republican**	**Democrat**	**Other**
		1	3	0

Data: National Governors Association; U.S. Senate, Office of the Clerk; U.S. House of Representatives

Business and Economic Agencies

Agency	Website Address
Arkansas State Chamber of Commerce	www.statechamber-aia.dina.org
Arkansas Department of Economic Development	www.1800arkansas.com
Arkansas Small Business Dev. Center	www.asbdc.ualr.edu
Arkansas Secretary of State	www.sos.arkansas.gov/corp_ucc.html

Data: Various agency websites

California

With a population of 36.6 million people, California was the most populous state in the United States in 2007. From 2000 to 2007 the state's population increased by 2.7 million people, and is projected to increase to 44.3 million by 2025. This 1.1% projected annual growth rate compares to the projected national average of 0.8%. From 2006 to 2007 the state's population grew by 0.3%. The state's 2007 per capita personal income of $41,580 was higher compared to $39,358 in 2006 and the seventh highest in the United States, some $3,016 above the national average. Per capita income in California grew at a compound annual rate of 3.6% from 2000 to 2007, compared to 3.7% nationally.

California's largest industry in terms of 2006 employment was retail trade, followed by health care and social assistance. The fastest growing industry was construction, with 5.6% annual growth from 1998 to 2006. The state's workforce is generally more educated than other states—29.5% hold a bachelor degree or higher (national average is 27.0%);

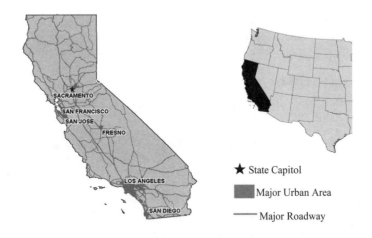

★ State Capitol

▓ Major Urban Area

—— Major Roadway

Demographic and Socioeconomic Profile

Demographics and Socioeconomic Figures			
Population and Households	**2000**	**2006**	**2007**
Total Population	33,871,648	36,457,549	36,553,215
Number of Households	11,502,870	12,151,227	12,200,672
Average Household Size	2.9	2.9	2.9
Age and Ethnicity			
Median Age	33.3	34.4	34.7
Population 18 Years of Age and Older	24,650,185	26,926,503	27,169,594
Population 65 Years of Age and Older	3,586,794	3,927,830	4,000,949
Caucasian Population	20,122,959	21,810,156	22,026,736
African-American Population	2,219,190	2,260,648	2,263,363
Hispanic Population	10,969,132	13,074,155	13,220,888
Asian Population	3,682,975	4,483,252	4,511,407
Foreign-Born Population (%)	26.2	27.2	27.4
Income			
Per Capita Personal Income (USD)	$32,463	$39,358	$41,580
Median Household Income (USD)	$47,493	$56,645	$59,948
Individuals below Poverty Level	14.2%	13.1%	12.4%

Data: U.S. Census, American Community Survey; U.S. Department of Commerce, Bureau of Economic Analysis

and 10.5% hold professional or graduate degrees compared to the national average of 10.1%; however, only 80.2% of the state's adult population has graduated from high school, compared to an 84.1% national average.

California's total tax revenue was $163.7 billion for fiscal year 2005–6, up from the 2004–5 total revenue of $146.6 billion. The largest share of tax revenue in 2005–6 was generated from sales and gross receipts taxes, followed by individual income taxes. On a per capita basis, residents of California paid taxes of $4,492, compared to the national average of $3,992 for 2005–6. In terms of business taxes, the state ranked thirty-first in a 2008 analysis by Anderson Economic Group. Forbes Magazine and the Tax Foundation ranked the state's business climate fortieth and forty-eighth, respectively.

Population Projections

Year	2010	2015	2020	2025
Total Population	38,067,134	40,123,232	42,206,743	44,305,177
Median Age	34.9	35.2	35.7	36.5
Population 18 Years of Age and Older	28,570,156	30,303,080	31,792,635	33,473,509
Population 65 Years of Age and Older	4,392,708	5,227,964	6,199,126	7,284,978

Data: U.S. Census Bureau

Workforce and Industry Profile

Workforce

	2000	2006	2007
Civilian Labor Force	16,857,578	17,901,874	18,077,963
Labor Force Participation Rate	67.1%	65.4%	65.6%
Unemployment Rate	4.9%	4.9%	5.4%
Average Wage Per Job (USD)	$41,186	$44,180	$45,990
Education Attainment (Population 25 Years and Older)	(%)	(%)	(%)
High School Graduate or Higher	76.8	80.1	80.2
Bachelors Degree or Higher	26.6	29.0	29.5
Graduate or Professional Degree	9.5	10.4	10.5

Data: U.S. Census Bureau, American Community Survey; U.S. Department of Commerce, Bureau of Economic Analysis; U.S. Department of Labor, Bureau of Labor Statistics

Industry Overview

	1998	2005	2006
Total Employees	12,026,989	13,382,470	13,834,264
Total Payroll ($1,000)	406,481,070	588,450,315	633,801,812
Total Establishments	773,925	860,866	878,128
Establishments with 1–19 Employees	662,920	738,392	750,600
Establishments with 20–49 Employees	69,203	75,940	79,234
Establishments with 50–249 Employees	36,809	40,949	42,506
Establishments with 250–999 Employees	4,372	4,837	4,988
Establishments with 1,000+ Employees	621	748	800

Data: U.S. Census Bureau, County Business Patterns

Major Industries (Ranked by 2006 Employment; Payroll in $1,000s)				
Industry	1998 Employment	2006 Employment	1998 Payroll	2006 Payroll
Retail Trade	1,382,460	1,700,802	29,103,980	45,771,768
Health Care and Social Assistance	1,269,893	1,556,748	39,962,820	67,945,691
Manufacturing	1,827,350	1,449,769	73,353,460	75,714,222
Accommodation and Food Services	1,052,065	1,321,880	13,134,254	21,243,809
Professional, Scientific, Technical Services	923,030	1,224,939	42,291,124	83,745,958
Admin., Support, Waste Mngt., Remediation Services	992,229	1,153,010	21,527,208	34,730,071
Construction	621,722	958,436	22,673,205	43,808,271
Wholesale Trade	769,617	825,742	32,448,343	50,038,361
Finance and Insurance	599,859	733,723	32,773,849	59,106,693
Other Services (except Public Admin.)	517,331	581,428	10,684,352	15,652,198

Data: U.S. Census Bureau, County Business Patterns

Taxes and Business Climate

State and Local Taxes		
Combined Revenues ($1,000)	2004–5	2005–6
Revenue from Property Taxes	34,058,299	37,225,196
Revenue from Sales and Gross Receipts Taxes	49,026,218	52,019,380
Revenue from Individual Income Taxes	42,992,007	51,219,823
Revenue from Corporate Income Taxes	8,670,066	10,316,468
Revenue from Other Taxes	11,870,297	12,968,136
Total Tax Revenue	146,616,887	163,749,003
Per Capita Taxes		
Property Tax Per Capita	946	1,021
Sales and Gross Receipts Tax Per Capita	1,362	1,427
Individual Income Tax Per Capita	1,195	1,405
Corporate Income Tax Per Capita	241	283
Other Taxes Per Capita	330	356
Total Taxes Per Capita	4,074	4,492

Data: U.S. Census Bureau; Anderson Economic Group, LLC

Business Climate Measures	
Anderson Economic Group: 2008 Business Tax Ranking (1 is Best)	31
Forbes Magazine: 2008 Best States for Business Ranking (1 is Best)	40
Tax Foundation: 2009 Business Tax Climate Ranking (1 is Best)	48
2004–5 Employer Firm Births	96,241
2004–5 Employer Firm Terminations	83,155

Data: Anderson Economic Group; Tax Foundation; Forbes Magazine; U.S. Census, Statistics of U.S. Businesses

Voting Behavior and Elected Officials

Voter Registration and Turnout (%)				
	1996	2000	2004	2008
Registered Voters Who Voted	64.0	69.8	75.0	78.5
Population Age 18+ Who Voted	43.9	44.5	47.7	50.0

Data: Dave Leip's Atlas of U.S. Presidential Elections

Presidential Election Results (Nationwide Winner Listed First)		
2008	Popular Vote (%)	Electoral Votes
Barack Obama (Democrat)	61.0	55
John McCain (Republican)	36.9	0
Other	2.1	0
2004		
George W. Bush (Republican, Incumbent)	44.4	0
John Kerry (Democrat)	54.3	55
Other	1.3	0
2000		
George W. Bush (Republican)	41.7	0
Albert Gore (Democrat)	53.5	54
Ralph Nader (Green)	3.8	0
Other	1.1	0
1996		
William Clinton (Democrat, Incumbent)	51.1	54
Robert Dole (Republican)	38.2	0
H. Ross Perot (Reformist)	7.0	0
Other	3.7	0

Data: Dave Leip's Atlas of U.S. Presidential Elections

Governor and U.S. Congressional Seats				
Governor	**Party**	**Year Term Began**	**Term**	**Max. Consecutive Terms**
Arnold Schwarzenegger	R	2007	Second	2
U.S. Senators	**Party**	**Year Elected**	**Term Expires**	
Barbara Boxer	D	1992	2011	
Dianne Feinstein	D	1992	2013	
U.S. Representatives		**Republican**	**Democrat**	**Other**
		19	34	0

Data: National Governors Association; U.S. Senate, Office of the Clerk; U.S. House of Representatives

Business and Economic Agencies

Agency	Website Address
California Chamber of Commerce	www.calchamber.com
California Association for Local Economic Development	www.caled.org
California Small Business Dev. Center	sbdc.ucmerced.edu
California Secretary of State	www.ss.ca.gov

Data: Various agency websites

Colorado

Colorado is located in the Mountain region of the United States. Colorado has a population of 4.9 million people, making it the twenty-ninth least populous state in 2007. The state's population increased by 560,254 people from 2000 to 2007, and is projected to increase to 5.5 million by 2025. This 0.7% projected annual growth rate is below the national average of 0.8%. From 2006 to 2007 the state's population grew by 2.3%. Per capita personal income in Colorado was $41,019 in 2007, up from $39,587 in 2006. For 2007, this was $2,455 above the national average and the eleventh highest in the country. The state's per capita income grew at a compound annual rate of 3.0% from 2000 to 2007, compared to 3.7% nationally.

The state's workforce generally has more education than other states—88.9% of the state's adult population has graduated from high school, compared to an 84.1% national average; 35.0% hold a bachelor degree or higher (national average is 27.0%); and 12.5% hold professional or graduate degrees

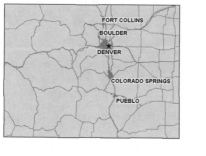

★ State Capitol

▮ Major Urban Area

— Major Roadway

Demographic and Socioeconomic Profile

Demographics and Socioeconomic Figures			
Population and Households	**2000**	**2006**	**2007**
Total Population	4,301,261	4,753,377	4,861,515
Number of Households	1,658,238	1,846,988	1,859,965
Average Household Size	2.5	2.5	2.6
Age and Ethnicity			
Median Age	34.3	35.4	35.7
Population 18 Years of Age and Older	3,204,471	3,583,734	3,669,376
Population 65 Years of Age and Older	415,782	476,885	493,393
Caucasian Population	3,558,579	3,934,971	4,061,059
African-American Population	159,279	177,902	189,217
Hispanic Population	735,099	934,410	965,884
Asian Population	93,306	133,079	131,699
Foreign-Born Population (%)	8.6	10.3	10.0
Income			
Per Capita Personal Income (USD)	$33,371	$39,587	$41,019
Median Household Income (USD)	$47,203	$52,015	$55,212
Individuals below Poverty Level	9.3%	12.0%	12.0%

Data: U.S. Census, American Community Survey; U.S. Department of Commerce, Bureau of Economic Analysis

(national average is 10.1%). In 2006, the state's largest industry in terms of employment was health care and social assistance, followed by accommodation and food services. The fastest growing industry was mining, with 6.5% annual growth from 1998 to 2006.

In fiscal year 2005–6, Colorado had total tax revenues of $17.2 billion. The largest share was generated from sales and gross receipts taxes, followed by property taxes. The per capita tax burden in Colorado was $3,623 for 2005–6, some $369 below the national average, and a $268 increase from the 2004–5 per capita tax burden. In terms of business taxes, Colorado ranked seventeenth in a 2008 report by Anderson Economic Group. The state's business climate was ranked sixth by Forbes Magazine and thirteenth by the Tax Foundation.

Population Projections

Year	2010	2015	2020	2025
Total Population	4,831,554	5,049,493	5,278,867	5,522,803
Median Age	35.7	35.9	36.0	36.0
Population 18 Years of Age and Older	3,642,971	3,793,139	3,951,400	4,128,803
Population 65 Years of Age and Older	517,419	627,408	750,903	869,646

Data: U.S. Census Bureau

Workforce and Industry Profile

Workforce

	2000	2006	2007
Civilian Labor Force	2,364,990	2,651,718	2,686,427
Labor Force Participation Rate	72.4%	72.8%	72.6%
Unemployment Rate	2.7%	4.3%	3.9%
Average Wage Per Job (USD)	$37,168	$41,450	$43,100
Education Attainment (Population 25 Years and Older)	(%)	(%)	(%)
High School Graduate or Higher	86.9	88.1	88.9
Bachelors Degree or Higher	32.7	34.4	35.0
Graduate or Professional Degree	11.1	12.4	12.5

Data: U.S. Census Bureau, American Community Survey; U.S. Department of Commerce, Bureau of Economic Analysis; U.S. Department of Labor, Bureau of Labor Statistics

Industry Overview

	1998	2005	2006
Total Employees	1,757,628	1,936,264	2,019,125
Total Payroll ($1,000)	53,790,978	75,525,841	82,344,137
Total Establishments	130,354	151,070	154,536
Establishments with 1–19 Employees	114,141	133,125	135,793
Establishments with 20–49 Employees	10,144	11,317	11,812
Establishments with 50–249 Employees	5,370	5,876	6,155
Establishments with 250–999 Employees	602	648	666
Establishments with 1,000+ Employees	97	104	110

Data: U.S. Census Bureau, County Business Patterns

Major Industries (Ranked by 2006 Employment; Payroll in $1,000s)

Industry	1998 Employment	2006 Employment	1998 Payroll	2006 Payroll
Retail Trade	232,581	256,958	4,667,472	6,395,857
Health Care and Social Assistance	180,801	229,705	5,267,467	8,851,683
Accommodation and Food Services	192,632	229,478	2,208,219	3,327,152
Admin., Support, Waste Mngt., Remediation Services	150,768	187,190	3,550,768	6,126,661
Construction	132,921	167,527	4,582,355	7,235,357
Professional, Scientific, Technical Services	117,740	164,123	5,631,574	10,379,831
Manufacturing	173,403	134,598	6,555,826	6,476,695
Finance and Insurance	97,679	107,432	4,292,298	6,771,577
Wholesale Trade	92,992	100,022	3,735,494	5,680,594
Other Services (except Public Admin.)	83,161	95,106	1,666,738	2,409,932

Data: U.S. Census Bureau, County Business Patterns

Taxes and Business Climate

State and Local Taxes		
Combined Revenues ($1,000)	**2004–5**	**2005–6**
Revenue from Property Taxes	4,940,398	5,269,089
Revenue from Sales and Gross Receipts Taxes	5,696,742	6,216,229
Revenue from Individual Income Taxes	3,770,736	4,258,944
Revenue from Corporate Income Taxes	315,834	457,673
Revenue from Other Taxes	957,111	1,021,605
Total Tax Revenue	15,680,821	17,223,540
Per Capita Taxes		
Property Tax Per Capita	1,057	1,108
Sales and Gross Receipts Tax Per Capita	1,219	1,308
Individual Income Tax Per Capita	807	896
Corporate Income Tax Per Capita	68	96
Other Taxes Per Capita	205	215
Total Taxes Per Capita	3,355	3,623

Data: U.S. Census Bureau; Anderson Economic Group, LLC

Business Climate Measures

Anderson Economic Group: 2008 Business Tax Ranking (1 is Best)	17
Forbes Magazine: 2008 Best States for Business Ranking (1 is Best)	6
Tax Foundation: 2009 Business Tax Climate Ranking (1 is Best)	13
2004–5 Employer Firm Births	17,673
2004–5 Employer Firm Terminations	14,744

Data: Anderson Economic Group; Tax Foundation; Forbes Magazine; U.S. Census, Statistics of U.S. Businesses

Voting Behavior and Elected Officials

Voter Registration and Turnout (%)

	1996	2000	2004	2008
Registered Voters Who Voted	66.1	65.9	88.6	91.1
Population Age 18+ Who Voted	52.8	54.3	62.7	65.4

Data: Dave Leip's Atlas of U.S. Presidential Elections

Presidential Election Results (Nationwide Winner Listed First)

2008	Popular Vote (%)	Electoral Votes
Barack Obama (Democrat)	53.7	9
John McCain (Republican)	44.7	0
Other	1.6	0
2004		
George W. Bush (Republican, Incumbent)	51.7	9
John Kerry (Democrat)	47.0	0
Other	1.3	0
2000		
George W. Bush (Republican)	50.8	8
Albert Gore (Democrat)	42.4	0
Ralph Nader (Green)	5.3	0
Other	1.6	0
1996		
William Clinton (Democrat, Incumbent)	44.4	0
Robert Dole (Republican)	45.8	8
H. Ross Perot (Reformist)	6.6	0
Other	3.2	0

Data: Dave Leip's Atlas of U.S. Presidential Elections

Governor and U.S. Congressional Seats

Governor	Party	Year Term Began	Term	Max. Consecutive Terms
Bill Ritter Jr.	D	2007	First	2

U.S. Senators	Party	Year Elected	Term Expires	
Mark Udall	D	2008	2015	
Michael Bennet	D	2008	2011	

U.S. Representatives	Republican	Democrat	Other
	2	5	0

Data: National Governors Association; U.S. Senate, Office of the Clerk; U.S. House of Representatives

Business and Economic Agencies

Agency	Website Address
Colorado Association of Commerce and Industry	www.cochamber.com
Colorado Office of Economic Development	www.state.co.us/oed
Colorado Small Business Dev. Center	www.coloradosbdc.org
Colorado Secretary of State	www.sos.state.co.us

Data: Various agency websites

Connecticut

Connecticut, located in the Northeast, New England region of the United States, has a population of 3.5 million people, making it the twenty-second least populous state in 2007. The state's population increased by 96,744 people from 2000 to 2007, and is projected to increase to 3.7 million by 2025. This 0.3% projected annual growth rate compares to the projected national average of 0.8%. From 2006 to 2007 the state's population declined by 0.1%. Per capita personal income in Connecticut was $54,984 in 2007, up from $50,787 in 2006. For 2007, this was the highest in the country and $16,420 above the national average. From 2000 to 2007 the per capita income in Connecticut grew at a compound annual rate of 4.1%, compared to 3.7% nationally.

In 2006, the state's largest industry in terms of employment was retail trade, followed by manufacturing. The fastest growing industry was mining, with 5.7% annual growth from 1998 to 2006. The state's workforce is generally more educated than other states—88.0% of the state's adult population

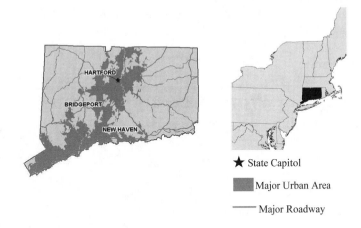

★ State Capitol

▮ Major Urban Area

— Major Roadway

Demographic and Socioeconomic Profile

Demographics and Socioeconomic Figures			
Population and Households	**2000**	**2006**	**2007**
Total Population	3,405,565	3,504,809	3,502,309
Number of Households	1,301,670	1,325,443	1,320,714
Average Household Size	2.5	2.6	2.6
Age and Ethnicity			
Median Age	37.4	39.1	39.1
Population 18 Years of Age and Older	2,565,991	2,686,943	2,683,259
Population 65 Years of Age and Older	469,287	470,465	471,460
Caucasian Population	2,777,794	2,800,344	2,786,401
African-American Population	305,902	332,711	328,401
Hispanic Population	318,947	391,935	403,375
Asian Population	82,277	117,054	118,216
Foreign-Born Population (%)	10.9	12.9	12.8
Income			
Per Capita Personal Income (USD)	$41,489	$50,787	$54,984
Median Household Income (USD)	$53,935	$63,422	$65,967
Individuals below Poverty Level	7.9%	8.3%	7.9%

Data: U.S. Census, American Community Survey; U.S. Department of Commerce, Bureau of Economic Analysis

has graduated from high school, compared to an 84.1% national average. Nationally, an average of 27.0% hold a bachelor degree or higher compared to 34.7% in Connecticut; and 15.4% hold professional or graduate degrees (national average is 10.1%).

In fiscal year 2005–6, Connecticut had total tax revenues of $19.9 billion. The largest share was generated from property taxes, followed by individual income taxes. The per capita tax burden in Connecticut was $5,670 for 2005–6, some $1,678 above the national average. In terms of business taxes, the state ranked tenth in a 2008 analysis by Anderson Economic Group. Forbes Magazine and the Tax Foundation ranked the state's business climate thirty-third and thirty-seventh, respectively.

Population Projections

Year	2010	2015	2020	2025
Total Population	3,577,490	3,635,414	3,675,650	3,691,016
Median Age	39.6	39.6	39.7	40.3
Population 18 Years of Age and Older	2,763,482	2,828,539	2,859,305	2,864,095
Population 65 Years of Age and Older	515,621	577,083	642,541	723,326

Data: U.S. Census Bureau

Workforce and Industry Profile

Workforce

	2000	2006	2007
Civilian Labor Force	1,736,831	1,844,235	1,850,345
Labor Force Participation Rate	66.9%	67.7%	68.2%
Unemployment Rate	2.3%	4.3%	4.6%
Average Wage Per Job (USD)	$45,486	$45,970	$47,680
Education Attainment (Population 25 Years and Older)	**(%)**	**(%)**	**(%)**
High School Graduate or Higher	84.0	88.0	88.0
Bachelors Degree or Higher	31.4	33.7	34.7
Graduate or Professional Degree	13.3	14.4	15.4

Data: U.S. Census Bureau, American Community Survey; U.S. Department of Commerce, Bureau of Economic Analysis; U.S. Department of Labor, Bureau of Labor Statistics

Industry Overview

	1998	2005	2006
Total Employees	1,493,964	1,529,827	1,585,843
Total Payroll ($1,000)	58,225,763	75,605,605	78,835,063
Total Establishments	92,362	93,561	93,421
Establishments with 1–19 Employees	79,965	80,422	79,873
Establishments with 20–49 Employees	7,451	7,992	8,242
Establishments with 50–249 Employees	4,315	4,549	4,730
Establishments with 250–999 Employees	538	508	482
Establishments with 1,000+ Employees	93	90	94

Data: U.S. Census Bureau, County Business Patterns

Major Industries (Ranked by 2006 Employment; Payroll in $1,000s)				
Industry	1998 Employment	2006 Employment	1998 Payroll	2006 Payroll
Health Care and Social Assistance	211,359	245,242	6,617,997	9,859,983
Retail Trade	189,957	200,828	3,989,688	5,312,658
Manufacturing	246,125	182,138	10,779,212	9,940,763
Finance and Insurance	122,463	169,053	9,087,074	16,257,029
Accommodation and Food Services	95,866	133,164	1,208,849	2,507,459
Admin., Support, Waste Mngt., Remediation Services	98,890	107,244	2,434,799	3,391,223
Professional, Scientific, Technical Services	78,060	103,307	4,410,149	6,931,486
Wholesale Trade	73,082	80,323	3,804,026	5,242,926
Construction	60,041	65,767	2,531,796	3,590,665
Other Services (except Public Admin.)	61,578	65,234	1,356,837	1,758,126

Data: U.S. Census Bureau, County Business Patterns

Taxes and Business Climate

State and Local Taxes		
Combined Revenues ($1,000)	2004–5	2005–6
Revenue from Property Taxes	7,155,644	7,566,269
Revenue from Sales and Gross Receipts Taxes	5,128,163	4,970,746
Revenue from Individual Income Taxes	5,033,442	5,777,636
Revenue from Corporate Income Taxes	574,984	634,990
Revenue from Other Taxes	1,004,579	922,326
Total Tax Revenue	18,896,812	19,871,967
Per Capita Taxes		
Property Tax Per Capita	2,052	2,159
Sales and Gross Receipts Tax Per Capita	1,471	1,418
Individual Income Tax Per Capita	1,444	1,648
Corporate Income Tax Per Capita	165	181
Other Taxes Per Capita	288	263
Total Taxes Per Capita	5,420	5,670

Data: U.S. Census Bureau; Anderson Economic Group, LLC

Business Climate Measures

Anderson Economic Group: 2008 Business Tax Ranking (1 is Best)	10
Forbes Magazine: 2008 Best States for Business Ranking (1 is Best)	33
Tax Foundation: 2009 Business Tax Climate Ranking (1 is Best)	37
2004–5 Employer Firm Births	8,221
2004–5 Employer Firm Terminations	7,776

Data: Anderson Economic Group; Tax Foundation; Forbes Magazine; U.S. Census, Statistics of U.S. Businesses

Voting Behavior and Elected Officials

Voter Registration and Turnout (%)

	1996	2000	2004	2008
Registered Voters Who Voted	74.0	76.8	77.2	78.2
Population Age 18+ Who Voted	56.2	56.9	59.6	61.4

Data: Dave Leip's Atlas of U.S. Presidential Elections

Presidential Election Results (Nationwide Winner Listed First)

2008	Popular Vote (%)	Electoral Votes
Barack Obama (Democrat)	60.6	7
John McCain (Republican)	38.2	0
Other	1.2	0
2004		
George W. Bush (Republican, Incumbent)	44.0	0
John Kerry (Democrat)	54.3	7
Other	1.7	0
2000		
George W. Bush (Republican)	38.4	0
Albert Gore (Democrat)	55.9	8
Ralph Nader (Green)	4.4	0
Other	1.2	0
1996		
William Clinton (Democrat, Incumbent)	52.8	8
Robert Dole (Republican)	34.7	0
H. Ross Perot (Reformist)	10.0	0
Other	2.5	0

Data: Dave Leip's Atlas of U.S. Presidential Elections

Governor and U.S. Congressional Seats

Governor	Party	Year Term Began	Term	Max. Consecutive Terms
M. Jodi Rell	R	2007	Second	No limit

U.S. Senators	Party	Year Elected	Term Expires	
Christopher Dodd	D	1980	2011	
Joseph Lieberman	D	1988	2013	

U.S. Representatives		Republican	Democrat	Other
		0	5	0

Data: National Governors Association; U.S. Senate, Office of the Clerk; U.S. House of Representatives

Business and Economic Agencies

Agency	Website Address
Connecticut Business and Industry Association, Inc.	www.cbia.com
Department of Economic and Community Development	www.ct.gov/ecd
Connecticut Small Business Dev. Center	www.sbdc.uconn.edu
Connecticut Secretary of State, Commercial Recording Division	www.sots.ct.gov/CommercialRecording/Crdindex.html

Data: Various agency websites

Delaware

With a population of 864,764 people, Delaware was the sixth least populous state in the United States in 2007. From 2000 to 2007 the state's population increased by 81,164 people, and is projected to increase to 990,694 people by 2025. This 0.8% projected annual growth rate compares to the projected national average of 0.8%. From 2006 to 2007 the state's population grew by 1.3%. The state's 2007 per capita personal income of $40,058 was higher compared to $38,984 in 2006 and was the fourteenth highest in the United States, some $1,494 above the national average. Per capita income in Delaware grew at a compound annual rate of 3.8% from 2000 to 2007, compared to 3.7% nationally.

Delaware's largest industry in terms of 2006 employment was health care and social assistance. The fastest growing industry was transportation and warehousing, with 9.2% annual growth from 1998 to 2006. The second fastest growing industry was mining. The state's workforce is generally more educated than other states— 87.4% of the state's adult

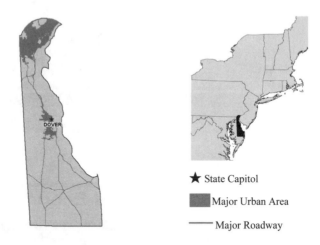

★ State Capitol

■ Major Urban Area

—— Major Roadway

Demographic and Socioeconomic Profile

Demographics and Socioeconomic Figures			
Population and Households	**2000**	**2006**	**2007**
Total Population	783,600	853,476	864,764
Number of Households	298,736	320,110	328,477
Average Household Size	2.5	2.6	2.6
Age and Ethnicity			
Median Age	36.0	37.5	37.8
Population 18 Years of Age and Older	589,638	649,740	659,132
Population 65 Years of Age and Older	101,670	114,554	117,081
Caucasian Population	584,684	615,638	625,354
African-American Population	148,823	176,845	175,682
Hispanic Population	37,321	53,836	56,153
Asian Population	16,053	24,413	25,372
Foreign-Born Population (%)	5.7	8.1	7.6
Income			
Per Capita Personal Income (USD)	$30,869	$38,984	$40,058
Median Household Income (USD)	$47,381	$52,833	$54,610
Individuals below Poverty Level	9.2%	11.1%	10.5%

Data: U.S. Census, American Community Survey; U.S. Department of Commerce, Bureau of Economic Analysis

population has graduated from high school, compared to an 84.1% national average; 26.1% hold a bachelor degree or higher (national average is 27.0%); and 10.4% hold professional or graduate degrees compared to the national average of 10.1%.

Delaware's total tax revenue was $3.6 billion for fiscal year 2005–6, up from the 2004–5 total revenue of $3.3 billion. The largest share of tax revenue in 2005–6 was generated from motor and other taxes, followed by individual income taxes. On a per capita basis, residents of Delaware paid taxes of $4,240, compared to the national average of $3,992 for 2005–6. In terms of business taxes, the state ranked second in a 2008 analysis by Anderson Economic Group. Forbes Magazine and the Tax Foundation ranked the state's business climate twelfth and tenth, respectively.

Population Projections

Year	2010	2015	2020	2025
Total Population	884,342	927,400	963,209	990,694
Median Age	39.4	40.5	41.5	42.8
Population 18 Years of Age and Older	682,134	717,862	747,886	772,682
Population 65 Years of Age and Older	124,972	148,682	176,121	208,599

Data: U.S. Census Bureau

Workforce and Industry Profile

Workforce

	2000	2006	2007
Civilian Labor Force	416,503	440,322	440,912
Labor Force Participation Rate	69.7%	66.9%	66.2%
Unemployment Rate	3.3%	3.6%	3.4%
Average Wage Per Job (USD)	$36,533	$41,680	$43,020
Education Attainment (Population 25 Years and Older)	(%)	(%)	(%)
High School Graduate or Higher	82.6	85.5	87.4
Bachelors Degree or Higher	25.0	27.0	26.1
Graduate or Professional Degree	9.4	10.5	10.4

Data: U.S. Census Bureau, American Community Survey; U.S. Department of Commerce, Bureau of Economic Analysis; U.S. Department of Labor, Bureau of Labor Statistics

Industry Overview

	1998	2005	2006
Total Employees	354,643	392,840	388,250
Total Payroll ($1,000)	11,831,134	16,875,311	17,448,593
Total Establishments	22,871	25,319	25,613
Establishments with 1–19 Employees	19,941	21,983	22,110
Establishments with 20–49 Employees	1,777	2,047	2,191
Establishments with 50–249 Employees	985	1,118	1,152
Establishments with 250–999 Employees	146	139	131
Establishments with 1,000+ Employees	22	32	29

Data: U.S. Census Bureau, County Business Patterns

Major Industries (Ranked by 2006 Employment; Payroll in $1,000s)				
Industry	1998 Employment	2006 Employment	1998 Payroll	2006 Payroll
Retail Trade	47,631	56,439	871,384	1,375,275
Health Care and Social Assistance	41,202	53,502	1,279,822	2,215,136
Finance and Insurance	41,611	35,487	1,909,720	2,558,826
Manufacturing	43,511	33,155	1,632,155	1,702,900
Accommodation and Food Services	25,867	32,049	313,948	505,404
Professional, Scientific, Technical Services	17,043	27,575	824,062	2,045,456
Construction	20,367	25,695	676,309	1,102,355
Admin., Support, Waste Mngt., Remediation Services	26,117	24,074	488,195	683,040
Wholesale Trade	14,839	20,165	789,212	1,510,516
Other Services (except Public Admin.)	15,412	17,421	273,095	393,709

Data: U.S. Census Bureau, County Business Patterns

Taxes and Business Climate

State and Local Taxes		
Combined Revenues ($1,000)	2004–5	2005–6
Revenue from Property Taxes	485,848	530,764
Revenue from Sales and Gross Receipts Taxes	405,451	440,551
Revenue from Individual Income Taxes	932,254	1,076,552
Revenue from Corporate Income Taxes	248,869	295,577
Revenue from Other Taxes	1,204,965	1,274,992
Total Tax Revenue	3,277,387	3,618,436
Per Capita Taxes		
Property Tax Per Capita	578	622
Sales and Gross Receipts Tax Per Capita	482	516
Individual Income Tax Per Capita	1,109	1,261
Corporate Income Tax Per Capita	296	346
Other Taxes Per Capita	1,434	1,494
Total Taxes Per Capita	3,899	4,240

Data: U.S. Census Bureau; Anderson Economic Group, LLC

Business Climate Measures

Anderson Economic Group: 2008 Business Tax Ranking (1 is Best)	2
Forbes Magazine: 2008 Best States for Business Ranking (1 is Best)	12
Tax Foundation: 2009 Business Tax Climate Ranking (1 is Best)	10
2004–5 Employer Firm Births	2,480
2004–5 Employer Firm Terminations	2,420

Data: Anderson Economic Group; Tax Foundation; Forbes Magazine; U.S. Census, Statistics of U.S. Businesses

Voting Behavior and Elected Officials

Voter Registration and Turnout (%)

	1996	2000	2004	2008
Registered Voters Who Voted	64.2	65.1	67.7	NaN
Population Age 18+ Who Voted	49.4	55.6	60.6	62.6

Data: Dave Leip's Atlas of U.S. Presidential Elections

Presidential Election Results (Nationwide Winner Listed First)

2008	Popular Vote (%)	Electoral Votes
Barack Obama (Democrat)	61.9	3
John McCain (Republican)	37.0	0
Other	1.1	0
2004		
George W. Bush (Republican, Incumbent)	45.8	0
John Kerry (Democrat)	53.4	3
Other	0.9	0
2000		
George W. Bush (Republican)	41.9	0
Albert Gore (Democrat)	55.0	3
Ralph Nader (Green)	2.5	0
Other	0.6	0
1996		
William Clinton (Democrat, Incumbent)	51.8	3
Robert Dole (Republican)	36.6	0
H. Ross Perot (Reformist)	10.6	0
Other	1.0	0

Data: Dave Leip's Atlas of U.S. Presidential Elections

Governor and U.S. Congressional Seats				
Governor	**Party**	**Year Term Began**	**Term**	**Max. Consecutive Terms**
Jack Markell	D	2009	First	2
U.S. Senators	**Party**	**Year Elected**	**Term Expires**	
Thomas Carper	D	2000	2013	
Edward Kaufmann	D	2008	2015	
U.S. Representatives		**Republican**	**Democrat**	**Other**
		1	0	0

Data: National Governors Association; U.S. Senate, Office of the Clerk; U.S. House of Representatives

Business and Economic Agencies

Agency	Website Address
Delaware State Chamber of Commerce	www.dscc.com
Delaware Economic Development Office	www.state.de.us/dedo/default.shtml
Delaware Small Business Dev. Center	www.delawaresbdc.org
Delaware Division of Corporations	www.state.de.us/corp

Data: Various agency websites

Florida

Florida is located in the South Atlantic region of the United States. Florida has a population of 18.3 million people, making it the fourth most populous state in 2007. The state's population increased by 2.3 million people from 2000 to 2007, and is projected to increase to 25.9 million by 2025. This 2.0% projected annual growth rate is above the national average of 0.8%. From 2006 to 2007 the state's population grew by 0.9%. Per capita personal income in Florida was $38,316 in 2007, up from $36,665 in 2006. For 2007, this was $248 below the national average and the twentieth highest in the country. The state's per capita income grew at a compound annual rate of 4.3% from 2000 to 2007, compared to 3.7% nationally.

The state's workforce generally has less education than other states—25.8% hold a bachelor degree or higher (national average is 27.0%); and 8.9% hold professional or graduate degrees (national average is 10.1%); however, 84.9% of the state's adult population has graduated from high school, compared to an 84.1%

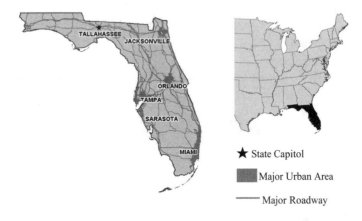

★ State Capitol

▮ Major Urban Area

— Major Roadway

Demographic and Socioeconomic Profile

Demographics and Socioeconomic Figures			
Population and Households	**2000**	**2006**	**2007**
Total Population	15,982,378	18,089,889	18,251,243
Number of Households	6,337,929	7,106,042	7,088,960
Average Household Size	2.5	2.5	2.5
Age and Ethnicity			
Median Age	38.7	39.8	40.0
Population 18 Years of Age and Older	12,347,806	14,071,245	14,208,574
Population 65 Years of Age and Older	2,806,137	3,034,117	3,096,575
Caucasian Population	12,463,302	13,767,248	13,921,401
African-American Population	2,312,105	2,778,549	2,800,374
Hispanic Population	2,680,314	3,642,989	3,757,424
Asian Population	264,377	393,427	409,144
Foreign-Born Population (%)	16.7	18.9	18.9
Income			
Per Capita Personal Income (USD)	$28,509	$36,665	$38,316
Median Household Income (USD)	$38,819	$45,495	$47,804
Individuals below Poverty Level	12.5%	12.6%	12.1%

Data: U.S. Census, American Community Survey; U.S. Department of Commerce, Bureau of Economic Analysis

national average. In 2006, the state's largest industry in terms of employment was administrative, support, waste management, and remediation services, followed by retail trade. The fastest growing industry was administrative, support, waste management, and remediation services, with 9.0% annual growth from 1998 to 2006.

In fiscal year 2005–6, Florida had total tax revenues of $66.7 billion. The largest share was generated from sales and gross receipts taxes, followed by property taxes. The per capita tax burden in Florida was $3,687 for 2005–6, some $305 below the national average, and a $312 increase from the 2004–5 per capita tax burden. In terms of business taxes, Florida ranked forty-forth in a 2008 report by Anderson Economic Group. The state's business climate was ranked eighth by Forbes Magazine and fifth by the Tax Foundation.

Population Projections

Year	2010	2015	2020	2025
Total Population	19,251,691	21,204,132	23,406,525	25,912,458
Median Age	41.9	43.2	44.1	44.8
Population 18 Years of Age and Older	15,165,568	16,749,420	18,518,914	20,611,286
Population 65 Years of Age and Older	3,418,697	4,133,945	5,106,857	6,387,843

Data: U.S. Census Bureau

Workforce and Industry Profile

Workforce

	2000	2006	2007
Civilian Labor Force	7,869,690	8,988,611	9,088,439
Labor Force Participation Rate	63.0%	62.9%	63.5%
Unemployment Rate	3.8%	3.3%	4.1%
Average Wage Per Job (USD)	$30,560	$35,820	$37,260
Education Attainment (Population 25 Years and Older)	**(%)**	**(%)**	**(%)**
High School Graduate or Higher	79.9	84.6	84.9
Bachelors Degree or Higher	22.3	25.3	25.8
Graduate or Professional Degree	8.1	9.2	8.9

Data: U.S. Census Bureau, American Community Survey; U.S. Department of Commerce, Bureau of Economic Analysis; U.S. Department of Labor, Bureau of Labor Statistics

Industry Overview

	1998	2005	2006
Total Employees	5,756,353	7,107,378	7,535,515
Total Payroll ($1,000)	149,936,849	239,197,889	260,444,393
Total Establishments	420,638	504,662	517,069
Establishments with 1–19 Employees	371,384	447,764	457,059
Establishments with 20–49 Employees	29,930	34,320	36,186
Establishments with 50–249 Employees	17,086	19,890	21,011
Establishments with 250–999 Employees	1,890	2,291	2,396
Establishments with 1,000+ Employees	348	397	417

Data: U.S. Census Bureau, County Business Patterns

Major Industries (Ranked by 2006 Employment; Payroll in $1,000s)				
Industry	1998 Employment	2006 Employment	1998 Payroll	2006 Payroll
Admin., Support, Waste Mngt., Remediation Services	705,898	1,408,215	13,287,683	38,945,336
Retail Trade	872,391	1,056,865	15,636,653	25,287,461
Health Care and Social Assistance	740,828	877,821	21,829,102	34,465,717
Accommodation and Food Services	596,481	742,060	6,994,893	11,626,249
Construction	341,673	542,849	9,674,731	21,000,933
Professional, Scientific, Technical Services	318,814	455,324	13,047,144	24,343,275
Finance and Insurance	302,704	388,417	12,522,788	22,007,335
Manufacturing	428,642	372,151	13,514,960	15,487,613
Wholesale Trade	298,551	319,971	10,388,706	15,022,725
Other Services (except Public Admin.)	288,705	319,579	5,192,259	7,334,733

Data: U.S. Census Bureau, County Business Patterns

Taxes and Business Climate

State and Local Taxes		
Combined Revenues ($1,000)	2004–5	2005–6
Revenue from Property Taxes	20,389,149	23,044,982
Revenue from Sales and Gross Receipts Taxes	29,785,839	32,343,761
Revenue from Individual Income Taxes	0	0
Revenue from Corporate Income Taxes	1,785,623	2,406,225
Revenue from Other Taxes	7,903,273	8,900,256
Total Tax Revenue	59,863,884	66,695,224
Per Capita Taxes		
Property Tax Per Capita	1,150	1,274
Sales and Gross Receipts Tax Per Capita	1,679	1,788
Individual Income Tax Per Capita	0	0
Corporate Income Tax Per Capita	101	133
Other Taxes Per Capita	446	492
Total Taxes Per Capita	3,375	3,687

Data: U.S. Census Bureau; Anderson Economic Group, LLC

Business Climate Measures	
Anderson Economic Group: 2008 Business Tax Ranking (1 is Best)	44
Forbes Magazine: 2008 Best States for Business Ranking (1 is Best)	8
Tax Foundation: 2009 Business Tax Climate Ranking (1 is Best)	5
2004–5 Employer Firm Births	67,451
2004–5 Employer Firm Terminations	51,044

Data: Anderson Economic Group; Tax Foundation; Forbes Magazine; U.S. Census, Statistics of U.S. Businesses

Voting Behavior and Elected Officials

Voter Registration and Turnout (%)				
	1996	2000	2004	2008
Registered Voters Who Voted	65.7	68.1	73.9	74.8
Population Age 18+ Who Voted	48.0	48.3	58.1	59.2

Data: Dave Leip's Atlas of U.S. Presidential Elections

Presidential Election Results (Nationwide Winner Listed First)		
2008	Popular Vote (%)	Electoral Votes
Barack Obama (Democrat)	50.9	27
John McCain (Republican)	48.1	0
Other	1.0	0
2004		
George W. Bush (Republican, Incumbent)	52.1	27
John Kerry (Democrat)	47.1	0
Other	0.8	0
2000		
George W. Bush (Republican)	48.9	25
Albert Gore (Democrat)	48.8	0
Ralph Nader (Green)	1.6	0
Other	0.7	0
1996		
William Clinton (Democrat, Incumbent)	48.0	25
Robert Dole (Republican)	42.3	0
H. Ross Perot (Reformist)	9.1	0
Other	0.5	0

Data: Dave Leip's Atlas of U.S. Presidential Elections

Governor and U.S. Congressional Seats				
Governor	**Party**	**Year Term Began**	**Term**	**Max. Consecutive Terms**
Charlie Crist	R	2007	First	2
U.S. Senators	**Party**	**Year Elected**	**Term Expires**	
Mel Martinez	R	2004	2011	
Bill Nelson	D	2000	2013	
U.S. Representatives		**Republican**	**Democrat**	**Other**
		15	10	0

Data: National Governors Association; U.S. Senate, Office of the Clerk; U.S. House of Representatives

Business and Economic Agencies

Agency	Website Address
Florida Chamber of Commerce	www.flchamber.com
Governor's Office of Trade, Tourism, and Economic Development	www.flgov.com/otted_home
Florida Small Business Dev. Center	www.floridasbdc.com
Florida Department of State, Division of Corporations	www.sunbiz.org

Data: Various agency websites

Georgia

Georgia, located in the South Atlantic region of the United States, has a population of 9.5 million people, making it the ninth most populous state in 2007. The state's population increased by 1.4 million people from 2000 to 2007, and is projected to increase to 11.4 million by 2025. This 1.0% projected annual growth rate compares to the projected national average of 0.8%. From 2006 to 2007 the state's population increased by 1.9%. Per capita personal income in Georgia was $33,416 in 2007, up from $32,025 in 2006. For 2007, this was fourteenth lowest in the country and $5,148 below the national average. From 2000 to 2007 the per capita income in Georgia grew at a compound annual rate of 2.6%, compared to 3.7% nationally.

In 2006, the state's largest industry in terms of employment was retail trade, followed by manufacturing. The fastest growing industry was transportation and warehousing, with 4.3% annual growth from 1998 to 2006. The state's workforce is generally less educated than other states—82.9% of the state's adult population has

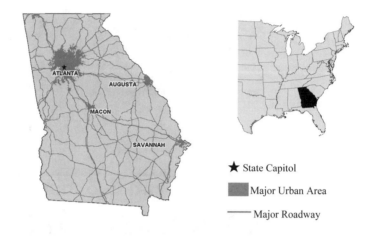

★ State Capitol

▨ Major Urban Area

— Major Roadway

Demographic and Socioeconomic Profile

Demographics and Socioeconomic Figures			
Population and Households	**2000**	**2006**	**2007**
Total Population	8,186,453	9,363,941	9,544,750
Number of Households	3,006,369	3,376,763	3,417,115
Average Household Size	2.6	2.7	2.7
Age and Ethnicity			
Median Age	33.4	34.6	34.8
Population 18 Years of Age and Older	6,020,679	6,911,716	7,017,887
Population 65 Years of Age and Older	787,906	906,879	940,461
Caucasian Population	5,327,175	5,816,513	5,918,880
African-American Population	2,342,110	2,794,300	2,855,189
Hispanic Population	429,976	696,146	729,116
Asian Population	171,463	254,899	265,188
Foreign-Born Population (%)	7.1	9.2	9.1
Income			
Per Capita Personal Income (USD)	$27,989	$32,025	$33,416
Median Household Income (USD)	$42,433	$46,832	$49,136
Individuals below Poverty Level	13.0%	14.7%	14.3%

Data: U.S. Census, American Community Survey; U.S. Department of Commerce, Bureau of Economic Analysis

graduated from high school, compared to an 84.1% national average. Nationally, an average of 27.0% hold a bachelor degree or higher compared to 27.1% in Georgia; and 9.5% hold professional or graduate degrees (national average is 10.1%).

In fiscal year 2005–6, Georgia had total tax revenues of $31.0 billion. The largest share was generated from sales and gross receipts taxes, followed by property taxes. The per capita tax burden in Georgia was $3,313 for 2005–6, some $679 below the national average. In terms of business taxes, the state ranked thirteenth in a 2008 analysis by Anderson Economic Group. Forbes Magazine and the Tax Foundation ranked the state's business climate fifth and twenty-seventh, respectively.

Population Projections

Year	2010	2015	2020	2025
Total Population	9,589,080	10,230,578	10,843,753	11,438,622
Median Age	34.7	35.1	35.4	35.5
Population 18 Years of Age and Older	7,086,694	7,551,789	8,006,490	8,453,077
Population 65 Years of Age and Older	980,824	1,187,576	1,409,923	1,659,679

Data: U.S. Census Bureau

Workforce and Industry Profile

Workforce

	2000	2006	2007
Civilian Labor Force	4,242,889	4,741,860	4,798,003
Labor Force Participation Rate	69.6%	68.3%	67.8%
Unemployment Rate	3.5%	4.6%	4.6%
Average Wage Per Job (USD)	$34,214	$37,150	$38,320
Education Attainment (Population 25 Years and Older)	**(%)**	**(%)**	**(%)**
High School Graduate or Higher	78.6	82.2	82.9
Bachelors Degree or Higher	24.3	26.6	27.1
Graduate or Professional Degree	8.3	9.8	9.5

Data: U.S. Census Bureau, American Community Survey; U.S. Department of Commerce, Bureau of Economic Analysis; U.S. Department of Labor, Bureau of Labor Statistics

Industry Overview

	1998	2005	2006
Total Employees	3,198,950	3,489,046	3,623,210
Total Payroll ($1,000)	94,687,270	128,827,270	137,926,543
Total Establishments	194,213	220,528	225,996
Establishments with 1–19 Employees	166,186	189,331	193,348
Establishments with 20–49 Employees	17,122	19,192	20,037
Establishments with 50–249 Employees	9,306	10,363	10,944
Establishments with 250–999 Employees	1,403	1,442	1,457
Establishments with 1,000+ Employees	196	200	210

Data: U.S. Census Bureau, County Business Patterns

Major Industries (Ranked by 2006 Employment; Payroll in $1,000s)				
Industry	1998 Employment	2006 Employment	1998 Payroll	2006 Payroll
Retail Trade	431,806	478,499	7,798,334	11,044,779
Manufacturing	535,051	430,697	16,722,306	16,604,747
Health Care and Social Assistance	331,889	408,413	9,810,907	15,496,774
Admin., Support, Waste Mngt., Remediation Services	261,555	355,047	5,596,097	9,890,228
Accommodation and Food Services	273,389	354,332	3,035,725	4,653,558
Professional, Scientific, Technical Services	166,535	222,435	7,679,090	12,935,102
Construction	174,774	213,778	5,527,052	8,648,832
Wholesale Trade	193,112	207,204	8,167,514	10,882,268
Finance and Insurance	154,798	179,263	6,662,088	10,757,328
Transportation and Warehousing	117,455	164,058	3,755,017	6,801,876

Data: U.S. Census Bureau, County Business Patterns

Taxes and Business Climate

State and Local Taxes		
Combined Revenues ($1,000)	2004–5	2005–6
Revenue from Property Taxes	8,214,542	8,946,070
Revenue from Sales and Gross Receipts Taxes	10,137,348	12,031,213
Revenue from Individual Income Taxes	7,326,225	8,040,366
Revenue from Corporate Income Taxes	712,310	890,732
Revenue from Other Taxes	1,095,684	1,117,076
Total Tax Revenue	27,486,109	31,025,457
Per Capita Taxes		
Property Tax Per Capita	902	955
Sales and Gross Receipts Tax Per Capita	1,113	1,285
Individual Income Tax Per Capita	804	859
Corporate Income Tax Per Capita	78	95
Other Taxes Per Capita	120	119
Total Taxes Per Capita	3,018	3,313

Data: U.S. Census Bureau; Anderson Economic Group, LLC

Business Climate Measures

Anderson Economic Group: 2008 Business Tax Ranking (1 is Best)	13
Forbes Magazine: 2008 Best States for Business Ranking (1 is Best)	5
Tax Foundation: 2009 Business Tax Climate Ranking (1 is Best)	27
2004–5 Employer Firm Births	25,055
2004–5 Employer Firm Terminations	20,743

Data: Anderson Economic Group; Tax Foundation; Forbes Magazine; U.S. Census, Statistics of U.S. Businesses

Voting Behavior and Elected Officials

Voter Registration and Turnout (%)

	1996	2000	2004	2008
Registered Voters Who Voted	60.3	67.3	79.4	NaN
Population Age 18+ Who Voted	42.4	43.1	51.7	56.0

Data: Dave Leip's Atlas of U.S. Presidential Elections

Presidential Election Results (Nationwide Winner Listed First)

2008	Popular Vote (%)	Electoral Votes
Barack Obama (Democrat)	46.9	0
John McCain (Republican)	52.1	15
Other	1.0	0
2004		
George W. Bush (Republican, Incumbent)	58.0	15
John Kerry (Democrat)	41.4	0
Other	0.7	0
2000		
George W. Bush (Republican)	54.7	13
Albert Gore (Democrat)	43.0	0
Ralph Nader (Green)	.5	0
Other	1.8	0
1996		
William Clinton (Democrat, Incumbent)	45.8	0
Robert Dole (Republican)	47.0	13
H. Ross Perot (Reformist)	6.4	0
Other	0.8	0

Data: Dave Leip's Atlas of U.S. Presidential Elections

Governor and U.S. Congressional Seats				
Governor	**Party**	**Year Term Began**	**Term**	**Max. Consecutive Terms**
Sonny Perdue	R	2007	Second	2
U.S. Senators	**Party**	**Year Elected**	**Term Expires**	
Saxby Chambliss	R	2002	2015	
Johnny Isakson	R	2004	2011	
U.S. Representatives		**Republican**	**Democrat**	**Other**
		7	6	0

Data: National Governors Association; U.S. Senate, Office of the Clerk; U.S. House of Representatives

Business and Economic Agencies

Agency	Website Address
Georgia Chamber of Commerce	www.gachamber.com
Georgia Department of Economic Development	www.georgia.org
Georgia Small Business Dev. Center	www.sbdc.uga.edu
Georgia Secretary of State, Corporations Division	www.sos.state.ga.us/corporations

Data: Various agency websites

Hawaii

With a population of 1.3 million people, Hawaii was the ninth least populous state in the United States in 2007. From 2000 to 2007 the state's population increased by 71,851 people, and is projected to increase to 1.4 million by 2025. This 0.6% projected annual growth rate compares to the projected national average of 0.8%. From 2006 to 2007 the state's population declined by 0.2%. The state's 2007 per capita personal income of $39,060 was higher compared to $36,826 in 2006 and the eighteenth highest in the United States, some $496 above the national average. Per capita income in Hawaii grew at a compound annual rate of 4.6% from 2000 to 2007, compared to 3.7% nationally.

Hawaii's largest industry in terms of 2006 employment was retail trade. The fastest growing industry was construction, with 5.3% annual growth from 1998 to 2006. The second fastest growing industry was professional, scientific, and technical services. The state's workforce is generally more educated than other states—89.4% of the state's adult population

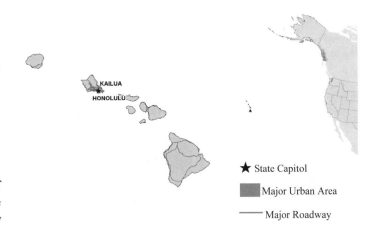

★ State Capitol

▮ Major Urban Area

— Major Roadway

Demographic and Socioeconomic Profile

Demographics and Socioeconomic Figures			
Population and Households	**2000**	**2006**	**2007**
Total Population	1,211,537	1,285,498	1,283,388
Number of Households	403,240	432,632	439,685
Average Household Size	2.9	2.9	2.8
Age and Ethnicity			
Median Age	36.2	37.2	38.1
Population 18 Years of Age and Older	917,212	988,265	997,623
Population 65 Years of Age and Older	161,141	179,012	184,492
Caucasian Population	292,457	337,507	341,779
African-American Population	20,945	28,062	27,836
Hispanic Population	87,582	99,664	105,171
Asian Population	503,950	512,995	498,468
Foreign-Born Population (%)	17.5	16.3	17.3
Income			
Per Capita Personal Income (USD)	$28,422	$36,826	$39,060
Median Household Income (USD)	$49,820	$61,160	$63,746
Individuals below Poverty Level	10.7%	9.3%	8.0%

Data: U.S. Census, American Community Survey; U.S. Department of Commerce, Bureau of Economic Analysis

has graduated from high school, compared to an 84.1% national average; 29.2% hold a bachelor degree or higher (national average is 27.0%); however, 9.9% hold professional or graduate degrees compared to the national average of 10.1%.

Hawaii's total tax revenue was $6.2 billion for fiscal year 2005–6, up from the 2004–5 total revenue of $5.5 billion. The largest share of tax revenue in 2005–6 was generated from sales and gross receipts taxes, followed by individual income taxes. On a per capita basis, residents of Hawaii paid taxes of $4,823, compared to the national average of $3,992 for 2005–6. In terms of business taxes, the state ranked forty-seventh in a 2008 analysis by Anderson Economic Group. Forbes Magazine and the Tax Foundation ranked the state's business climate twenty-seventh and twenty-fourth, respectively.

Population Projections

Year	2010	2015	2020	2025
Total Population	1,340,674	1,385,952	1,412,373	1,438,720
Median Age	37.4	37.3	37.5	38.1
Population 18 Years of Age and Older	1,024,411	1,055,684	1,073,236	1,105,783
Population 65 Years of Age and Older	191,065	226,189	264,527	300,743

Data: U.S. Census Bureau

Workforce and Industry Profile

Workforce

	2000	2006	2007
Civilian Labor Force	609,018	643,486	645,947
Labor Force Participation Rate	67.6%	66.2%	65.8%
Unemployment Rate	4.0%	2.4%	2.6%
Average Wage Per Job (USD)	$30,628	$38,630	$40,200
Education Attainment (Population 25 Years and Older)	**(%)**	**(%)**	**(%)**
High School Graduate or Higher	84.6	89.0	89.4
Bachelors Degree or Higher	26.2	29.7	29.2
Graduate or Professional Degree	8.4	7.1	9.9

Data: U.S. Census Bureau, American Community Survey; U.S. Department of Commerce, Bureau of Economic Analysis; U.S. Department of Labor, Bureau of Labor Statistics

Industry Overview

	1998	2005	2006
Total Employees	416,571	490,682	512,543
Total Payroll ($1,000)	11,291,978	16,163,137	17,287,011
Total Establishments	29,603	32,244	33,118
Establishments with 1–19 Employees	25,653	27,711	28,355
Establishments with 20–49 Employees	2,498	2,730	2,884
Establishments with 50–249 Employees	1,287	1,581	1,669
Establishments with 250–999 Employees	142	194	184
Establishments with 1,000+ Employees	23	28	26

Data: U.S. Census Bureau, County Business Patterns

Major Industries (Ranked by 2006 Employment; Payroll in $1,000s)				
Industry	1998 Employment	2006 Employment	1998 Payroll	2006 Payroll
Accommodation and Food Services	83,261	101,183	1,519,689	2,305,129
Retail Trade	60,620	72,579	1,179,640	1,770,009
Health Care and Social Assistance	47,389	61,904	1,670,402	2,503,184
Admin., Support, Waste Mngt., Remediation Services	31,342	41,752	649,096	1,090,532
Construction	21,265	32,120	862,290	1,740,944
Transportation and Warehousing	23,635	29,976	773,653	1,031,257
Professional, Scientific, Technical Services	17,140	25,820	690,001	1,286,264
Other Services (except Public Admin.)	22,790	25,661	456,924	632,678
Wholesale Trade	18,442	20,799	602,585	818,908
Finance and Insurance	20,050	20,097	807,310	1,103,330

Data: U.S. Census Bureau, County Business Patterns

Taxes and Business Climate

State and Local Taxes		
Combined Revenues ($1,000)	2004–5	2005–6
Revenue from Property Taxes	818,239	982,653
Revenue from Sales and Gross Receipts Taxes	2,895,269	3,168,154
Revenue from Individual Income Taxes	1,381,481	1,550,757
Revenue from Corporate Income Taxes	124,125	148,084
Revenue from Other Taxes	304,633	349,756
Total Tax Revenue	5,523,747	6,199,404
Per Capita Taxes		
Property Tax Per Capita	646	764
Sales and Gross Receipts Tax Per Capita	2,284	2,465
Individual Income Tax Per Capita	1,090	1,206
Corporate Income Tax Per Capita	98	115
Other Taxes Per Capita	240	272
Total Taxes Per Capita	4,358	4,823

Data: U.S. Census Bureau; Anderson Economic Group, LLC

Business Climate Measures	
Anderson Economic Group: 2008 Business Tax Ranking (1 is Best)	47
Forbes Magazine: 2008 Best States for Business Ranking (1 is Best)	27
Tax Foundation: 2009 Business Tax Climate Ranking (1 is Best)	24
2004–5 Employer Firm Births	2,965
2004–5 Employer Firm Terminations	2,460

Data: Anderson Economic Group; Tax Foundation; Forbes Magazine; U.S. Census, Statistics of U.S. Businesses

Voting Behavior and Elected Officials

Voter Registration and Turnout (%)				
	1996	2000	2004	2008
Registered Voters Who Voted	66.1	57.7	66.3	65.6
Population Age 18+ Who Voted	40.5	40.1	44.7	45.5

Data: Dave Leip's Atlas of U.S. Presidential Elections

Presidential Election Results (Nationwide Winner Listed First)		
2008	Popular Vote (%)	Electoral Votes
Barack Obama (Democrat)	71.9	4
John McCain (Republican)	26.6	0
Other	1.6	0
2004		
George W. Bush (Republican, Incumbent)	45.3	0
John Kerry (Democrat)	54.0	4
Other	0.7	0
2000		
George W. Bush (Republican)	37.5	0
Albert Gore (Democrat)	55.8	4
Ralph Nader (Green)	5.9	0
Other	0.9	0
1996		
William Clinton (Democrat, Incumbent)	56.9	4
Robert Dole (Republican)	31.6	0
H. Ross Perot (Reformist)	7.6	0
Other	3.8	0

Data: Dave Leip's Atlas of U.S. Presidential Elections

Governor and U.S. Congressional Seats

Governor	Party	Year Term Began	Term	Max. Consecutive Terms
Linda Lingle	R	2006	Second	2

U.S. Senators	Party	Year Elected	Term Expires	
Daniel K. Akaka	D	1990	2013	
Daniel K. Inouye	D	1962	2011	

U.S. Representatives	Republican	Democrat	Other
	0	2	0

Data: National Governors Association; U.S. Senate, Office of the Clerk; U.S. House of Representatives

Business and Economic Agencies

Agency	Website Address
Chamber of Commerce of Hawaii	www.cochawaii.com
Department of Business, Economic Development & Tourism	www.hawaii.gov/dbedt
Hawaii Small Business Dev. Center	www.hawaii-sbdc.org
Department of Commerce and Consumer Affairs	www.hawaii.gov/dcca

Data: Various agency websites

Idaho

Idaho is located in the Mountain region of the United States. Idaho has a population of 1.5 million people, making it the twelfth least populous state in 2007. The state's population increased by 205,449 people from 2000 to 2007, and is projected to increase to 1.9 million by 2025. This 1.2% projected annual growth rate is above the national average of 0.8%. From 2006 to 2007 the state's population grew by 2.3%. Per capita personal income in Idaho was $31,703 in 2007, up from $29,948 in 2006. For 2007, this was $6,861 below the national average and the eighth lowest in the country. The state's per capita income grew at a compound annual rate of 4.0% from 2000 to 2007, compared to 3.7% nationally.

The state's workforce generally has less education than other states—24.5% hold a bachelor degree or higher (national average is 27.0%); and 7.6% hold professional or graduate degrees (national average is 10.1%); however, 88.4% of the state's adult population has graduated from high school, compared to an 84.1%

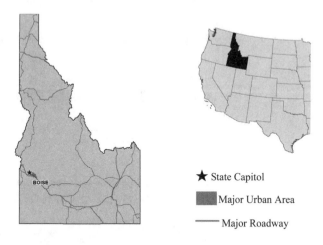

★ State Capitol

▇ Major Urban Area

── Major Roadway

Demographic and Socioeconomic Profile

Demographics and Socioeconomic Figures			
Population and Households	**2000**	**2006**	**2007**
Total Population	1,293,953	1,466,465	1,499,402
Number of Households	469,645	548,555	560,567
Average Household Size	2.7	2.6	2.6
Age and Ethnicity			
Median Age	33.2	34.3	34.3
Population 18 Years of Age and Older	925,822	1,072,150	1,091,585
Population 65 Years of Age and Older	145,945	169,391	174,901
Caucasian Population	1,176,568	1,357,129	1,386,347
African-American Population	5,244	6,842	9,011
Hispanic Population	101,594	138,871	147,427
Asian Population	11,321	15,335	16,810
Foreign-Born Population (%)	5.0	5.6	5.6
Income			
Per Capita Personal Income (USD)	$24,075	$29,948	$31,703
Median Household Income (USD)	$37,572	$42,865	$46,253
Individuals below Poverty Level	11.8%	12.6%	12.1%

Data: U.S. Census, American Community Survey; U.S. Department of Commerce, Bureau of Economic Analysis

national average. In 2006, the state's largest industry in terms of employment was health care and social assistance, followed by manufacturing. The fastest growing industry was administrative, support, waste management, and remediation services, with 8.2% annual growth from 1998 to 2006.

In fiscal year 2005–6, Idaho had total tax revenues of $4.5 billion. The largest share was generated from sales and gross receipts taxes, followed by property taxes. The per capita tax burden in Idaho was $3,070 for 2005–6, some $922 below the national average, and a $137 increase from the 2004–5 per capita tax burden. In terms of business taxes, Idaho ranked forty-first in a 2008 report by Anderson Economic Group. The state's business climate was ranked seventh by Forbes Magazine and twenty-ninth by the Tax Foundation.

Population Projections

Year	2010	2015	2020	2025
Total Population	1,517,291	1,630,045	1,741,333	1,852,627
Median Age	34.8	35.9	37.5	38.6
Population 18 Years of Age and Older	1,117,054	1,202,945	1,292,913	1,385,569
Population 65 Years of Age and Older	181,416	220,113	269,439	320,205

Data: U.S. Census Bureau

Workforce and Industry Profile

Workforce

	2000	2006	2007
Civilian Labor Force	662,958	749,244	748,709
Labor Force Participation Rate	69.7%	68.0%	67.5%
Unemployment Rate	4.6%	3.4%	3.0%
Average Wage Per Job (USD)	$27,701	$34,810	$35,310
Education Attainment (Population 25 Years and Older)	(%)	(%)	(%)
High School Graduate or Higher	84.7	87.3	88.4
Bachelors Degree or Higher	21.7	23.3	24.5
Graduate or Professional Degree	6.8	10.8	7.6

Data: U.S. Census Bureau, American Community Survey; U.S. Department of Commerce, Bureau of Economic Analysis; U.S. Department of Labor, Bureau of Labor Statistics

Industry Overview

	1998	2005	2006
Total Employees	423,615	519,319	546,251
Total Payroll ($1,000)	10,595,285	15,397,889	17,215,691
Total Establishments	35,961	43,346	45,739
Establishments with 1–19 Employees	32,152	38,744	40,789
Establishments with 20–49 Employees	2,562	3,061	3,336
Establishments with 50–249 Employees	1,105	1,349	1,421
Establishments with 250–999 Employees	125	168	172
Establishments with 1,000+ Employees	17	24	21

Data: U.S. Census Bureau, County Business Patterns

Major Industries (Ranked by 2006 Employment; Payroll in $1,000s)				
Industry	1998 Employment	2006 Employment	1998 Payroll	2006 Payroll
Retail Trade	65,665	80,795	1,173,071	1,874,867
Health Care and Social Assistance	50,674	72,261	1,285,725	2,312,786
Manufacturing	66,719	64,212	2,214,164	2,751,219
Accommodation and Food Services	44,106	54,345	389,942	643,933
Construction	35,446	52,804	1,064,026	1,958,258
Admin., Support, Waste Mngt., Remediation Services	25,398	47,835	452,844	1,079,740
Professional, Scientific, Technical Services	22,338	34,258	902,270	1,497,294
Wholesale Trade	23,488	23,809	699,924	975,846
Finance and Insurance	16,285	22,162	531,207	928,345
Other Services (except Public Admin.)	16,899	19,910	249,420	402,990

Data: U.S. Census Bureau, County Business Patterns

Taxes and Business Climate

State and Local Taxes		
Combined Revenues ($1,000)	2004–5	2005–6
Revenue from Property Taxes	1,153,841	1,238,724
Revenue from Sales and Gross Receipts Taxes	1,523,808	1,496,642
Revenue from Individual Income Taxes	1,040,512	1,222,569
Revenue from Corporate Income Taxes	140,585	198,302
Revenue from Other Taxes	323,800	346,369
Total Tax Revenue	4,182,546	4,502,606
Per Capita Taxes		
Property Tax Per Capita	809	845
Sales and Gross Receipts Tax Per Capita	1,069	1,021
Individual Income Tax Per Capita	730	834
Corporate Income Tax Per Capita	99	135
Other Taxes Per Capita	227	236
Total Taxes Per Capita	2,933	3,070

Data: U.S. Census Bureau; Anderson Economic Group, LLC

Business Climate Measures

Anderson Economic Group: 2008 Business Tax Ranking (1 is Best)	41
Forbes Magazine: 2008 Best States for Business Ranking (1 is Best)	7
Tax Foundation: 2009 Business Tax Climate Ranking (1 is Best)	29
2004–5 Employer Firm Births	5,194
2004–5 Employer Firm Terminations	3,629

Data: Anderson Economic Group; Tax Foundation; Forbes Magazine; U.S. Census, Statistics of U.S. Businesses

Voting Behavior and Elected Officials

Voter Registration and Turnout (%)

	1996	2000	2004	2008
Registered Voters Who Voted	70.2	68.9	75.0	76.3
Population Age 18+ Who Voted	57.3	54.2	60.2	60.2

Data: Dave Leip's Atlas of U.S. Presidential Elections

Presidential Election Results (Nationwide Winner Listed First)

2008	Popular Vote (%)	Electoral Votes
Barack Obama (Democrat)	36.0	0
John McCain (Republican)	61.3	4
Other	2.7	0
2004		
George W. Bush (Republican, Incumbent)	68.4	4
John Kerry (Democrat)	30.3	0
Other	1.4	0
2000		
George W. Bush (Republican)	67.2	4
Albert Gore (Democrat)	27.6	0
Ralph Nader (Green)	2.5	0
Other	2.7	0
1996		
William Clinton (Democrat, Incumbent)	33.7	0
Robert Dole (Republican)	52.2	4
H. Ross Perot (Reformist)	12.7	0
Other	1.5	0

Data: Dave Leip's Atlas of U.S. Presidential Elections

Governor and U.S. Congressional Seats				
Governor	Party	Year Term Began	Term	Max. Consecutive Terms
C.L. "Butch" Otter	R	2007	First	2
U.S. Senators	**Party**	**Year Elected**	**Term Expires**	
Michael Crapo	R	1998	2011	
James Risch	R	2008	2015	
U.S. Representatives		**Republican**	**Democrat**	**Other**
		1	1	0

Data: National Governors Association; U.S. Senate, Office of the Clerk; U.S. House of Representatives

Business and Economic Agencies

Agency	Website Address
Boise Metro Chamber of Commerce	www.boisechamber.org
Idaho Department of Commerce and Labor	www.cl.idaho.gov
Idaho Small Business Dev. Center	www.idahosbdc.org
Idaho Secretary of State	www.idsos.state.id.us

Data: Various agency websites

Illinois

Illinois, located in the East North Central region of the United States, has a population of 12.9 million people, making it the fifth most populous state in 2007. The state's population increased by 433,255 people from 2000 to 2007, and is projected to increase to 13.3 million by 2025. This 0.2% projected annual growth rate compares to the projected national average of 0.8%. From 2006 to 2007 the state's population grew by 0.2%. Per capita personal income in Illinois was $40,919 in 2007, up from $38,297 in 2006. For 2007, this was thirteenth highest in the country and $2,355 above the national average. From 2000 to 2007 the per capita income in Illinois grew at a compound annual rate of 3.5%, compared to 3.7% nationally.

In 2006, the state's largest industry in terms of employment was health care and social assistance, followed by manufacturing. The fastest growing industry was educational services with 2.8% annual growth from 1998 to 2006. The state's workforce is generally more educated than other states—85.7% of the state's adult population

★ State Capitol

▨ Major Urban Area

— Major Roadway

Demographic and Socioeconomic Profile

Demographics and Socioeconomic Figures			
Population and Households	**2000**	**2006**	**2007**
Total Population	12,419,293	12,831,970	12,852,548
Number of Households	4,591,779	4,724,252	4,759,579
Average Household Size	2.6	2.7	2.6
Age and Ethnicity			
Median Age	34.7	35.7	35.9
Population 18 Years of Age and Older	9,180,064	9,615,583	9,654,392
Population 65 Years of Age and Older	1,498,929	1,532,373	1,548,083
Caucasian Population	9,123,564	9,074,653	9,057,076
African-American Population	1,864,619	1,898,346	1,884,069
Hispanic Population	1,529,141	1,888,439	1,917,420
Asian Population	423,440	536,992	551,835
Foreign-Born Population (%)	12.3	13.8	13.8
Income			
Per Capita Personal Income (USD)	$32,185	$38,297	$40,919
Median Household Income (USD)	$46,590	$52,006	$54,124
Individuals below Poverty Level	10.7%	12.3%	11.9%

Data: U.S. Census, American Community Survey; U.S. Department of Commerce, Bureau of Economic Analysis

has graduated from high school, compared to an 84.1% national average. Nationally, an average of 27.0% hold a bachelor degree or higher compared to 29.5% in Illinois; and 11.0% hold professional or graduate degrees (national average is 10.1%).

In fiscal year 2005–6, Illinois had total tax revenues of $52.1 billion. The largest share was generated from property taxes, followed by sales and gross receipts taxes. The per capita tax burden in Illinois was $4,064 for 2005–6, some $72 above the national average. In terms of business taxes, the state ranked thirty-fourth in a 2008 analysis by Anderson Economic Group. Forbes Magazine and the Tax Foundation ranked the state's business climate thirty-fifth and twenty-third, respectively.

Population Projections

Year	2010	2015	2020	2025
Total Population	12,916,894	13,097,218	13,236,720	13,340,507
Median Age	36.0	36.3	37.0	37.4
Population 18 Years of Age and Older	9,719,988	9,882,541	9,980,950	10,075,188
Population 65 Years of Age and Older	1,600,863	1,777,487	1,988,764	2,226,431

Data: U.S. Census Bureau

Workforce and Industry Profile

Workforce

	2000	2006	2007
Civilian Labor Force	6,467,692	6,613,346	6,689,636
Labor Force Participation Rate	69.2%	67.4%	68.2%
Unemployment Rate	4.5%	4.5%	5.1%
Average Wage Per Job (USD)	$38,044	$40,910	$43,050
Education Attainment (Population 25 Years and Older)	(%)	(%)	(%)
High School Graduate or Higher	81.4	85.0	85.7
Bachelors Degree or Higher	26.1	28.9	29.5
Graduate or Professional Degree	9.5	8.0	11.0

Data: U.S. Census Bureau, American Community Survey; U.S. Department of Commerce, Bureau of Economic Analysis; U.S. Department of Labor, Bureau of Labor Statistics

Industry Overview

	1998	2005	2006
Total Employees	5,221,782	5,235,866	5,357,466
Total Payroll ($1,000)	175,703,556	217,221,786	231,106,738
Total Establishments	304,533	318,927	321,356
Establishments with 1–19 Employees	259,572	273,249	274,642
Establishments with 20–49 Employees	26,877	27,331	27,925
Establishments with 50–249 Employees	15,634	15,984	16,364
Establishments with 250–999 Employees	2,124	2,022	2,086
Establishments with 1,000+ Employees	326	341	339

Data: U.S. Census Bureau, County Business Patterns

Major Industries (Ranked by 2006 Employment; Payroll in $1,000s)

Industry	1998 Employment	2006 Employment	1998 Payroll	2006 Payroll
Health Care and Social Assistance	612,855	702,964	17,914,037	26,672,803
Manufacturing	883,472	666,711	33,319,088	31,246,293
Retail Trade	632,626	652,262	11,503,179	15,411,589
Admin., Support, Waste Mngt., Remediation Services	407,556	460,768	9,080,901	12,628,969
Accommodation and Food Services	395,322	457,399	4,554,156	6,762,211
Professional, Scientific, Technical Services	311,731	376,748	16,023,793	24,308,041
Finance and Insurance	338,042	352,619	17,736,564	27,363,581
Wholesale Trade	330,787	315,469	15,093,685	18,387,429
Construction	225,301	261,871	10,004,410	14,505,524
Other Services (except Public Admin.)	247,420	260,050	5,247,616	6,995,828

Data: U.S. Census Bureau, County Business Patterns

Taxes and Business Climate

State and Local Taxes

Combined Revenues ($1,000)	2004–5	2005–6
Revenue from Property Taxes	18,690,132	19,555,118
Revenue from Sales and Gross Receipts Taxes	16,693,556	17,892,547
Revenue from Individual Income Taxes	7,936,884	8,635,104
Revenue from Corporate Income Taxes	2,183,126	2,400,323
Revenue from Other Taxes	3,634,797	3,661,242
Total Tax Revenue	49,138,495	52,144,334

Per Capita Taxes

	2004–5	2005–6
Property Tax Per Capita	1,469	1,524
Sales and Gross Receipts Tax Per Capita	1,312	1,394
Individual Income Tax Per Capita	624	673
Corporate Income Tax Per Capita	172	187
Other Taxes Per Capita	286	285
Total Taxes Per Capita	3,863	4,064

Data: U.S. Census Bureau; Anderson Economic Group, LLC

Business Climate Measures

Anderson Economic Group: 2008 Business Tax Ranking (1 is Best)	34
Forbes Magazine: 2008 Best States for Business Ranking (1 is Best)	35
Tax Foundation: 2009 Business Tax Climate Ranking (1 is Best)	23
2004–5 Employer Firm Births	30,156
2004–5 Employer Firm Terminations	27,499

Data: Anderson Economic Group; Tax Foundation; Forbes Magazine; U.S. Census, Statistics of U.S. Businesses

Voting Behavior and Elected Officials

Voter Registration and Turnout (%)

	1996	2000	2004	2008
Registered Voters Who Voted	64.7	66.5	70.3	70.9
Population Age 18+ Who Voted	49.3	51.7	56.0	57.2

Data: Dave Leip's Atlas of U.S. Presidential Elections

Presidential Election Results (Nationwide Winner Listed First)

2008	Popular Vote (%)	Electoral Votes
Barack Obama (Democrat)	61.9	21
John McCain (Republican)	36.8	0
Other	1.3	0
2004		
George W. Bush (Republican, Incumbent)	44.5	0
John Kerry (Democrat)	54.8	21
Other	0.7	0
2000		
George W. Bush (Republican)	42.6	0
Albert Gore (Democrat)	54.6	22
Ralph Nader (Green)	2.2	0
Other	0.6	0
1996		
William Clinton (Democrat, Incumbent)	54.3	22
Robert Dole (Republican)	36.8	0
H. Ross Perot (Reformist)	8.0	0
Other	0.8	0

Data: Dave Leip's Atlas of U.S. Presidential Elections

Governor and U.S. Congressional Seats				
Governor	**Party**	**Year Term Began**	**Term**	**Max. Consecutive Terms**
Pat Quinn	D	2009	First	No limit
U.S. Senators	**Party**	**Year Elected**	**Term Expires**	
Richard Durbin	D	1996	2009	
Roland Burris	D	2009	2015	
U.S. Representatives		**Republican**	**Democrat**	**Other**
		7	11	1

Data: National Governors Association; U.S. Senate, Office of the Clerk; U.S. House of Representatives

Business and Economic Agencies

Agency	Website Address
Illinois State Chamber of Commerce	www.ilchamber.org
Department of Commerce and Economic Opportunity	www.commerce.state.il.us/dceo
Illinois Small Business Dev. Center	www.ilsbdc.biz
Illinois Secretary of State	www.sos.state.il.us

Data: Various agency websites

Indiana

With a population of 6.3 million people, Indiana was the fifteenth most populous state in the United States in 2007. From 2000 to 2007 the state's population increased by 264,804 people, and is projected to increase to 6.7 million by 2025. This 0.3% projected annual growth rate compares to the projected national average of 0.8%. From 2006 to 2007 the state's population grew by 0.5%. The state's 2007 per capita personal income of $33,152 was higher compared to $32,226 in 2006 and the twelfth lowest in the United States, some $5,412 below the national average. Per capita income in Indiana grew at a compound annual rate of 2.9% from 2000 to 2007, compared to 3.7% nationally.

Indiana's largest industry in terms of 2006 employment was health care and social assistance. The fastest growing industry was transportation and warehousing, with 4.2% annual growth from 1998 to 2006. The second fastest growing industry was professional, scientific, and technical services. The state's workforce is generally less educated than other

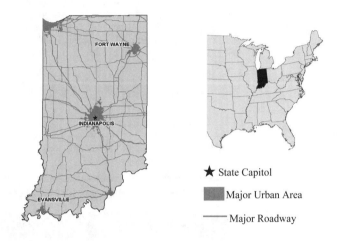

★ State Capitol

▮ Major Urban Area

— Major Roadway

Demographic and Socioeconomic Profile

Demographics and Socioeconomic Figures			
Population and Households	**2000**	**2006**	**2007**
Total Population	6,080,485	6,313,520	6,345,289
Number of Households	2,336,306	2,435,274	2,462,278
Average Household Size	2.5	2.5	2.5
Age and Ethnicity			
Median Age	35.2	36.3	36.5
Population 18 Years of Age and Older	4,507,679	4,733,923	4,758,979
Population 65 Years of Age and Older	752,885	780,992	793,156
Caucasian Population	5,317,334	5,427,561	5,436,898
African-American Population	504,449	551,864	551,215
Hispanic Population	210,538	299,398	312,863
Asian Population	57,193	81,054	83,200
Foreign-Born Population (%)	3.1	4.2	4.2
Income			
Per Capita Personal Income (USD)	$27,132	$32,226	$33,152
Median Household Income (USD)	$41,567	$45,394	$47,448
Individuals below Poverty Level	9.5%	12.7%	12.3%

Data: U.S. Census, American Community Survey; U.S. Department of Commerce, Bureau of Economic Analysis

states—22.1% hold a bachelor degree or higher (national average is 27.0%); and 7.9% hold professional or graduate degrees compared to the national average of 10.1%; however, 85.8% of the state's adult population has graduated from high school, compared to an 84.1% national average.

Indiana's total tax revenue was $23.0 billion for fiscal year 2005–6, up from the 2004–5 total revenue of $21.3 billion. The largest share of tax revenue in 2005–6 was generated from property taxes, followed by sales and gross receipts taxes. On a per capita basis, residents of Indiana paid taxes of $3,635, compared to the national average of $3,992 for 2005–6. In terms of business taxes, the state ranked thirtieth in a 2008 analysis by Anderson Economic Group. Forbes Magazine and the Tax Foundation ranked the state's business climate twenty-fifth and fourteenth, respectively.

Population Projections

Year	2010	2015	2020	2025
Total Population	6,392,139	6,517,631	6,627,008	6,721,322
Median Age	36.5	36.8	37.4	37.5
Population 18 Years of Age and Older	4,795,954	4,903,401	4,992,020	5,055,039
Population 65 Years of Age and Older	811,290	906,361	1,019,707	1,140,690

Data: U.S. Census Bureau

Workforce and Industry Profile

Workforce

	2000	2006	2007
Civilian Labor Force	3,144,379	3,271,496	3,221,054
Labor Force Participation Rate	68.3%	67.5%	66.6%
Unemployment Rate	2.9%	5.0%	4.6%
Average Wage Per Job (USD)	$31,017	$35,190	$36,410
Education Attainment (Population 25 Years and Older)	(%)	(%)	(%)
High School Graduate or Higher	82.1	85.2	85.8
Bachelors Degree or Higher	19.4	21.7	22.1
Graduate or Professional Degree	7.2	7.4	7.9

Data: U.S. Census Bureau, American Community Survey; U.S. Department of Commerce, Bureau of Economic Analysis; U.S. Department of Labor, Bureau of Labor Statistics

Industry Overview

	1998	2005	2006
Total Employees	2,540,866	2,610,899	2,673,010
Total Payroll ($1,000)	71,435,864	88,145,224	92,334,415
Total Establishments	146,197	149,871	151,283
Establishments with 1–19 Employees	123,653	126,655	127,477
Establishments with 20–49 Employees	13,836	14,106	14,482
Establishments with 50–249 Employees	7,559	7,882	8,079
Establishments with 250–999 Employees	987	1,056	1,065
Establishments with 1,000+ Employees	162	172	180

Data: U.S. Census Bureau, County Business Patterns

Major Industries (Ranked by 2006 Employment; Payroll in $1,000s)

Industry	1998 Employment	2006 Employment	1998 Payroll	2006 Payroll
Manufacturing	635,658	557,359	23,729,035	24,933,084
Health Care and Social Assistance	313,865	366,768	8,403,195	13,024,517
Retail Trade	344,444	350,633	5,719,109	7,144,426
Accommodation and Food Services	216,578	254,282	2,066,860	3,096,809
Admin., Support, Waste Mngt., Remediation Services	136,135	176,391	2,782,884	4,435,217
Construction	138,326	146,907	4,770,384	6,383,900
Other Services (except Public Admin.)	124,828	132,781	2,097,725	2,852,146
Wholesale Trade	115,519	118,402	4,082,819	5,368,633
Transportation and Warehousing	81,360	113,377	2,510,293	3,948,600
Professional, Scientific, Technical Services	81,704	112,824	2,789,896	5,352,462

Data: U.S. Census Bureau, County Business Patterns

Taxes and Business Climate

State and Local Taxes		
Combined Revenues ($1,000)	**2004–5**	**2005–6**
Revenue from Property Taxes	7,638,992	8,407,529
Revenue from Sales and Gross Receipts Taxes	7,279,831	7,660,357
Revenue from Individual Income Taxes	4,811,592	4,994,800
Revenue from Corporate Income Taxes	824,803	1,043,875
Revenue from Other Taxes	781,859	843,820
Total Tax Revenue	21,337,077	22,950,381
Per Capita Taxes		
Property Tax Per Capita	1,221	1,332
Sales and Gross Receipts Tax Per Capita	1,163	1,213
Individual Income Tax Per Capita	769	791
Corporate Income Tax Per Capita	132	165
Other Taxes Per Capita	125	134
Total Taxes Per Capita	3,410	3,635

Data: U.S. Census Bureau; Anderson Economic Group, LLC

Business Climate Measures

Anderson Economic Group: 2008 Business Tax Ranking (1 is Best)	30
Forbes Magazine: 2008 Best States for Business Ranking (1 is Best)	25
Tax Foundation: 2009 Business Tax Climate Ranking (1 is Best)	14
2004–5 Employer Firm Births	12,979
2004–5 Employer Firm Terminations	12,793

Data: Anderson Economic Group; Tax Foundation; Forbes Magazine; U.S. Census, Statistics of U.S. Businesses

Voting Behavior and Elected Officials

Voter Registration and Turnout (%)

	1996	2000	2004	2008
Registered Voters Who Voted	61.2	55.1	57.4	61.0
Population Age 18+ Who Voted	48.8	48.8	53.7	57.9

Data: Dave Leip's Atlas of U.S. Presidential Elections

Presidential Election Results (Nationwide Winner Listed First)

2008	Popular Vote (%)	Electoral Votes
Barack Obama (Democrat)	49.9	11
John McCain (Republican)	48.9	0
Other	1.2	0
2004		
George W. Bush (Republican, Incumbent)	59.9	11
John Kerry (Democrat)	39.3	0
Other	0.8	0
2000		
George W. Bush (Republican)	56.7	12
Albert Gore (Democrat)	41.0	0
Ralph Nader (Green)	.8	0
Other	1.5	0
1996		
William Clinton (Democrat, Incumbent)	41.6	0
Robert Dole (Republican)	47.1	12
H. Ross Perot (Reformist)	10.5	0
Other	0.8	0

Data: Dave Leip's Atlas of U.S. Presidential Elections

Governor and U.S. Congressional Seats

Governor	Party	Year Term Began	Term	Max. Consecutive Terms
Mitch Daniels	R	2009	Second	2

U.S. Senators	Party	Year Elected	Term Expires
Evan Bayh	D	1998	2011
Richard G. Lugar	R	1976	2013

U.S. Representatives	Republican	Democrat	Other
	4	5	0

Data: National Governors Association; U.S. Senate, Office of the Clerk; U.S. House of Representatives

Business and Economic Agencies

Agency	Website Address
Indiana Chamber of Commerce	www.indianachamber.com
Indiana Economic Development Corporation	www.in.gov/iedc
Indiana Small Business Dev. Center	www.isbdc.org
Indiana Secretary of State	www.state.in.us/sos/business

Data: Various agency websites

Iowa

Iowa is located in the West North Central region of the United States. Iowa has a population of 3.0 million people, making it the twenty-first least populous state in 2007. The state's population increased by 61,723 people from 2000 to 2007, and is projected to increase only slightly by 2025. This is below the national average of the 0.8% projected growth. From 2006 to 2007 the state's population grew by 0.2%. Per capita personal income in Iowa was $34,796 in 2007, up from $33,017 in 2006. For 2007, this was $3,768 below the national average and the twentieth lowest in the country. The state's per capita income grew at a compound annual rate of 3.9% from 2000 to 2007, compared to 3.7% nationally.

The state's workforce generally has less education than other states—24.3% hold a bachelor degree or higher (national average is 27.0%); and 7.5% hold professional or graduate degrees (national average is 10.1%); however, 89.6% of the state's adult population has graduated from high school, compared to an 84.1% national average.

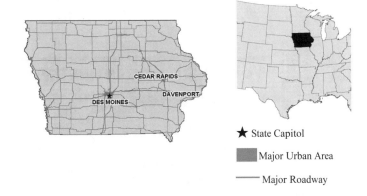

★ State Capitol

▨ Major Urban Area

— Major Roadway

Demographic and Socioeconomic Profile

Demographics and Socioeconomic Figures			
Population and Households	**2000**	**2006**	**2007**
Total Population	2,926,324	2,982,085	2,988,047
Number of Households	1,149,276	1,208,765	1,214,353
Average Household Size	2.5	2.4	2.4
Age and Ethnicity			
Median Age	36.6	37.8	38.0
Population 18 Years of Age and Older	2,193,990	2,267,565	2,276,363
Population 65 Years of Age and Older	436,377	435,373	438,600
Caucasian Population	2,749,737	2,772,535	2,766,081
African-American Population	59,758	67,297	70,018
Hispanic Population	81,501	112,987	119,716
Asian Population	35,023	45,647	47,849
Foreign-Born Population (%)	3.1	3.8	3.9
Income			
Per Capita Personal Income (USD)	$26,554	$33,017	$34,796
Median Household Income (USD)	$39,469	$44,491	$47,292
Individuals below Poverty Level	9.1%	11.0%	11.0%

Data: U.S. Census, American Community Survey; U.S. Department of Commerce, Bureau of Economic Analysis

In 2006, the state's largest industry in terms of employment was health care and social assistance, followed by retail trade. The fastest growing industry was transportation and warehousing, with 4.4% annual growth from 1998 to 2006.

In fiscal year 2005–6, Iowa had total tax revenues of $10.3 billion. The largest share was generated from property taxes, followed by sales and gross receipts taxes. The per capita tax burden in Iowa was $3,439 for 2005–6, some $553 below the national average, and a $20 increase from the 2004–5 per capita tax burden. In terms of business taxes, Iowa ranked nineteenth in a 2008 report by Anderson Economic Group. The state's business climate was ranked twenty-second by Forbes Magazine and forty-fourth by the Tax Foundation.

Population Projections

Year	2010	2015	2020	2025
Total Population	3,009,907	3,026,380	3,020,496	2,993,222
Median Age	38.3	38.9	40.1	41.3
Population 18 Years of Age and Older	2,298,851	2,319,340	2,323,127	2,311,474
Population 65 Years of Age and Older	449,887	494,565	556,540	619,227

Data: U.S. Census Bureau

Workforce and Industry Profile

Workforce

	2000	2006	2007
Civilian Labor Force	1,601,920	1,664,339	1,664,431
Labor Force Participation Rate	71.7%	72.3%	72.1%
Unemployment Rate	2.8%	3.7%	3.7%
Average Wage Per Job (USD)	$27,929	$33,250	$34,650
Education Attainment (Population 25 Years and Older)	**(%)**	**(%)**	**(%)**
High School Graduate or Higher	86.1	88.9	89.6
Bachelors Degree or Higher	21.2	24.0	24.3
Graduate or Professional Degree	6.5	9.8	7.5

Data: U.S. Census Bureau, American Community Survey; U.S. Department of Commerce, Bureau of Economic Analysis; U.S. Department of Labor, Bureau of Labor Statistics

Industry Overview

	1998	2005	2006
Total Employees	1,213,285	1,261,108	1,295,258
Total Payroll ($1,000)	30,409,574	39,420,961	42,096,840
Total Establishments	80,838	82,087	82,698
Establishments with 1–19 Employees	70,187	70,958	71,261
Establishments with 20–49 Employees	6,524	6,877	7,077
Establishments with 50–249 Employees	3,598	3,688	3,765
Establishments with 250–999 Employees	462	487	514
Establishments with 1,000+ Employees	67	77	81

Data: U.S. Census Bureau, County Business Patterns

Major Industries (Ranked by 2006 Employment; Payroll in $1,000s)				
Industry	1998 Employment	2006 Employment	1998 Payroll	2006 Payroll
Manufacturing	245,282	227,492	8,193,004	9,581,667
Health Care and Social Assistance	172,793	194,580	4,111,821	6,571,371
Retail Trade	177,723	181,376	2,846,480	3,591,201
Accommodation and Food Services	103,641	111,777	907,513	1,189,408
Finance and Insurance	73,746	93,013	2,715,795	4,698,253
Admin., Support, Waste Mngt., Remediation Services	58,306	72,002	993,597	1,548,516
Construction	58,557	64,574	1,947,744	2,718,462
Wholesale Trade	64,101	64,474	1,991,922	2,686,421
Other Services (except Public Admin.)	52,875	55,132	790,560	1,064,685
Transportation and Warehousing	37,379	52,647	1,050,574	1,868,589

Data: U.S. Census Bureau, County Business Patterns

Taxes and Business Climate

State and Local Taxes		
Combined Revenues ($1,000)	2004–5	2005–6
Revenue from Property Taxes	3,302,265	3,391,938
Revenue from Sales and Gross Receipts Taxes	3,155,247	3,342,043
Revenue from Individual Income Taxes	2,312,898	2,482,891
Revenue from Corporate Income Taxes	186,469	284,976
Revenue from Other Taxes	747,982	754,608
Total Tax Revenue	9,704,861	10,256,456
Per Capita Taxes		
Property Tax Per Capita	1,117	1,137
Sales and Gross Receipts Tax Per Capita	1,068	1,121
Individual Income Tax Per Capita	783	833
Corporate Income Tax Per Capita	63	96
Other Taxes Per Capita	253	253
Total Taxes Per Capita	3,284	3,439

Data: U.S. Census Bureau; Anderson Economic Group, LLC

Business Climate Measures

Anderson Economic Group: 2008 Business Tax Ranking (1 is Best)	19
Forbes Magazine: 2008 Best States for Business Ranking (1 is Best)	22
Tax Foundation: 2009 Business Tax Climate Ranking (1 is Best)	44
2004–5 Employer Firm Births	6,564
2004–5 Employer Firm Terminations	6,200

Data: Anderson Economic Group; Tax Foundation; Forbes Magazine; U.S. Census, Statistics of U.S. Businesses

Voting Behavior and Elected Officials

Voter Registration and Turnout (%)

	1996	2000	2004	2008
Registered Voters Who Voted	69.5	71.4	75.9	NaN
Population Age 18+ Who Voted	57.7	60.0	66.9	67.5

Data: Dave Leip's Atlas of U.S. Presidential Elections

Presidential Election Results (Nationwide Winner Listed First)

2008	Popular Vote (%)	Electoral Votes
Barack Obama (Democrat)	53.9	7
John McCain (Republican)	44.4	0
Other	1.7	0
2004		
George W. Bush (Republican, Incumbent)	49.9	7
John Kerry (Democrat)	49.2	0
Other	0.9	0
2000		
George W. Bush (Republican)	48.2	0
Albert Gore (Democrat)	48.5	7
Ralph Nader (Green)	2.2	0
Other	1.0	0
1996		
William Clinton (Democrat, Incumbent)	50.3	7
Robert Dole (Republican)	39.9	0
H. Ross Perot (Reformist)	8.5	0
Other	1.3	0

Data: Dave Leip's Atlas of U.S. Presidential Elections

Governor and U.S. Congressional Seats

Governor	Party	Year Term Began	Term	Max. Consecutive Terms
Chet Culver	D	2007	First	No limit
U.S. Senators	**Party**	**Year Elected**	**Term Expires**	
Chuck Grassley	R	1980	2011	
Tom Harkin	D	1984	2015	
U.S. Representatives		**Republican**	**Democrat**	**Other**
		2	3	0

Data: National Governors Association; U.S. Senate, Office of the Clerk; U.S. House of Representatives

Business and Economic Agencies

Agency	Website Address
Iowa Chamber Alliance	www.iowachamberalliance.org
Iowa Department of Economic Development	www.iowalifechanging.com
Iowa Small Business Dev. Center	www.iowasbdc.org
Iowa Secretary of State	www.sos.state.ia.us

Data: Various agency websites

Kansas

Kansas, located in the West North Central region of the United States, has a population of 2.8 million people, making it the eighteenth least populous state in 2007. The state's population increased by 87,579 people from 2000 to 2007, and is projected to increase to 2.9 million by 2025. This 0.3% projected annual growth rate compares to the projected national average of 0.8%. From 2006 to 2007 the state's population grew by 0.4%. Per capita personal income in Kansas was $36,483 in 2007, up from $34,744 in 2006. For 2007, this was twenty-eighth lowest in the country and $2,081 below the national average. From 2000 to 2007 the per capita income in Kansas grew at a compound annual rate of 4.0%, compared to 3.7% nationally.

In 2006, the state's largest industry in terms of employment was health care and social assistance, followed by retail trade. The fastest growing industry was mining with 4.3% annual growth from 1998 to 2006. The state's workforce is generally more educated than other states— 89.1% of the state's adult population has graduated

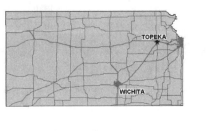

★ State Capitol

▨ Major Urban Area

— Major Roadway

Demographic and Socioeconomic Profile

Demographics and Socioeconomic Figures			
Population and Households	**2000**	**2006**	**2007**
Total Population	2,688,418	2,764,075	2,775,997
Number of Households	1,037,891	1,088,288	1,088,835
Average Household Size	2.5	2.5	2.5
Age and Ethnicity			
Median Age	35.2	36.3	36.3
Population 18 Years of Age and Older	1,977,198	2,069,408	2,079,051
Population 65 Years of Age and Older	355,681	355,664	358,875
Caucasian Population	2,312,119	2,361,047	2,374,824
African-American Population	150,584	153,560	159,268
Hispanic Population	186,299	236,351	242,787
Asian Population	44,772	60,646	59,948
Foreign-Born Population (%)	5.0	6.3	6.0
Income			
Per Capita Personal Income (USD)	$27,694	$34,744	$36,483
Median Household Income (USD)	$40,624	$45,478	$47,451
Individuals below Poverty Level	9.9%	12.4%	11.2%

Data: U.S. Census, American Community Survey; U.S. Department of Commerce, Bureau of Economic Analysis

from high school, compared to an 84.1% national average. Nationally, an average of 27.0% hold a bachelor degree or higher compared to 28.8% in Kansas; although 9.8% hold professional or graduate degrees (national average is 10.1%).

In fiscal year 2005–6, Kansas had total tax revenues of $10.5 billion. The largest share was generated from sales and gross receipts taxes, followed by property taxes. The per capita tax burden in Kansas was $3,781 for 2005–6, some $211 below the national average. In terms of business taxes, the state ranked thirty-third in a 2008 analysis by Anderson Economic Group. Forbes Magazine and the Tax Foundation ranked the state's business climate twenty-first and thirty-first, respectively.

Population Projections

Year	2010	2015	2020	2025
Total Population	2,805,470	2,852,690	2,890,566	2,919,002
Median Age	36.4	36.9	37.8	38.5
Population 18 Years of Age and Older	2,106,474	2,144,722	2,176,667	2,205,455
Population 65 Years of Age and Older	375,315	419,748	479,919	544,756

Data: U.S. Census Bureau

Workforce and Industry Profile

Workforce

	2000	2006	2007
Civilian Labor Force	1,405,104	1,466,004	1,485,237
Labor Force Participation Rate	70.2%	70.8%	70.7%
Unemployment Rate	3.8%	4.5%	4.1%
Average Wage Per Job (USD)	$29,360	$34,960	$36,300
Education Attainment (Population 25 Years and Older)	(%)	(%)	(%)
High School Graduate or Higher	86.0	88.5	89.1
Bachelors Degree or Higher	25.8	28.6	28.8
Graduate or Professional Degree	8.7	8.2	9.8

Data: U.S. Census Bureau, American Community Survey; U.S. Department of Commerce, Bureau of Economic Analysis; U.S. Department of Labor, Bureau of Labor Statistics

Industry Overview

	1998	2005	2006
Total Employees	1,081,941	1,116,216	1,142,680
Total Payroll ($1,000)	28,747,577	36,646,065	39,251,387
Total Establishments	74,019	76,173	76,446
Establishments with 1–19 Employees	64,030	65,796	65,764
Establishments with 20–49 Employees	6,304	6,512	6,637
Establishments with 50–249 Employees	3,263	3,409	3,562
Establishments with 250–999 Employees	373	407	434
Establishments with 1,000+ Employees	49	49	49

Data: U.S. Census Bureau, County Business Patterns

Major Industries (Ranked by 2006 Employment; Payroll in $1,000s)				
Industry	1998 Employment	2006 Employment	1998 Payroll	2006 Payroll
Manufacturing	196,519	176,444	6,666,326	7,621,873
Health Care and Social Assistance	154,002	174,519	3,801,133	5,814,218
Retail Trade	149,270	150,783	2,476,930	3,126,495
Accommodation and Food Services	90,431	106,234	842,346	1,185,280
Admin., Support, Waste Mngt., Remediation Services	54,086	67,478	1,076,557	1,800,846
Construction	60,896	67,107	1,947,778	2,700,351
Finance and Insurance	52,839	59,286	1,875,213	2,928,931
Professional, Scientific, Technical Services	49,417	57,742	1,762,448	2,655,690
Wholesale Trade	63,953	57,057	2,370,432	2,592,211
Other Services (except Public Admin.)	51,825	52,568	870,742	1,055,932

Data: U.S. Census Bureau, County Business Patterns

Taxes and Business Climate

State and Local Taxes		
Combined Revenues ($1,000)	2004–5	2005–6
Revenue from Property Taxes	3,090,403	3,273,931
Revenue from Sales and Gross Receipts Taxes	3,470,022	3,817,482
Revenue from Individual Income Taxes	2,050,562	2,402,083
Revenue from Corporate Income Taxes	248,135	381,273
Revenue from Other Taxes	526,374	577,096
Total Tax Revenue	9,385,496	10,451,865
Per Capita Taxes		
Property Tax Per Capita	1,127	1,184
Sales and Gross Receipts Tax Per Capita	1,266	1,381
Individual Income Tax Per Capita	748	869
Corporate Income Tax Per Capita	91	138
Other Taxes Per Capita	192	209
Total Taxes Per Capita	3,423	3,781

Data: U.S. Census Bureau; Anderson Economic Group, LLC

Business Climate Measures

Anderson Economic Group: 2008 Business Tax Ranking (1 is Best)	33
Forbes Magazine: 2008 Best States for Business Ranking (1 is Best)	21
Tax Foundation: 2009 Business Tax Climate Ranking (1 is Best)	31
2004–5 Employer Firm Births	6,753
2004–5 Employer Firm Terminations	6,297

Data: Anderson Economic Group; Tax Foundation; Forbes Magazine; U.S. Census, Statistics of U.S. Businesses

Voting Behavior and Elected Officials

Voter Registration and Turnout (%)

	1996	2000	2004	2008
Registered Voters Who Voted	74.6	66.0	70.1	NaN
Population Age 18+ Who Voted	56.6	54.2	58.6	59.6

Data: Dave Leip's Atlas of U.S. Presidential Elections

Presidential Election Results (Nationwide Winner Listed First)

2008	Popular Vote (%)	Electoral Votes
Barack Obama (Democrat)	41.6	0
John McCain (Republican)	56.5	6
Other	1.9	0
2004		
George W. Bush (Republican, Incumbent)	62.0	6
John Kerry (Democrat)	36.6	0
Other	1.4	0
2000		
George W. Bush (Republican)	58.0	6
Albert Gore (Democrat)	37.2	0
Ralph Nader (Green)	3.4	0
Other	1.4	0
1996		
William Clinton (Democrat, Incumbent)	36.1	0
Robert Dole (Republican)	54.3	6
H. Ross Perot (Reformist)	8.6	0
Other	1.0	0

Data: Dave Leip's Atlas of U.S. Presidential Elections

Governor and U.S. Congressional Seats				
Governor	Party	Year Term Began	Term	Max. Consecutive Terms
Kathleen Sebelius	D	2007	Second	2
U.S. Senators	**Party**	**Year Elected**	**Term Expires**	
Sam Brownback	R	1996	2011	
Pat Roberts	R	1996	2015	
U.S. Representatives		**Republican**	**Democrat**	**Other**
		3	1	0

Data: National Governors Association; U.S. Senate, Office of the Clerk; U.S. House of Representatives

Business and Economic Agencies

Agency	Website Address
Kansas Chamber of Commerce and Industry	www.kansaschamber.org
Kansas Department of Commerce	www.kansascommerce.com
Kansas Small Business Dev. Center	www.fhsu.edu/ksbdc
Kansas Secretary of State, Business Services	www.kssos.org/business/business.html

Data: Various agency websites

Kentucky

With a population of 4.2 million people, Kentucky was the twenty-sixth most populous state in the United States in 2007. From 2000 to 2007 the state's population increased by 199,705 people, and is projected to increase to 4.5 million by 2025. This 0.3% projected annual growth rate compares to the projected national average of 0.8%. From 2006 to 2007 the state's population grew by 0.8%. The state's 2007 per capita personal income of $30,787 was higher compared to $29,719 in 2006 and the sixth lowest in the United States, some $7,777 below the national average. Per capita income in Kentucky grew at a compound annual rate of 3.4% from 2000 to 2007, compared to 3.7% nationally.

Kentucky's largest industry in terms of 2006 employment was health care and social assistance. The fastest growing industry was transportation and warehousing, with 3.7% annual growth from 1998 to 2006. The state's workforce is generally less educated than other states—80.1% of the state's adult population has graduated from high school,

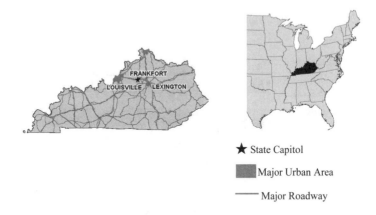

★ State Capitol

▨ Major Urban Area

── Major Roadway

Demographic and Socioeconomic Profile

Demographics and Socioeconomic Figures			
Population and Households	**2000**	**2006**	**2007**
Total Population	4,041,769	4,206,074	4,241,474
Number of Households	1,590,647	1,651,911	1,655,767
Average Household Size	2.5	2.5	2.5
Age and Ethnicity			
Median Age	35.9	37.3	37.4
Population 18 Years of Age and Older	3,047,928	3,205,733	3,236,045
Population 65 Years of Age and Older	503,668	535,303	546,014
Caucasian Population	3,639,168	3,762,571	3,781,361
African-American Population	293,915	310,146	322,149
Hispanic Population	56,414	83,015	89,771
Asian Population	28,994	38,835	39,749
Foreign-Born Population (%)	2.0	2.7	2.5
Income			
Per Capita Personal Income (USD)	$24,412	$29,719	$30,787
Median Household Income (USD)	$33,672	$39,372	$40,267
Individuals below Poverty Level	15.8%	17.0%	17.3%

Data: U.S. Census, American Community Survey; U.S. Department of Commerce, Bureau of Economic Analysis

compared to an 84.1% national average; 20.0% hold a bachelor degree or higher (national average is 27.0%); and 8.0% hold professional or graduate degrees compared to the national average of 10.1%.

Kentucky's total tax revenue was $13.6 billion for fiscal year 2005–6, up from the 2004–5 total revenue of $12.3 billion. The largest share of tax revenue in 2005–6 was generated from sales and gross receipts taxes, followed by individual income taxes. On a per capita basis, residents of Kentucky paid taxes of $3,224, compared to the national average of $3,992 for 2005–6. In terms of business taxes, the state ranked twenty-fifth in a 2008 analysis by Anderson Economic Group. Forbes Magazine and the Tax Foundation ranked the state's business climate forty-fourth and thirty-fourth, respectively.

Population Projections

Year	2010	2015	2020	2025
Total Population	4,265,117	4,351,188	4,424,431	4,489,662
Median Age	38.0	38.6	39.4	39.8
Population 18 Years of Age and Older	3,262,810	3,344,209	3,417,155	3,480,547
Population 65 Years of Age and Older	557,471	637,351	729,741	826,659

Data: U.S. Census Bureau

Workforce and Industry Profile

Workforce

	2000	2006	2007
Civilian Labor Force	1,949,013	2,038,971	2,036,459
Labor Force Participation Rate	63.1%	62.6%	62.3%
Unemployment Rate	4.2%	5.7%	5.5%
Average Wage Per Job (USD)	$28,801	$33,490	$34,950
Education Attainment (Population 25 Years and Older)	**(%)**	**(%)**	**(%)**
High School Graduate or Higher	74.1	79.6	80.1
Bachelors Degree or Higher	17.1	20.0	20.0
Graduate or Professional Degree	6.9	6.8	8.0

Data: U.S. Census Bureau, American Community Survey; U.S. Department of Commerce, Bureau of Economic Analysis; U.S. Department of Labor, Bureau of Labor Statistics

Industry Overview

	1998	2005	2006
Total Employees	1,443,015	1,514,199	1,552,012
Total Payroll ($1,000)	36,889,001	47,983,162	50,224,838
Total Establishments	89,593	92,176	92,829
Establishments with 1–19 Employees	76,564	78,359	78,623
Establishments with 20–49 Employees	8,100	8,550	8,806
Establishments with 50–249 Employees	4,227	4,533	4,656
Establishments with 250–999 Employees	638	664	668
Establishments with 1,000+ Employees	64	70	76

Data: U.S. Census Bureau, County Business Patterns

Major Industries (Ranked by 2006 Employment; Payroll in $1,000s)				
Industry	1998 Employment	2006 Employment	1998 Payroll	2006 Payroll
Manufacturing	290,665	256,670	9,829,745	10,842,448
Health Care and Social Assistance	194,305	231,177	5,052,060	8,103,816
Retail Trade	221,580	227,872	3,385,861	4,528,686
Accommodation and Food Services	127,561	150,307	1,245,296	1,760,904
Admin., Support, Waste Mngt., Remediation Services	70,020	91,667	1,103,006	1,906,014
Construction	77,191	85,789	2,263,487	3,088,318
Transportation and Warehousing	60,183	80,529	2,054,206	3,377,087
Other Services (except Public Admin.)	62,968	69,883	1,042,453	1,457,163
Wholesale Trade	69,862	69,149	2,214,967	2,891,433
Finance and Insurance	61,079	67,595	1,989,927	3,004,598

Data: U.S. Census Bureau, County Business Patterns

Taxes and Business Climate

State and Local Taxes		
Combined Revenues ($1,000)	2004–5	2005–6
Revenue from Property Taxes	2,246,867	2,420,696
Revenue from Sales and Gross Receipts Taxes	4,649,379	5,081,107
Revenue from Individual Income Taxes	3,792,231	3,921,908
Revenue from Corporate Income Taxes	478,505	1,113,124
Revenue from Other Taxes	1,094,830	1,021,617
Total Tax Revenue	12,261,812	13,558,452
Per Capita Taxes		
Property Tax Per Capita	539	576
Sales and Gross Receipts Tax Per Capita	1,115	1,208
Individual Income Tax Per Capita	909	932
Corporate Income Tax Per Capita	115	265
Other Taxes Per Capita	262	243
Total Taxes Per Capita	2,940	3,224

Data: U.S. Census Bureau; Anderson Economic Group, LLC

Business Climate Measures

Anderson Economic Group: 2008 Business Tax Ranking (1 is Best)	25
Forbes Magazine: 2008 Best States for Business Ranking (1 is Best)	44
Tax Foundation: 2009 Business Tax Climate Ranking (1 is Best)	34
2004–5 Employer Firm Births	8,328
2004–5 Employer Firm Terminations	7,751

Data: Anderson Economic Group; Tax Foundation; Forbes Magazine; U.S. Census, Statistics of U.S. Businesses

Voting Behavior and Elected Officials

Voter Registration and Turnout (%)

	1996	2000	2004	2008
Registered Voters Who Voted	58.1	60.4	64.3	62.9
Population Age 18+ Who Voted	47.4	50.7	57.5	56.5

Data: Dave Leip's Atlas of U.S. Presidential Elections

Presidential Election Results (Nationwide Winner Listed First)

2008	Popular Vote (%)	Electoral Votes
Barack Obama (Democrat)	41.2	0
John McCain (Republican)	57.4	8
Other	1.5	0
2004		
George W. Bush (Republican, Incumbent)	59.6	8
John Kerry (Democrat)	39.7	0
Other	0.8	0
2000		
George W. Bush (Republican)	56.5	8
Albert Gore (Democrat)	41.4	0
Ralph Nader (Green)	1.5	0
Other	0.6	0
1996		
William Clinton (Democrat, Incumbent)	45.8	8
Robert Dole (Republican)	44.9	0
H. Ross Perot (Reformist)	8.7	0
Other	0.6	0

Data: Dave Leip's Atlas of U.S. Presidential Elections

Governor and U.S. Congressional Seats				
Governor	**Party**	**Year Term Began**	**Term**	**Max. Consecutive Terms**
Steven Beshear	D	2007	First	2
U.S. Senators	**Party**	**Year Elected**	**Term Expires**	
Mitch McConnell	R	1984	2015	
Jim Bunning	R	1998	2011	
U.S. Representatives		**Republican**	**Democrat**	**Other**
		4	2	0

Data: National Governors Association; U.S. Senate, Office of the Clerk; U.S. House of Representatives

Business and Economic Agencies

Agency	Website Address
Kentucky Chamber of Commerce	www.kychamber.com
Kentucky Cabinet for Economic Development	www.thinkkentucky.com
Kentucky Small Business Dev. Center	www.ksbdc.org
Kentucky Secretary of State, Business Services	www.sos.ky.gov/business

Data: Various agency websites

Louisiana

Louisiana is located in the West South Central region of the United States. Louisiana has a population of 4.3 million people, making it the twenty-fifth most populous state in 2007. The state's population decreased by 175,772 people from 2000 to 2007. This is in-part due to those displaced after Hurricanes Katrina and Rita in 2005. However, Louisiana's population is projected to increase to 4.8 million by 2025. This 0.6% projected annual growth rate is only slightly below the national average of 0.8%. From 2006 to 2007 the state's population grew by 0.1%. Per capita personal income in Louisiana was $35,770 in 2007, up from $31,369 in 2006. For 2007, this was $2,794 below the national average and the twenty-fourth lowest in the country. The state's per capita income grew at a compound annual rate of 6.5% from 2000 to 2007, compared to 3.7% nationally.

The state's workforce generally has less education than other states—79.9% of the state's adult population has graduated from high school, compared to an

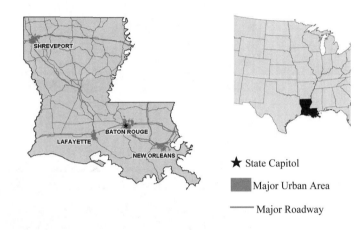

★ State Capitol

▨ Major Urban Area

— Major Roadway

Demographic and Socioeconomic Profile

Demographics and Socioeconomic Figures			
Population and Households	**2000**	**2006**	**2007**
Total Population	4,468,976	4,287,768	4,293,204
Number of Households	1,656,053	1,564,978	1,597,111
Average Household Size	2.6	2.7	2.6
Age and Ethnicity			
Median Age	34.0	35.6	35.7
Population 18 Years of Age and Older	3,250,523	3,198,771	3,214,672
Population 65 Years of Age and Older	518,097	522,874	522,181
Caucasian Population	2,855,964	2,760,233	2,756,277
African-American Population	1,444,566	1,356,981	1,357,893
Hispanic Population	107,854	123,281	134,085
Asian Population	55,492	57,084	59,825
Foreign-Born Population (%)	2.6	2.9	3.3
Income			
Per Capita Personal Income (USD)	$23,078	$31,369	$35,770
Median Household Income (USD)	$32,566	$39,337	$40,926
Individuals below Poverty Level	19.6%	19.0%	18.6%

Data: U.S. Census, American Community Survey; U.S. Department of Commerce, Bureau of Economic Analysis

84.1% national average; 20.4% hold a bachelor degree or higher (national average is 27.0%); and 6.6% hold professional or graduate degrees (national average is 10.1%). In 2006, the state's largest industry in terms of employment was health care and social assistance, followed by retail trade. The fastest growing industry was administrative, support, waste management, and remediation services, with 2.6% annual growth from 1998 to 2006.

In fiscal year 2005–6, Louisiana had total tax revenues of $15.7 billion. The largest share was generated from sales and gross receipts taxes, followed by individual income taxes. The per capita tax burden in Louisiana was $3,667 for 2005–6, some $325 below the national average, and a $486 increase from the 2004–5 per capita tax burden. In terms of business taxes, Louisiana ranked sixth in a 2008 report by Anderson Economic Group. The state's business climate was ranked forty-ninth by Forbes Magazine and thirty-third by the Tax Foundation.

Population Projections

Year	2010	2015	2020	2025
Total Population	4,612,679	4,673,721	4,719,160	4,762,398
Median Age	35.7	36.4	37.5	38.3
Population 18 Years of Age and Older	3,441,177	3,497,533	3,546,384	3,609,162
Population 65 Years of Age and Older	582,340	663,788	763,468	868,502

Data: U.S. Census Bureau

Workforce and Industry Profile

Workforce

	2000	2006	2007
Civilian Labor Force	2,031,292	1,990,120	2,025,777
Labor Force Participation Rate	61.7%	61.8%	61.5%
Unemployment Rate	5.0%	4.0%	3.8%
Average Wage Per Job (USD)	$27,889	$32,900	$34,060
Education Attainment (Population 25 Years and Older)	**(%)**	**(%)**	**(%)**
High School Graduate or Higher	74.8	79.4	79.9
Bachelors Degree or Higher	18.7	20.3	20.4
Graduate or Professional Degree	6.5	8.9	6.6

Data: U.S. Census Bureau, American Community Survey; U.S. Department of Commerce, Bureau of Economic Analysis; U.S. Department of Labor, Bureau of Labor Statistics

Industry Overview

	1998	2005	2006
Total Employees	1,577,220	1,617,507	1,593,033
Total Payroll ($1,000)	40,802,387	50,657,624	55,518,401
Total Establishments	100,667	102,790	101,802
Establishments with 1–19 Employees	85,803	87,638	86,838
Establishments with 20–49 Employees	9,421	9,535	9,305
Establishments with 50–249 Employees	4,775	4,986	5,029
Establishments with 250–999 Employees	580	537	538
Establishments with 1,000+ Employees	88	94	92

Data: U.S. Census Bureau, County Business Patterns

Major Industries (Ranked by 2006 Employment; Payroll in $1,000s)				
Industry	1998 Employment	2006 Employment	1998 Payroll	2006 Payroll
Health Care and Social Assistance	234,869	252,970	5,910,937	8,334,745
Retail Trade	226,586	230,212	3,610,877	5,113,606
Accommodation and Food Services	157,120	165,998	1,724,134	2,266,015
Manufacturing	171,549	141,459	6,373,959	7,084,902
Construction	124,838	132,693	3,622,058	5,334,565
Admin., Support, Waste Mngt., Remediation Services	90,251	110,565	1,688,891	2,901,170
Professional, Scientific, Technical Services	74,826	85,586	2,580,019	4,042,131
Other Services (except Public Admin.)	78,090	72,890	1,330,511	1,615,737
Wholesale Trade	79,877	72,015	2,592,307	3,311,837
Finance and Insurance	68,110	63,751	2,391,798	2,967,725

Data: U.S. Census Bureau, County Business Patterns

Taxes and Business Climate

State and Local Taxes		
Combined Revenues ($1,000)	2004–5	2005–6
Revenue from Property Taxes	2,429,386	2,469,740
Revenue from Sales and Gross Receipts Taxes	7,676,704	8,766,178
Revenue from Individual Income Taxes	2,392,727	2,501,120
Revenue from Corporate Income Taxes	352,136	506,174
Revenue from Other Taxes	1,451,042	1,480,753
Total Tax Revenue	14,301,995	15,723,965
Per Capita Taxes		
Property Tax Per Capita	540	576
Sales and Gross Receipts Tax Per Capita	1,708	2,044
Individual Income Tax Per Capita	532	583
Corporate Income Tax Per Capita	78	118
Other Taxes Per Capita	323	345
Total Taxes Per Capita	3,181	3,667

Data: U.S. Census Bureau; Anderson Economic Group, LLC

Business Climate Measures

Anderson Economic Group: 2008 Business Tax Ranking (1 is Best)	6
Forbes Magazine: 2008 Best States for Business Ranking (1 is Best)	49
Tax Foundation: 2009 Business Tax Climate Ranking (1 is Best)	33
2004–5 Employer Firm Births	9,193
2004–5 Employer Firm Terminations	9,111

Data: Anderson Economic Group; Tax Foundation; Forbes Magazine; U.S. Census, Statistics of U.S. Businesses

Voting Behavior and Elected Officials

Voter Registration and Turnout (%)

	1996	2000	2004	2008
Registered Voters Who Voted	69.7	63.1	66.5	NaN
Population Age 18+ Who Voted	57.0	54.3	58.5	61.0

Data: Dave Leip's Atlas of U.S. Presidential Elections

Presidential Election Results (Nationwide Winner Listed First)

2008	Popular Vote (%)	Electoral Votes
Barack Obama (Democrat)	39.9	0
John McCain (Republican)	58.6	9
Other	1.5	0
2004		
George W. Bush (Republican, Incumbent)	56.7	9
John Kerry (Democrat)	42.2	0
Other	1.1	0
2000		
George W. Bush (Republican)	52.6	9
Albert Gore (Democrat)	44.9	0
Ralph Nader (Green)	1.2	0
Other	1.4	0
1996		
William Clinton (Democrat, Incumbent)	52.0	9
Robert Dole (Republican)	39.9	0
H. Ross Perot (Reformist)	6.9	0
Other	1.1	0

Data: Dave Leip's Atlas of U.S. Presidential Elections

Governor and U.S. Congressional Seats				
Governor	**Party**	**Year Term Began**	**Term**	**Max. Consecutive Terms**
Bobby Jindal	R	2008	First	2
U.S. Senators	**Party**	**Year Elected**	**Term Expires**	
Mary L. Landrieu	D	1996	2015	
David Vitter	R	2004	2011	
U.S. Representatives		**Republican**	**Democrat**	**Other**
		6	1	0

Data: National Governors Association; U.S. Senate, Office of the Clerk; U.S. House of Representatives

Business and Economic Agencies

Agency	Website Address
Louisiana Association of Business and Industry	www.labi.org
Louisiana Economic Development	www.lded.state.la.us
Louisiana Small Business Dev. Center	www.lsbdc.org
Louisiana Secretary of State, Commercial Division	www.sos.louisiana.gov/tabid/66/Default.aspx

Data: Various agency websites

Maine

Maine, located in the New England, Northeast region of the United States, has a population of 1.3 million people, making it the eleventh least populous state in 2007. The state's population increased by 42,284 people from 2000 to 2007, and is projected to increase to 1.4 million by 2025. This 0.4% projected annual growth rate compares to the projected national average of 0.8%. From 2006 to 2007 the state's population declined by 0.3%. Per capita personal income in Maine was $33,962 in 2007, up from $31,931 in 2006. For 2007, this was sixteenth lowest in the country and $4,602 below the national average. From 2000 to 2007 the per capita income in Maine grew at a compound annual rate of 3.9%, compared to 3.7% nationally.

In 2006, the state's largest industry in terms of employment was retail trade, followed by manufacturing. The fastest growing industry was transportation and warehousing with 4.9% annual growth from 1998 to 2006. The state's workforce is generally less educated than other states—nationally, an average

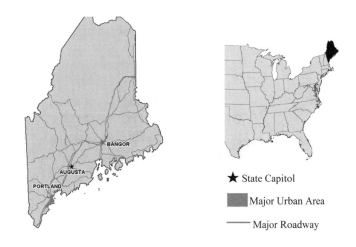

★ State Capitol

▩ Major Urban Area

— Major Roadway

Demographic and Socioeconomic Profile

Demographics and Socioeconomic Figures			
Population and Households	**2000**	**2006**	**2007**
Total Population	1,274,923	1,321,574	1,317,207
Number of Households	518,200	548,247	543,952
Average Household Size	2.4	2.3	2.4
Age and Ethnicity			
Median Age	38.6	41.0	41.7
Population 18 Years of Age and Older	973,945	1,039,702	1,037,541
Population 65 Years of Age and Older	183,642	192,434	194,951
Caucasian Population	1,236,422	1,265,541	1,254,460
African-American Population	6,047	13,669	14,652
Hispanic Population	9,226	12,622	14,953
Asian Population	8,259	12,004	12,718
Foreign-Born Population (%)	2.9	3.2	3.4
Income			
Per Capita Personal Income (USD)	$25,969	$31,931	$33,962
Median Household Income (USD)	$37,240	$43,439	$45,888
Individuals below Poverty Level	10.9%	12.9%	12.0%

Data: U.S. Census, American Community Survey; U.S. Department of Commerce, Bureau of Economic Analysis

of 27.0% hold a bachelor degree or higher compared to 26.7% in Maine; and 9.2% hold professional or graduate degrees (national average is 10.1%); however, 89.4% of the state's adult population has graduated from high school, compared to an 84.1% national average.

In fiscal year 2005–6, Maine had total tax revenues of $5.8 billion. The largest share was generated from property taxes, followed by sales and gross receipts taxes. The per capita tax burden in Maine was $4,393 for 2005–6, some $401 above the national average. In terms of business taxes, the state ranked fiftieth in a 2008 analysis by Anderson Economic Group. Forbes Magazine and the Tax Foundation ranked the state's business climate forty-sixth and fortieth, respectively.

Population Projections

Year	2010	2015	2020	2025
Total Population	1,357,134	1,388,878	1,408,665	1,414,402
Median Age	42.2	43.4	44.1	45.3
Population 18 Years of Age and Older	1,087,902	1,120,280	1,140,230	1,149,909
Population 65 Years of Age and Older	212,278	250,195	293,990	339,038

Data: U.S. Census Bureau

Workforce and Industry Profile

Workforce

	2000	2006	2007
Civilian Labor Force	672,440	711,376	702,549
Labor Force Participation Rate	67.6%	66.8%	66.5%
Unemployment Rate	3.3%	4.6%	4.6%
Average Wage Per Job (USD)	$27,664	$35,160	$36,450
Education Attainment (Population 25 Years and Older)	**(%)**	**(%)**	**(%)**
High School Graduate or Higher	85.4	88.7	89.4
Bachelors Degree or Higher	22.9	25.8	26.7
Graduate or Professional Degree	7.9	15.7	9.2

Data: U.S. Census Bureau, American Community Survey; U.S. Department of Commerce, Bureau of Economic Analysis; U.S. Department of Labor, Bureau of Labor Statistics

Industry Overview

	1998	2005	2006
Total Employees	456,715	497,387	508,163
Total Payroll ($1,000)	11,559,136	15,873,419	16,664,977
Total Establishments	38,334	41,933	42,038
Establishments with 1–19 Employees	34,326	74,273	37,321
Establishments with 20–49 Employees	2,516	3,030	3,072
Establishments with 50–249 Employees	1,312	1,398	1,451
Establishments with 250–999 Employees	162	171	176
Establishments with 1,000+ Employees	18	18	18

Data: U.S. Census Bureau, County Business Patterns

Major Industries (Ranked by 2006 Employment; Payroll in $1,000s)				
Industry	1998 Employment	2006 Employment	1998 Payroll	2006 Payroll
Health Care and Social Assistance	79,828	101,078	2,029,109	3,496,779
Retail Trade	74,220	84,934	1,263,051	1,899,144
Manufacturing	80,640	59,322	2,630,781	2,446,799
Accommodation and Food Services	41,273	47,104	512,859	758,006
Construction	23,766	28,862	729,676	1,117,040
Finance and Insurance	21,374	28,135	839,098	1,283,608
Admin., Support, Waste Mngt., Remediation Services	23,318	27,825	445,008	843,214
Professional, Scientific, Technical Services	16,708	23,974	584,864	1,142,682
Other Services (except Public Admin.)	17,445	19,990	294,070	421,472
Wholesale Trade	20,932	19,170	658,579	832,097

Data: U.S. Census Bureau, County Business Patterns

Taxes and Business Climate

State and Local Taxes		
Combined Revenues ($1,000)	2004–5	2005–6
Revenue from Property Taxes	2,151,968	2,210,504
Revenue from Sales and Gross Receipts Taxes	1,363,266	1,670,185
Revenue from Individual Income Taxes	1,299,252	1,368,927
Revenue from Corporate Income Taxes	135,863	188,016
Revenue from Other Taxes	269,359	367,928
Total Tax Revenue	5,219,708	5,805,560
Per Capita Taxes		
Property Tax Per Capita	1,640	1,673
Sales and Gross Receipts Tax Per Capita	1,039	1,264
Individual Income Tax Per Capita	990	1,036
Corporate Income Tax Per Capita	104	142
Other Taxes Per Capita	205	278
Total Taxes Per Capita	3,978	4,393

Data: U.S. Census Bureau; Anderson Economic Group, LLC

Business Climate Measures

Anderson Economic Group: 2008 Business Tax Ranking (1 is Best)	50
Forbes Magazine: 2008 Best States for Business Ranking (1 is Best)	46
Tax Foundation: 2009 Business Tax Climate Ranking (1 is Best)	40
2004–5 Employer Firm Births	3,731
2004–5 Employer Firm Terminations	3,336

Data: Anderson Economic Group; Tax Foundation; Forbes Magazine; U.S. Census, Statistics of U.S. Businesses

Voting Behavior and Elected Officials

Voter Registration and Turnout (%)

	1996	2000	2004	2008
Registered Voters Who Voted	60.5	68.8	72.3	NaN
Population Age 18+ Who Voted	64.1	66.9	72.7	70.5

Data: Dave Leip's Atlas of U.S. Presidential Elections

Presidential Election Results (Nationwide Winner Listed First)

2008	Popular Vote (%)	Electoral Votes
Barack Obama (Democrat)	57.7	4
John McCain (Republican)	40.4	0
Other	1.9	0
2004		
George W. Bush (Republican, Incumbent)	44.6	0
John Kerry (Democrat)	53.6	4
Other	1.9	0
2000		
George W. Bush (Republican)	44.0	0
Albert Gore (Democrat)	49.1	4
Ralph Nader (Green)	5.7	0
Other	1.2	0
1996		
William Clinton (Democrat, Incumbent)	51.6	4
Robert Dole (Republican)	30.8	0
H. Ross Perot (Reformist)	14.2	0
Other	3.4	0

Data: Dave Leip's Atlas of U.S. Presidential Elections

Governor and U.S. Congressional Seats

Governor	Party	Year Term Began	Term	Max. Consecutive Terms
John Baldacci	D	2007	Second	2
U.S. Senators	**Party**	**Year Elected**	**Term Expires**	
Susan M. Collins	R	1996	2015	
Olympia J. Snowe	R	1994	2013	
U.S. Representatives		**Republican**	**Democrat**	**Other**
		0	2	0

Data: National Governors Association; U.S. Senate, Office of the Clerk; U.S. House of Representatives

Business and Economic Agencies

Agency	Website Address
Maine State Chamber of Commerce	www.mainechamber.org
The Maine Department of Economic and Community Development	www.econdevmaine.com
Maine Small Business Dev. Center	www.mainesbdc.org
Maine Bureau of Corporations	www.state.me.us/sos/cec/index.html

Data: Various agency websites

Maryland

With a population of 5.6 million people, Maryland was the nineteenth most populous state in the United States in 2007. From 2000 to 2007 the state's population increased by 321,858 people, and is projected to increase to 6.8 million by 2025. This 1.0% projected annual growth rate compares to the projected national average of 0.8%. From 2006 to 2007 the state's population did not have significant growth. The state's 2007 per capita personal income of $46,646 was higher compared to $43,774 in 2006 and the sixth highest in the United States, some $8,082 above the national average. Per capita income in Maryland grew at a compound annual rate of 4.5% from 2000 to 2007, compared to 3.7% nationally.

Maryland's largest industry in terms of 2006 employment was health care and social assistance. The fastest growing industry was construction, with 4.1% annual growth from 1998 to 2006. The second fastest growing industry was transportation and warehousing. The state's workforce is generally more educated than other states— 87.4% of the state's adult

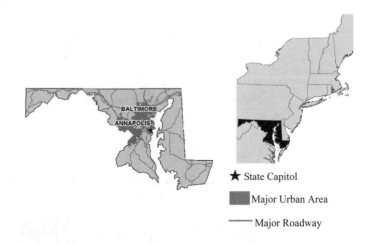

★ State Capitol

▆ Major Urban Area

— Major Roadway

Demographic and Socioeconomic Profile

Demographics and Socioeconomic Figures			
Population and Households	**2000**	**2006**	**2007**
Total Population	5,296,486	5,615,727	5,618,344
Number of Households	1,980,859	2,089,031	2,082,458
Average Household Size	2.6	2.6	2.6
Age and Ethnicity			
Median Age	36.0	37.3	37.4
Population 18 Years of Age and Older	3,943,067	4,253,595	4,259,768
Population 65 Years of Age and Older	598,004	647,332	661,293
Caucasian Population	3,391,021	3,441,497	3,402,960
African-American Population	1,468,243	1,624,858	1,626,017
Hispanic Population	227,105	336,390	354,969
Asian Population	209,713	276,362	275,002
Foreign-Born Population (%)	9.8	12.2	12.4
Income			
Per Capita Personal Income (USD)	$34,257	$43,774	$46,646
Median Household Income (USD)	$52,868	$65,144	$68,080
Individuals below Poverty Level	8.5%	7.8%	8.3%

Data: U.S. Census, American Community Survey; U.S. Department of Commerce, Bureau of Economic Analysis

population has graduated from high school, compared to an 84.1% national average; 35.2% hold a bachelor degree or higher (national average is 27.0%); and 15.7% hold professional or graduate degrees compared to the national average of 10.1%.

Maryland's total tax revenue was $25.8 billion for fiscal year 2005–6, up from the 2004–5 total revenue of $23.9 billion. The largest share of tax revenue in 2005–6 was generated from individual income taxes, followed by sales and gross receipts taxes. On a per capita basis, residents of Maryland paid taxes of $4,592, compared to the national average of $3,992 for 2005–6. In terms of business taxes, the state ranked twenty-third in a 2008 analysis by Anderson Economic Group. Forbes Magazine and the Tax Foundation ranked the state's business climate fourteenth and forty-fifth, respectively.

Population Projections

Year	2010	2015	2020	2025
Total Population	5,904,970	6,208,392	6,497,626	6,762,732
Median Age	36.8	36.1	36.4	36.9
Population 18 Years of Age and Older	4,498,676	4,721,718	4,911,565	5,098,221
Population 65 Years of Age and Older	717,987	837,124	962,160	1,104,757

Data: U.S. Census Bureau

Workforce and Industry Profile

Workforce

	2000	2006	2007
Civilian Labor Force	2,811,657	3,009,143	2,987,698
Labor Force Participation Rate	70.4%	69.4%	69.0%
Unemployment Rate	3.6%	3.9%	3.5%
Average Wage Per Job (USD)	$36,395	$44,030	$45,780
Education Attainment (Population 25 Years and Older)	(%)	(%)	(%)
High School Graduate or Higher	83.8	87.1	87.4
Bachelors Degree or Higher	31.4	35.1	35.2
Graduate or Professional Degree	13.4	15.6	15.7

Data: U.S. Census Bureau, American Community Survey; U.S. Department of Commerce, Bureau of Economic Analysis; U.S. Department of Labor, Bureau of Labor Statistics

Industry Overview

	1998	2005	2006
Total Employees	1,938,727	2,167,999	2,232,215
Total Payroll ($1,000)	59,817,673	88,964,728	93,718,780
Total Establishments	126,577	138,481	140,292
Establishments with 1–19 Employees	108,830	118,182	119,256
Establishments with 20–49 Employees	10,961	12,375	12,854
Establishments with 50–249 Employees	5,980	7,034	7,243
Establishments with 250–999 Employees	702	777	829
Establishments with 1,000+ Employees	104	113	110

Data: U.S. Census Bureau, County Business Patterns

Major Industries (Ranked by 2006 Employment; Payroll in $1,000s)

Industry	1998 Employment	2006 Employment	1998 Payroll	2006 Payroll
Health Care and Social Assistance	258,901	310,520	7,607,050	12,642,717
Retail Trade	273,016	307,080	5,245,293	7,543,790
Professional, Scientific, Technical Services	172,671	228,100	8,145,127	14,511,280
Construction	142,650	196,688	4,851,310	8,919,467
Accommodation and Food Services	160,294	193,867	1,838,370	2,895,919
Admin., Support, Waste Mngt., Remediation Services	160,362	176,588	3,665,695	5,482,713
Manufacturing	163,123	131,108	6,191,401	6,614,043
Finance and Insurance	104,336	125,459	4,556,298	8,796,054
Other Services (except Public Admin.)	105,452	116,200	2,288,378	3,332,454
Wholesale Trade	91,987	98,316	3,925,037	5,466,431

Data: U.S. Census Bureau, County Business Patterns

Taxes and Business Climate

State and Local Taxes

Combined Revenues ($1,000)	2004–5	2005–6
Revenue from Property Taxes	5,594,371	5,961,742
Revenue from Sales and Gross Receipts Taxes	5,758,944	6,222,644
Revenue from Individual Income Taxes	9,153,415	9,847,319
Revenue from Corporate Income Taxes	807,054	846,863
Revenue from Other Taxes	2,585,271	2,910,241
Total Tax Revenue	23,899,055	25,788,809

Per Capita Taxes

	2004–5	2005–6
Property Tax Per Capita	1,004	1,062
Sales and Gross Receipts Tax Per Capita	1,033	1,108
Individual Income Tax Per Capita	1,642	1,754
Corporate Income Tax Per Capita	145	151
Other Taxes Per Capita	464	518
Total Taxes Per Capita	4,288	4,592

Data: U.S. Census Bureau; Anderson Economic Group, LLC

Business Climate Measures

Anderson Economic Group: 2008 Business Tax Ranking (1 is Best)	23
Forbes Magazine: 2008 Best States for Business Ranking (1 is Best)	14
Tax Foundation: 2009 Business Tax Climate Ranking (1 is Best)	45
2004–5 Employer Firm Births	13,875
2004–5 Employer Firm Terminations	11,850

Data: Anderson Economic Group; Tax Foundation; Forbes Magazine; U.S. Census, Statistics of U.S. Businesses

Voting Behavior and Elected Officials

Voter Registration and Turnout (%)

	1996	2000	2004	2008
Registered Voters Who Voted	69.1	74.5	77.7	76.7
Population Age 18+ Who Voted	46.6	51.4	57.8	61.8

Data: Dave Leip's Atlas of U.S. Presidential Elections

Presidential Election Results (Nationwide Winner Listed First)

2008	Popular Vote (%)	Electoral Votes
Barack Obama (Democrat)	61.9	10
John McCain (Republican)	36.5	0
Other	1.6	0
2004		
George W. Bush (Republican, Incumbent)	42.9	0
John Kerry (Democrat)	55.9	10
Other	1.2	0
2000		
George W. Bush (Republican)	40.2	0
Albert Gore (Democrat)	56.6	10
Ralph Nader (Green)	2.7	0
Other	0.6	0
1996		
William Clinton (Democrat, Incumbent)	54.3	10
Robert Dole (Republican)	38.3	0
H. Ross Perot (Reformist)	6.5	0
Other	1.0	0

Data: Dave Leip's Atlas of U.S. Presidential Elections

Governor and U.S. Congressional Seats				
Governor	**Party**	**Year Term Began**	**Term**	**Max. Consecutive Terms**
Martin O'Malley	D	2007	First	2
U.S. Senators	**Party**	**Year Elected**	**Term Expires**	
Barbara A. Mikulski	D	1986	2011	
Ben Cardin	D	2006	2013	
U.S. Representatives		**Republican**	**Democrat**	**Other**
		1	7	0

Data: National Governors Association; U.S. Senate, Office of the Clerk; U.S. House of Representatives

Business and Economic Agencies

Agency	Website Address
Maryland Chamber of Commerce	www.mdchamber.org
Maryland Department of Business and Economic Development	www.dbed.state.md.us
Maryland Small Business Dev. Center	www.mdsbdc.umd.edu
Maryland Department of Assessments & Taxation	www.dat.state.md.us/sdatweb/charter.html

Data: Various agency websites

Massachusetts

Massachusetts is located in the New England region of the United States. Massachusetts has a population of 6.5 million people, making it the fourteenth most populous state in 2007. The state's population increased by 100,658 people from 2000 to 2007, and is projected to increase to 6.9 million by 2025. This 0.4% projected annual growth rate is below the national average of 0.8%. From 2006 to 2007 the state's population grew by 0.2%. Per capita personal income in Massachusetts was $49,142 in 2007, up from $46,255 in 2006. For 2007, this was $10,578 above the national average and the third highest in the country. The state's per capita income grew at a compound annual rate of 3.8% from 2000 to 2007, compared to 3.7% nationally.

The state's workforce generally has more education than other states—88.4% of the state's adult population has graduated from high school, compared to an 84.1% national average; 37.9% hold a bachelor degree or higher (national average is 27.0%); and 16.0% hold professional or graduate degrees (national average is 10.1%).

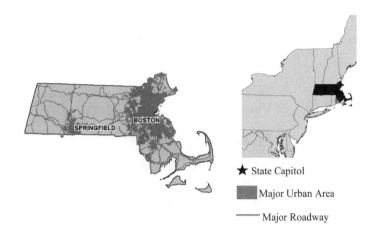

★ State Capitol

■ Major Urban Area

— Major Roadway

Demographic and Socioeconomic Profile

Demographics and Socioeconomic Figures			
Population and Households	**2000**	**2006**	**2007**
Total Population	6,349,097	6,437,193	6,449,755
Number of Households	2,443,580	2,446,485	2,449,133
Average Household Size	2.5	2.5	2.6
Age and Ethnicity			
Median Age	36.5	38.3	38.5
Population 18 Years of Age and Older	4,853,130	4,988,716	5,017,648
Population 65 Years of Age and Older	859,601	856,886	859,867
Caucasian Population	5,365,139	5,329,576	5,330,421
African-American Population	337,157	393,207	384,615
Hispanic Population	427,340	510,482	527,109
Asian Population	238,246	310,441	310,654
Foreign-Born Population (%)	12.2	14.1	14.2
Income			
Per Capita Personal Income (USD)	$37,756	$46,255	$49,142
Median Household Income (USD)	$50,502	$59,963	$62,365
Individuals below Poverty Level	9.3%	9.9%	9.9%

Data: U.S. Census, American Community Survey; U.S. Department of Commerce, Bureau of Economic Analysis

In 2006, the state's largest industry in terms of employment was retail trade, followed by manufacturing. The fastest growing industry was management of companies and enterprises, with 4.4% annual growth from 1998 to 2006.

In fiscal year 2005–6, Massachusetts had total tax revenues of $30.6 billion. The largest share was generated from property taxes, followed by individual income taxes. The per capita tax burden in Massachusetts was $4,759 for 2005–6, some $767 above the national average, and a $286 increase from the 2004–5 per capita tax burden. In terms of business taxes, Massachusetts ranked twenty-first in a 2008 report by Anderson Economic Group. The state's business climate was ranked thirty-sixth by Forbes Magazine and thirty-second by the Tax Foundation.

Population Projections

Year	2010	2015	2020	2025
Total Population	6,649,441	6,758,580	6,855,546	6,938,636
Median Age	38.8	39.2	39.5	39.7
Population 18 Years of Age and Older	5,165,588	5,284,629	5,362,379	5,419,996
Population 65 Years of Age and Older	908,565	1,025,448	1,159,817	1,317,940

Data: U.S. Census Bureau

Workforce and Industry Profile

Workforce

	2000	2006	2007
Civilian Labor Force	3,365,573	3,404,394	3,415,613
Labor Force Participation Rate	68.3%	67.1%	66.8%
Unemployment Rate	2.7%	5.0%	4.5%
Average Wage Per Job (USD)	$44,329	$47,340	$49,070
Education Attainment (Population 25 Years and Older)	(%)	(%)	(%)
High School Graduate or Higher	84.8	87.9	88.4
Bachelors Degree or Higher	33.2	37.0	37.9
Graduate or Professional Degree	13.7	9.2	16.0

Data: U.S. Census Bureau, American Community Survey; U.S. Department of Commerce, Bureau of Economic Analysis; U.S. Department of Labor, Bureau of Labor Statistics

Industry Overview

	1998	2005	2006
Total Employees	2,924,913	2,996,347	3,044,080
Total Payroll ($1,000)	105,871,311	140,580,627	148,086,017
Total Establishments	167,929	175,291	175,463
Establishments with 1–19 Employees	143,459	150,120	149,989
Establishments with 20–49 Employees	14,454	15,068	15,280
Establishments with 50–249 Employees	8,658	8,838	8,915
Establishments with 250–999 Employees	1,148	1,062	1,071
Establishments with 1,000+ Employees	210	203	208

Data: U.S. Census Bureau, County Business Patterns

Major Industries (Ranked by 2006 Employment; Payroll in $1,000s)				
Industry	1998 Employment	2006 Employment	1998 Payroll	2006 Payroll
Health Care and Social Assistance	452,465	499,919	13,494,246	21,082,419
Retail Trade	340,548	368,028	6,558,993	9,263,247
Manufacturing	409,938	275,180	17,170,367	15,696,243
Professional, Scientific, Technical Services	201,084	260,770	11,773,454	20,219,705
Accommodation and Food Services	232,603	247,654	2,994,758	4,335,245
Finance and Insurance	214,807	211,046	13,055,694	19,672,861
Admin., Support, Waste Mngt., Remediation Services	179,590	186,355	4,639,257	6,700,850
Educational Services	152,797	182,257	4,016,307	6,239,085
Wholesale Trade	147,661	144,638	7,145,803	9,924,237
Construction	106,184	132,559	4,591,611	7,371,503

Data: U.S. Census Bureau, County Business Patterns

Taxes and Business Climate

State and Local Taxes		
Combined Revenues ($1,000)	2004–5	2005–6
Revenue from Property Taxes	10,341,126	10,828,955
Revenue from Sales and Gross Receipts Taxes	5,932,045	6,092,350
Revenue from Individual Income Taxes	9,690,270	10,483,437
Revenue from Corporate Income Taxes	1,332,796	1,859,009
Revenue from Other Taxes	1,460,725	1,371,900
Total Tax Revenue	28,756,962	30,635,651
Per Capita Taxes		
Property Tax Per Capita	1,608	1,682
Sales and Gross Receipts Tax Per Capita	923	946
Individual Income Tax Per Capita	1,507	1,629
Corporate Income Tax Per Capita	207	289
Other Taxes Per Capita	227	213
Total Taxes Per Capita	4,473	4,759

Data: U.S. Census Bureau; Anderson Economic Group, LLC

Business Climate Measures	
Anderson Economic Group: 2008 Business Tax Ranking (1 is Best)	21
Forbes Magazine: 2008 Best States for Business Ranking (1 is Best)	36
Tax Foundation: 2009 Business Tax Climate Ranking (1 is Best)	32
2004–5 Employer Firm Births	15,351
2004–5 Employer Firm Terminations	15,744

Data: Anderson Economic Group; Tax Foundation; Forbes Magazine; U.S. Census, Statistics of U.S. Businesses

Voting Behavior and Elected Officials

Voter Registration and Turnout (%)				
	1996	2000	2004	2008
Registered Voters Who Voted	73.8	67.4	71.1	73.0
Population Age 18+ Who Voted	55.0	55.7	58.9	61.4

Data: Dave Leip's Atlas of U.S. Presidential Elections

Presidential Election Results (Nationwide Winner Listed First)		
2008	Popular Vote (%)	Electoral Votes
Barack Obama (Democrat)	61.8	12
John McCain (Republican)	36.0	0
Other	2.2	0
2004		
George W. Bush (Republican, Incumbent)	36.8	0
John Kerry (Democrat)	61.9	12
Other	1.3	0
2000		
George W. Bush (Republican)	32.5	0
Albert Gore (Democrat)	59.8	12
Ralph Nader (Green)	6.4	0
Other	1.3	0
1996		
William Clinton (Democrat, Incumbent)	61.5	12
Robert Dole (Republican)	28.1	0
H. Ross Perot (Reformist)	8.9	0
Other	1.6	0

Data: Dave Leip's Atlas of U.S. Presidential Elections

Governor and U.S. Congressional Seats

Governor	Party	Year Term Began	Term	Max. Consecutive Terms
Deveal Patrick	D	2007	First	No limit
U.S. Senators	**Party**	**Year Elected**	**Term Expires**	
John Kerry	D	1984	2015	
Edward Kennedy	D	1962	2013	
U.S. Representatives		**Republican**	**Democrat**	**Other**
		0	10	0

Data: National Governors Association; U.S. Senate, Office of the Clerk; U.S. House of Representatives

Business and Economic Agencies

Agency	Website Address
n/a	n/a
Massachusetts Economic Development	www.mass.gov
Massachusetts Small Business Dev. Center	www.msbdc.org
Massachusetts Corporations Division	www.sec.state.ma.us/cor/coridx.htm

Data: Various agency websites

Michigan

Michigan, located in the East North Central region of the United States, has a population of 10.1 million people, making it the eighth most populous state in 2007. The state's population increased by 133,378 people from 2000 to 2007, and is projected to increase to 10.7 million by 2025. This 0.3% projected annual growth rate compares to the projected national average of 0.8%. From 2006 to 2007 the state's population declined by 0.2%. Per capita personal income in Michigan was $34,342 in 2007, up from $33,784 in 2006. For 2007, this was eighteenth lowest in the country and $4,222 below the national average. From 2000 to 2007 the per capita income in Michigan grew at a compound annual rate of 2.2%, compared to 3.7% nationally.

In 2006, the state's largest industry in terms of employment was manufacturing, followed by health care and social assistance. The fastest growing industry was professional, scientific, and technical services with 5.8% annual growth from 1998 to 2006. The state's workforce is generally less educated than other states—nationally,

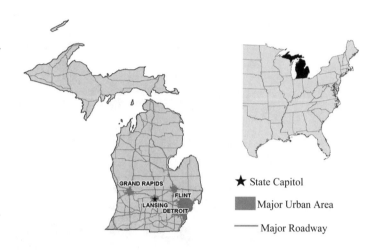

★ State Capitol

■ Major Urban Area

— Major Roadway

Demographic and Socioeconomic Profile

Demographics and Socioeconomic Figures			
Population and Households	**2000**	**2006**	**2007**
Total Population	9,938,444	10,095,643	10,071,822
Number of Households	3,785,661	3,869,117	3,849,007
Average Household Size	2.6	2.5	2.6
Age and Ethnicity			
Median Age	35.5	37.3	37.6
Population 18 Years of Age and Older	7,345,849	7,618,222	7,621,612
Population 65 Years of Age and Older	1,219,232	1,260,367	1,279,034
Caucasian Population	7,960,342	8,026,545	8,001,673
African-American Population	1,401,723	1,426,809	1,416,635
Hispanic Population	322,160	392,770	401,009
Asian Population	174,824	236,972	240,214
Foreign-Born Population (%)	5.3	5.9	6.1
Income			
Per Capita Personal Income (USD)	$29,552	$33,784	$34,342
Median Household Income (USD)	$44,667	$47,182	$47,950
Individuals below Poverty Level	10.5%	13.5%	14.0%

Data: U.S. Census, American Community Survey; U.S. Department of Commerce, Bureau of Economic Analysis

an average of 27.0% hold a bachelor degree or higher compared to 24.7% in Michigan; and 9.5% hold professional or graduate degrees (national average is 10.1%); however, 87.4% of the state's adult population has graduated from high school, compared to an 84.1% national average.

In fiscal year 2005–6, Michigan had total tax revenues of $36.0 billion. The largest share was generated from property taxes, followed by sales and gross receipts taxes. The per capita tax burden in Michigan was $3,568 for 2005–6, some $424 below the national average. In terms of business taxes, the state ranked twenty-second in a 2008 analysis by Anderson Economic Group. Forbes Magazine and the Tax Foundation ranked the state's business climate forty-seventh and twentieth, respectively.

Population Projections

Year	2010	2015	2020	2025
Total Population	10,428,683	10,599,122	10,695,993	10,713,730
Median Age	37.4	37.8	38.6	39.4
Population 18 Years of Age and Older	7,941,625	8,120,199	8,216,729	8,241,856
Population 65 Years of Age and Older	1,334,491	1,506,856	1,711,476	1,926,396

Data: U.S. Census Bureau

Workforce and Industry Profile

Workforce

	2000	2006	2007
Civilian Labor Force	5,143,916	5,081,336	5,023,910
Labor Force Participation Rate	68.4%	65.2%	64.5%
Unemployment Rate	3.7%	6.9%	7.1%
Average Wage Per Job (USD)	$37,011	$41,230	$42,210
Education Attainment (Population 25 Years and Older)	**(%)**	**(%)**	**(%)**
High School Graduate or Higher	83.4	87.2	87.4
Bachelors Degree or Higher	21.8	24.5	24.7
Graduate or Professional Degree	8.1	9.6	9.5

Data: U.S. Census Bureau, American Community Survey; U.S. Department of Commerce, Bureau of Economic Analysis; U.S. Department of Labor, Bureau of Labor Statistics

Industry Overview

	1998	2005	2006
Total Employees	3,919,567	3,796,876	3,819,537
Total Payroll ($1,000)	128,649,484	148,456,286	151,504,380
Total Establishments	235,403	237,523	235,750
Establishments with 1–19 Employees	201,308	204,045	202,081
Establishments with 20–49 Employees	21,230	20,492	20,602
Establishments with 50–249 Employees	11,163	11,338	11,467
Establishments with 250–999 Employees	1,456	1,432	1,373
Establishments with 1,000+ Employees	246	216	227

Data: U.S. Census Bureau, County Business Patterns

Major Industries (Ranked by 2006 Employment; Payroll in $1,000s)				
Industry	1998 Employment	2006 Employment	1998 Payroll	2006 Payroll
Manufacturing	828,751	614,888	35,615,528	30,905,187
Health Care and Social Assistance	486,987	541,170	14,340,634	20,439,729
Retail Trade	537,895	489,183	9,629,527	10,428,674
Admin., Support, Waste Mngt., Remediation Services	271,928	341,956	6,276,011	10,933,114
Accommodation and Food Services	320,768	338,092	3,167,701	4,040,346
Professional, Scientific, Technical Services	192,200	302,222	8,926,124	18,992,195
Other Services (except Public Admin.)	178,300	173,930	3,419,688	3,964,184
Wholesale Trade	191,469	173,601	8,163,387	9,337,832
Finance and Insurance	164,990	167,343	6,929,849	8,659,620
Construction	179,122	156,318	7,147,499	7,343,055

Data: U.S. Census Bureau, County Business Patterns

Taxes and Business Climate

State and Local Taxes		
Combined Revenues ($1,000)	2004–5	2005–6
Revenue from Property Taxes	12,918,887	13,525,071
Revenue from Sales and Gross Receipts Taxes	11,784,107	11,862,951
Revenue from Individual Income Taxes	6,565,176	6,698,913
Revenue from Corporate Income Taxes	1,907,190	1,886,168
Revenue from Other Taxes	2,119,798	2,043,791
Total Tax Revenue	35,295,158	36,016,894
Per Capita Taxes		
Property Tax Per Capita	1,278	1,340
Sales and Gross Receipts Tax Per Capita	1,166	1,175
Individual Income Tax Per Capita	650	664
Corporate Income Tax Per Capita	189	187
Other Taxes Per Capita	210	202
Total Taxes Per Capita	3,492	3,568

Data: U.S. Census Bureau; Anderson Economic Group, LLC

Business Climate Measures

Anderson Economic Group: 2008 Business Tax Ranking (1 is Best)	22
Forbes Magazine: 2008 Best States for Business Ranking (1 is Best)	47
Tax Foundation: 2009 Business Tax Climate Ranking (1 is Best)	20
2004–5 Employer Firm Births	21,034
2004–5 Employer Firm Terminations	20,982

Data: Anderson Economic Group; Tax Foundation; Forbes Magazine; U.S. Census, Statistics of U.S. Businesses

Voting Behavior and Elected Officials

Voter Registration and Turnout (%)

	1996	2000	2004	2008
Registered Voters Who Voted	57.6	61.7	67.5	67.0
Population Age 18+ Who Voted	54.4	57.6	64.2	65.7

Data: Dave Leip's Atlas of U.S. Presidential Elections

Presidential Election Results (Nationwide Winner Listed First)

2008	Popular Vote (%)	Electoral Votes
Barack Obama (Democrat)	57.4	17
John McCain (Republican)	40.9	0
Other	1.7	0
2004		
George W. Bush (Republican, Incumbent)	47.8	0
John Kerry (Democrat)	51.2	17
Other	1.0	0
2000		
George W. Bush (Republican)	46.1	0
Albert Gore (Democrat)	51.3	18
Ralph Nader (Green)	2.0	0
Other	0.6	0
1996		
William Clinton (Democrat, Incumbent)	51.7	18
Robert Dole (Republican)	38.5	0
H. Ross Perot (Reformist)	8.8	0
Other	1.1	0

Data: Dave Leip's Atlas of U.S. Presidential Elections

Governor and U.S. Congressional Seats

Governor	Party	Year Term Began	Term	Max. Consecutive Terms
Jennifer Granholm	D	2007	Second	2

U.S. Senators	Party	Year Elected	Term Expires	
Carl Levin	D	1978	2015	
Debbie Stabenow	D	2000	2013	

U.S. Representatives		Republican	Democrat	Other
		7	8	0

Data: National Governors Association; U.S. Senate, Office of the Clerk; U.S. House of Representatives

Business and Economic Agencies

Agency	Website Address
Michigan Chamber of Commerce	www.michamber.com
Michigan Economic Development Corporation	www.themedc.org
Michigan Small Business & Tech Dev. Center	www.misbtdc.org
Michigan Department of Labor and Economic Growth	www.michigan.gov/dleg

Data: Various agency websites

Minnesota

With a population of 5.2 million people, Minnesota was the twenty-first most populous state in the United States in 2007. From 2000 to 2007 the state's population increased by 278,142 people, and is projected to increase to 6.1 million by 2025. This 0.9% projected annual growth rate compares to the projected national average of 0.8%. From 2006 to 2007 the state's population grew by 0.6%. The state's 2007 per capita personal income of $40,969 was higher compared to $38,751 in 2006 and the twelfth highest in the United States, some $2,405 above the national average. Per capita income in Minnesota grew at a compound annual rate of 3.6% from 2000 to 2007, compared to 3.7% nationally.

Minnesota's largest industry in terms of 2006 employment was manufacturing. The fastest growing industry was educational services, with 4.2% annual growth from 1998 to 2006. The second fastest growing industry was construction. The state's workforce is generally more educated than other states—91.0% of the state's adult

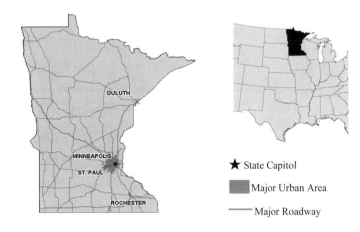

★ State Capitol

Major Urban Area

Major Roadway

Demographic and Socioeconomic Profile

Demographics and Socioeconomic Figures			
Population and Households	**2000**	**2006**	**2007**
Total Population	4,919,479	5,167,101	5,197,621
Number of Households	1,895,127	2,042,297	2,062,681
Average Household Size	2.5	2.5	2.5
Age and Ethnicity			
Median Age	35.4	36.8	37.1
Population 18 Years of Age and Older	3,632,940	3,909,171	3,938,165
Population 65 Years of Age and Older	593,415	628,105	635,764
Caucasian Population	4,402,124	4,538,957	4,570,486
African-American Population	167,857	228,354	225,798
Hispanic Population	141,786	195,138	204,789
Asian Population	139,245	179,295	180,700
Foreign-Born Population (%)	5.3	6.6	6.6
Income			
Per Capita Personal Income (USD)	$32,017	$38,751	$40,969
Median Household Income (USD)	$47,111	$54,023	$55,802
Individuals below Poverty Level	7.9%	9.8%	9.5%

Data: U.S. Census, American Community Survey; U.S. Department of Commerce, Bureau of Economic Analysis

population has graduated from high school, compared to an 84.1% national average; 31.0% hold a bachelor degree or higher (national average is 27.0%); and 10.0% hold professional or graduate degrees compared to the national average of 10.1%.

Minnesota's total tax revenue was $22.5 billion for fiscal year 2005–6, up from the 2004–5 total revenue of $21.0 billion. The largest share of tax revenue in 2005–6 was generated from sales and gross receipt taxes, followed by individual income taxes. On a per capita basis, residents of Minnesota paid taxes of $4,353, compared to the national average of $3,992 for 2005–6. In terms of business taxes, the state ranked eighth in a 2008 analysis by Anderson Economic Group. Forbes Magazine and the Tax Foundation ranked the state's business climate eleventh and forty-first, respectively.

Population Projections

Year	2010	2015	2020	2025
Total Population	5,420,636	5,668,211	5,900,769	6,108,787
Median Age	36.5	36.7	37.5	38.4
Population 18 Years of Age and Older	4,130,673	4,318,787	4,484,545	4,636,987
Population 65 Years of Age and Older	670,429	774,390	909,950	1,063,116

Data: U.S. Census Bureau

Workforce and Industry Profile

Workforce

	2000	2006	2007
Civilian Labor Force	2,807,668	2,939,304	2,910,811
Labor Force Participation Rate	75.3%	72.9%	72.6%
Unemployment Rate	3.1%	4.0%	4.6%
Average Wage Per Job (USD)	$35,413	$41,510	$42,820
Education Attainment (Population 25 Years and Older)	(%)	(%)	(%)
High School Graduate or Higher	87.9	90.7	91.0
Bachelors Degree or Higher	27.4	30.4	31.0
Graduate or Professional Degree	8.3	6.1	10.0

Data: U.S. Census Bureau, American Community Survey; U.S. Department of Commerce, Bureau of Economic Analysis; U.S. Department of Labor, Bureau of Labor Statistics

Industry Overview

	1998	2005	2006
Total Employees	2,271,671	2,430,853	2,476,354
Total Payroll ($1,000)	70,094,975	96,992,711	100,645,287
Total Establishments	134,981	150,231	151,150
Establishments with 1–19 Employees	115,369	128,700	129,181
Establishments with 20–49 Employees	11,910	13,126	13,400
Establishments with 50–249 Employees	6,637	7,293	7,461
Establishments with 250–999 Employees	918	964	957
Establishments with 1,000+ Employees	147	148	151

Data: U.S. Census Bureau, County Business Patterns

Major Industries (Ranked by 2006 Employment; Payroll in $1,000s)				
Industry	1998 Employment	2006 Employment	1998 Payroll	2006 Payroll
Health Care and Social Assistance	304,550	390,109	8,290,432	14,307,275
Manufacturing	378,392	336,776	13,760,626	15,787,627
Retail Trade	295,669	312,998	5,089,588	7,164,549
Accommodation and Food Services	181,104	217,588	1,923,350	2,901,562
Finance and Insurance	129,833	152,310	6,191,235	10,674,976
Admin., Support, Waste Mngt., Remediation Services	140,086	147,928	2,847,993	4,371,391
Professional, Scientific, Technical Services	110,695	138,683	4,944,905	8,158,990
Wholesale Trade	133,590	136,824	5,616,725	8,438,012
Construction	98,539	126,560	4,227,371	6,807,015
Other Services (except Public Admin.)	115,687	116,369	2,015,766	2,494,831

Data: U.S. Census Bureau, County Business Patterns

Taxes and Business Climate

State and Local Taxes		
Combined Revenues ($1,000)	2004–5	2005–6
Revenue from Property Taxes	5,250,869	5,340,562
Revenue from Sales and Gross Receipts Taxes	6,832,316	7,438,897
Revenue from Individual Income Taxes	6,341,164	6,862,953
Revenue from Corporate Income Taxes	933,981	1,071,953
Revenue from Other Taxes	1,598,309	1,776,218
Total Tax Revenue	20,956,639	22,490,583
Per Capita Taxes		
Property Tax Per Capita	1,027	1,034
Sales and Gross Receipts Tax Per Capita	1,336	1,440
Individual Income Tax Per Capita	1,240	1,328
Corporate Income Tax Per Capita	183	207
Other Taxes Per Capita	313	344
Total Taxes Per Capita	4,098	4,353

Data: U.S. Census Bureau; Anderson Economic Group, LLC

Business Climate Measures

Anderson Economic Group: 2008 Business Tax Ranking (1 is Best)	8
Forbes Magazine: 2008 Best States for Business Ranking (1 is Best)	11
Tax Foundation: 2009 Business Tax Climate Ranking (1 is Best)	41
2004–5 Employer Firm Births	13,655
2004–5 Employer Firm Terminations	12,122

Data: Anderson Economic Group; Tax Foundation; Forbes Magazine; U.S. Census, Statistics of U.S. Businesses

Voting Behavior and Elected Officials

Voter Registration and Turnout (%)

	1996	2000	2004	2008
Registered Voters Who Voted	71.5	74.7	79.5	NaN
Population Age 18+ Who Voted	64.3	67.1	74.2	73.9

Data: Dave Leip's Atlas of U.S. Presidential Elections

Presidential Election Results (Nationwide Winner Listed First)

2008	Popular Vote (%)	Electoral Votes
Barack Obama (Democrat)	54.1	10
John McCain (Republican)	43.8	0
Other	2.1	0
2004		
George W. Bush (Republican, Incumbent)	47.6	0
John Kerry (Democrat)	51.1	9
Other	1.3	0
2000		
George W. Bush (Republican)	45.5	0
Albert Gore (Democrat)	47.9	10
Ralph Nader (Green)	5.2	0
Other	1.4	0
1996		
William Clinton (Democrat, Incumbent)	51.1	10
Robert Dole (Republican)	35.0	0
H. Ross Perot (Reformist)	11.8	0
Other	2.2	0

Data: Dave Leip's Atlas of U.S. Presidential Elections

Governor and U.S. Congressional Seats				
Governor	**Party**	**Year Term Began**	**Term**	**Max. Consecutive Terms**
Tim Pawlenty	R	2007	Second	No limit
U.S. Senators	**Party**	**Year Elected**	**Term Expires**	
Amy Klobuchar	D	2006	2013	
n/a vacant	n/a	n/a	n/a	
U.S. Representatives		**Republican**	**Democrat**	**Other**
		3	5	0

Data: National Governors Association; U.S. Senate, Office of the Clerk; U.S. House of Representatives

Business and Economic Agencies

Agency	Website Address
Minnesota Chamber of Commerce	www.mnchamber.com
Minnesota Department of Commerce	www.commerce.state.mn.us
Minnesota Small Business Dev. Center	www.mnsbdc.com
Minnesota Secretary of State	www.sos.state.mn.us/home/index.asp?page=3

Data: Various agency websites

Mississippi

Mississippi is located in the East South Central region of the United States. Mississippi has a population of 2.9 million people, making it the twentieth least populous state in 2007. The state's population increased by 74,127 people from 2000 to 2007, and is projected to increase to 3.1 million by 2025. This 0.3% projected annual growth rate is below the national average of 0.8%. From 2006 to 2007 the state's population grew by 0.3%. Per capita personal income in Mississippi was $28,527 in 2007, up from $26,908 in 2006. For 2007, this was $10,037 below the national average and the lowest in the country. The state's per capita income grew at a compound annual rate of 4.5% from 2000 to 2007, compared to 3.7% nationally.

The state's workforce generally has less education than other states—78.5% of the state's adult population has graduated from high school, compared to an 84.1% national average; 18.9% hold a bachelor degree or higher (national average is 27.0%); and 6.4% hold professional or graduate degrees (national average is 10.1%).

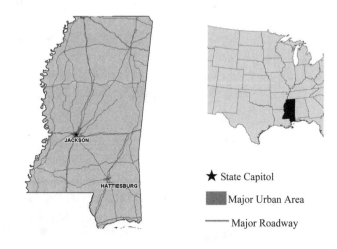

★ State Capitol

▨ Major Urban Area

— Major Roadway

Demographic and Socioeconomic Profile

Demographics and Socioeconomic Figures			
Population and Households	**2000**	**2006**	**2007**
Total Population	2,844,658	2,910,540	2,918,785
Number of Households	1,046,434	1,075,521	1,080,039
Average Household Size	2.6	2.6	2.6
Age and Ethnicity			
Median Age	33.8	35.4	35.4
Population 18 Years of Age and Older	2,070,254	2,151,613	2,152,342
Population 65 Years of Age and Older	344,288	360,693	361,741
Caucasian Population	1,745,353	1,749,296	1,745,130
African-American Population	1,033,437	1,087,114	1,095,051
Hispanic Population	37,790	46,348	52,515
Asian Population	17,709	22,116	20,207
Foreign-Born Population (%)	1.4	1.8	1.7
Income			
Per Capita Personal Income (USD)	$21,005	$26,908	$28,527
Median Household Income (USD)	$31,330	$34,473	$36,338
Individuals below Poverty Level	19.9%	21.1%	20.6%

Data: U.S. Census, American Community Survey; U.S. Department of Commerce, Bureau of Economic Analysis

In 2006, the state's largest industry in terms of employment was retail trade, followed by health care and social assistance. The fastest growing industry was professional, scientific, and technical services, with 3.4% annual growth from 1998 to 2006.

In fiscal year 2005–6, Mississippi had total tax revenues of $8.2 billion. The largest share was generated from sales and gross receipts taxes, followed by property taxes. The per capita tax burden in Mississippi was $2,811 for 2005–6, some $1,181 below the national average, and a $228 increase from the 2004–5 per capita tax burden. In terms of business taxes, Mississippi ranked thirty-sixth in a 2008 report by Anderson Economic Group. The state's business climate was ranked forty-second by Forbes Magazine and nineteenth by the Tax Foundation.

Population Projections

Year	2010	2015	2020	2025
Total Population	2,971,412	3,014,409	3,044,812	3,069,420
Median Age	36.5	37.8	39.4	40.6
Population 18 Years of Age and Older	2,211,962	2,261,862	2,307,758	2,351,380
Population 65 Years of Age and Older	379,025	433,428	499,190	573,543

Data: U.S. Census Bureau

Workforce and Industry Profile

Workforce

	2000	2006	2007
Civilian Labor Force	1,314,154	1,307,347	1,306,633
Labor Force Participation Rate	62.7%	60.3%	60.1%
Unemployment Rate	5.7%	6.8%	6.3%
Average Wage Per Job (USD)	$25,205	$30,460	$31,730
Education Attainment (Population 25 Years and Older)	**(%)**	**(%)**	**(%)**
High School Graduate or Higher	72.9	77.9	78.5
Bachelors Degree or Higher	16.9	18.8	18.9
Graduate or Professional Degree	5.8	8.7	6.4

Data: U.S. Census Bureau, American Community Survey; U.S. Department of Commerce, Bureau of Economic Analysis; U.S. Department of Labor, Bureau of Labor Statistics

Industry Overview

	1998	2005	2006
Total Employees	937,023	926,952	940,609
Total Payroll ($1,000)	21,066,790	25,796,066	27,439,442
Total Establishments	59,771	60,542	60,590
Establishments with 1–19 Employees	51,949	52,370	52,179
Establishments with 20–49 Employees	4,921	5,236	5,312
Establishments with 50–249 Employees	2,430	2,533	2,691
Establishments with 250–999 Employees	405	344	348
Establishments with 1,000+ Employees	66	59	60

Data: U.S. Census Bureau, County Business Patterns

Major Industries (Ranked by 2006 Employment; Payroll in $1,000s)				
Industry	1998 Employment	2006 Employment	1998 Payroll	2006 Payroll
Manufacturing	230,175	172,656	5,882,128	5,875,896
Retail Trade	138,422	149,045	2,156,337	2,974,920
Health Care and Social Assistance	126,613	143,368	3,309,588	4,997,068
Accommodation and Food Services	93,376	112,012	1,163,591	1,575,194
Construction	49,854	54,762	1,291,418	2,000,606
Admin., Support, Waste Mngt., Remediation Services	43,815	49,315	703,619	992,817
Other Services (except Public Admin.)	39,511	40,829	585,933	787,510
Wholesale Trade	39,464	37,852	1,123,409	1,476,862
Finance and Insurance	34,047	34,550	1,049,663	1,417,183
Transportation and Warehousing	25,871	33,031	693,395	1,136,284

Data: U.S. Census Bureau, County Business Patterns

Taxes and Business Climate

State and Local Taxes		
Combined Revenues ($1,000)	2004–5	2005–6
Revenue from Property Taxes	1,967,447	2,076,028
Revenue from Sales and Gross Receipts Taxes	3,584,852	3,990,126
Revenue from Individual Income Taxes	1,174,065	1,254,733
Revenue from Corporate Income Taxes	283,242	316,994
Revenue from Other Taxes	481,075	542,568
Total Tax Revenue	7,490,681	8,180,449
Per Capita Taxes		
Property Tax Per Capita	678	713
Sales and Gross Receipts Tax Per Capita	1,236	1,371
Individual Income Tax Per Capita	405	431
Corporate Income Tax Per Capita	98	109
Other Taxes Per Capita	166	186
Total Taxes Per Capita	2,583	2,811

Data: U.S. Census Bureau; Anderson Economic Group, LLC

Business Climate Measures

Anderson Economic Group: 2008 Business Tax Ranking (1 is Best)	36
Forbes Magazine: 2008 Best States for Business Ranking (1 is Best)	42
Tax Foundation: 2009 Business Tax Climate Ranking (1 is Best)	19
2004–5 Employer Firm Births	5,730
2004–5 Employer Firm Terminations	5,636

Data: Anderson Economic Group; Tax Foundation; Forbes Magazine; U.S. Census, Statistics of U.S. Businesses

Voting Behavior and Elected Officials

Voter Registration and Turnout (%)

	1996	2000	2004	2008
Registered Voters Who Voted	52.1	57.2	63.9	NaN
Population Age 18+ Who Voted	45.4	48.1	54.4	59.9

Data: Dave Leip's Atlas of U.S. Presidential Elections

Presidential Election Results (Nationwide Winner Listed First)

2008	Popular Vote (%)	Electoral Votes
Barack Obama (Democrat)	43.0	0
John McCain (Republican)	56.2	6
Other	0.8	0
2004		
George W. Bush (Republican, Incumbent)	59.4	6
John Kerry (Democrat)	39.7	0
Other	0.8	0
2000		
George W. Bush (Republican)	57.6	7
Albert Gore (Democrat)	40.7	0
Ralph Nader (Green)	.8	0
Other	0.9	0
1996		
William Clinton (Democrat, Incumbent)	44.1	0
Robert Dole (Republican)	49.2	7
H. Ross Perot (Reformist)	5.8	0
Other	0.9	0

Data: Dave Leip's Atlas of U.S. Presidential Elections

Governor and U.S. Congressional Seats				
Governor	Party	Year Term Began	Term	Max. Consecutive Terms
Haley Barbour	R	2008	Second	2
U.S. Senators	Party	Year Elected	Term Expires	
Thad Cochran	R	1978	2015	
Roger Wicker	R	2007	2013	
U.S. Representatives		Republican	Democrat	Other
		1	3	0

Data: National Governors Association; U.S. Senate, Office of the Clerk; U.S. House of Representatives

Business and Economic Agencies

Agency	Website Address
Mississippi Economic Council	www.msmec.com
Mississippi Development Authority	www.mississippi.org
Mississippi Small Business Dev. Center	www.olemiss.edu/depts/mssbdc
Mississippi Secretary of State, Business Services	www.sos.state.ms.us/busserv

Data: Various agency websites

Missouri

Missouri, located in the West North Central region of the United States, has a population of 5.9 million people, making it the eighteenth most populous state in 2007. The state's population increased by 283,204 people from 2000 to 2007, and is projected to increase to 6.3 million by 2025. This 0.4% projected annual growth rate compares to the projected national average of 0.8%. From 2006 to 2007 the state's population grew by 0.6%. Per capita personal income in Missouri was $33,984 in 2007, up from $32,793 in 2006. For 2007, this was seventeenth lowest in the country and $4,580 below the national average. From 2000 to 2007 the per capita income in Missouri grew at a compound annual rate of 3.2%, compared to 3.7% nationally.

In 2006, the state's largest industry in terms of employment was retail trade, followed by manufacturing. The fastest growing industry was construction with 3.1% annual growth from 1998 to 2006. The state's workforce is generally less educated than other states—nationally, an average of 27.0% hold a bachelor degree or higher

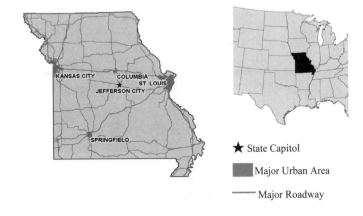

★ State Capitol

■ Major Urban Area

— Major Roadway

Demographic and Socioeconomic Profile

Demographics and Socioeconomic Figures			
Population and Households	**2000**	**2006**	**2007**
Total Population	5,595,211	5,842,713	5,878,415
Number of Households	2,194,594	2,305,027	2,309,626
Average Household Size	2.5	2.5	2.5
Age and Ethnicity			
Median Age	36.1	37.2	37.5
Population 18 Years of Age and Older	4,169,109	4,420,284	4,451,113
Population 65 Years of Age and Older	756,038	779,605	786,201
Caucasian Population	4,746,952	4,905,832	4,930,507
African-American Population	622,087	661,535	664,022
Hispanic Population	116,373	160,898	176,878
Asian Population	60,429	86,010	81,621
Foreign-Born Population (%)	2.7	3.3	3.5
Income			
Per Capita Personal Income (USD)	$27,241	$32,793	$33,984
Median Household Income (USD)	$37,934	$42,841	$45,114
Individuals below Poverty Level	11.7%	13.6%	13.0%

Data: U.S. Census, American Community Survey; U.S. Department of Commerce, Bureau of Economic Analysis

compared to 24.5% in Missouri; and 8.9% hold professional or graduate degrees (national average is 10.1%); however, 85.6% of the state's adult population has graduated from high school, compared to an 84.1% national average.

In fiscal year 2005–6, Missouri had total tax revenues of $18.3 billion. The largest share was generated from sales and gross receipts taxes, followed by property taxes. The per capita tax burden in Missouri was $3,134 for 2005–6, some $858 below the national average. In terms of business taxes, the state ranked fifth in a 2008 analysis by Anderson Economic Group. Forbes Magazine and the Tax Foundation ranked the state's business climate thirtieth and sixteenth, respectively.

Population Projections

Year	2010	2015	2020	2025
Total Population	5,922,078	6,069,556	6,199,882	6,315,366
Median Age	37.6	37.9	38.6	39.2
Population 18 Years of Age and Older	4,510,684	4,633,827	4,739,310	4,839,119
Population 65 Years of Age and Older	821,645	922,418	1,047,071	1,189,605

Data: U.S. Census Bureau

Workforce and Industry Profile

Workforce

	2000	2006	2007
Civilian Labor Force	2,973,092	3,032,434	3,023,106
Labor Force Participation Rate	70.2%	67.4%	67.0%
Unemployment Rate	3.3%	4.8%	5.1%
Average Wage Per Job (USD)	$31,385	$35,670	$37,240
Education Attainment (Population 25 Years and Older)	**(%)**	**(%)**	**(%)**
High School Graduate or Higher	81.3	84.8	85.6
Bachelors Degree or Higher	21.6	24.3	24.5
Graduate or Professional Degree	7.6	8.4	8.9

Data: U.S. Census Bureau, American Community Survey; U.S. Department of Commerce, Bureau of Economic Analysis; U.S. Department of Labor, Bureau of Labor Statistics

Industry Overview

	1998	2005	2006
Total Employees	2,310,122	2,425,403	2,468,035
Total Payroll ($1,000)	64,669,474	82,340,359	87,735,211
Total Establishments	143,912	154,306	154,546
Establishments with 1–19 Employees	123,828	132,741	132,345
Establishments with 20–49 Employees	12,250	16,654	13,835
Establishments with 50–249 Employees	6,801	7,157	7,283
Establishments with 250–999 Employees	885	906	934
Establishments with 1,000+ Employees	148	148	149

Data: U.S. Census Bureau, County Business Patterns

Major Industries (Ranked by 2006 Employment; Payroll in $1,000s)

Industry	1998 Employment	2006 Employment	1998 Payroll	2006 Payroll
Health Care and Social Assistance	320,300	362,926	8,508,854	12,476,845
Retail Trade	304,009	326,498	5,452,695	7,041,920
Manufacturing	382,003	305,447	12,487,544	12,983,861
Accommodation and Food Services	203,301	239,793	2,165,787	3,049,350
Admin., Support, Waste Mngt., Remediation Services	126,561	157,337	2,345,691	3,954,732
Construction	120,864	154,628	4,279,334	6,629,988
Professional, Scientific, Technical Services	108,911	137,901	4,351,928	7,448,468
Finance and Insurance	123,925	136,916	4,878,339	7,331,686
Wholesale Trade	126,722	127,755	4,638,609	5,504,284
Other Services (except Public Admin.)	112,331	120,644	1,957,301	2,714,542

Data: U.S. Census Bureau, County Business Patterns

Taxes and Business Climate

State and Local Taxes

Combined Revenues ($1,000)	2004–5	2005–6
Revenue from Property Taxes	4,695,477	4,984,531
Revenue from Sales and Gross Receipts Taxes	7,031,545	7,074,313
Revenue from Individual Income Taxes	4,318,505	4,821,082
Revenue from Corporate Income Taxes	237,476	364,023
Revenue from Other Taxes	1,091,261	1,067,787
Total Tax Revenue	17,374,264	18,311,736
Per Capita Taxes		
Property Tax Per Capita	811	853
Sales and Gross Receipts Tax Per Capita	1,215	1,211
Individual Income Tax Per Capita	746	825
Corporate Income Tax Per Capita	41	62
Other Taxes Per Capita	189	183
Total Taxes Per Capita	3,002	3,134

Data: U.S. Census Bureau; Anderson Economic Group, LLC

Business Climate Measures

Anderson Economic Group: 2008 Business Tax Ranking (1 is Best)	5
Forbes Magazine: 2008 Best States for Business Ranking (1 is Best)	30
Tax Foundation: 2009 Business Tax Climate Ranking (1 is Best)	16
2004–5 Employer Firm Births	16,245
2004–5 Employer Firm Terminations	14,639

Data: Anderson Economic Group; Tax Foundation; Forbes Magazine; U.S. Census, Statistics of U.S. Businesses

Voting Behavior and Elected Officials

Voter Registration and Turnout (%)

	1996	2000	2004	2008
Registered Voters Who Voted	64.6	61.1	65.1	NaN
Population Age 18+ Who Voted	54.0	56.6	63.6	65.8

Data: Dave Leip's Atlas of U.S. Presidential Elections

Presidential Election Results (Nationwide Winner Listed First)

2008	Popular Vote (%)	Electoral Votes
Barack Obama (Democrat)	49.3	0
John McCain (Republican)	49.4	11
Other	1.4	0
2004		
George W. Bush (Republican, Incumbent)	53.3	11
John Kerry (Democrat)	46.1	0
Other	0.6	0
2000		
George W. Bush (Republican)	50.4	11
Albert Gore (Democrat)	47.1	0
Ralph Nader (Green)	1.6	0
Other	0.9	0
1996		
William Clinton (Democrat, Incumbent)	47.5	11
Robert Dole (Republican)	41.2	0
H. Ross Perot (Reformist)	10.1	0
Other	1.2	0

Data: Dave Leip's Atlas of U.S. Presidential Elections

Governor and U.S. Congressional Seats				
Governor	**Party**	**Year Term Began**	**Term**	**Max. Consecutive Terms**
Jay Nixon	D	2009	First	2
U.S. Senators	**Party**	**Year Elected**	**Term Expires**	
Claire McCaskill	D	2006	2013	
Christopher Bond	R	1986	2011	
U.S. Representatives		**Republican**	**Democrat**	**Other**
		5	4	0

Data: National Governors Association; U.S. Senate, Office of the Clerk; U.S. House of Representatives

Business and Economic Agencies

Agency	Website Address
Missouri Chamber of Commerce & Industry	www.mochamber.org
Missouri Department of Economic Development	www.ded.mo.gov
Missouri Small Business Dev. Center	www.missouribusiness.net/sbdc
Missouri Secretary of State, Corporations Division	www.sos.mo.gov/business/corporations

Data: Various agency websites

Montana

With a population of 957,861 people, Montana was the seventh least populous state in the United States in 2007. From 2000 to 2007 the state's population increased by 55,666 people, and is projected to increase to 1.0 million by 2025. This 0.4% projected annual growth rate compares to the projected national average of 0.8%. From 2006 to 2007 the state's population grew by 1.4%. The state's 2007 per capita personal income of $33,145 was higher compared to $30,886 in 2006 and the eleventh lowest in the United States, some $5,419 below the national average. Per capita income in Montana grew at a compound annual rate of 5.4% from 2000 to 2007, compared to 3.7% nationally.

Montana's largest industry in terms of 2006 employment was health care and social assistance. The fastest growing industry was professional, scientific, and technical services, with 7.9% annual growth from 1998 to 2006. The second fastest growing industry was construction. The state's workforce is generally more educated than other

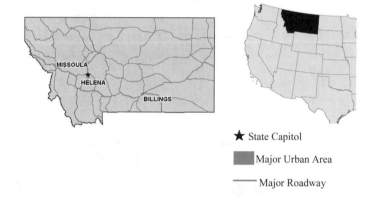

★ State Capitol

▇ Major Urban Area

— Major Roadway

Demographic and Socioeconomic Profile

Demographics and Socioeconomic Figures			
Population and Households	**2000**	**2006**	**2007**
Total Population	902,195	944,632	957,861
Number of Households	358,667	372,190	371,954
Average Household Size	2.4	2.5	2.5
Age and Ethnicity			
Median Age	37.5	39.5	39.1
Population 18 Years of Age and Older	672,251	726,534	737,810
Population 65 Years of Age and Older	120,931	131,318	131,467
Caucasian Population	817,604	847,192	858,205
African-American Population	2,359	4,470	5,961
Hispanic Population	18,490	20,513	25,513
Asian Population	4,363	5,525	5,040
Foreign-Born Population (%)	1.8	1.9	1.7
Income			
Per Capita Personal Income (USD)	$22,929	$30,886	$33,145
Median Household Income (USD)	$33,024	$40,627	$43,531
Individuals below Poverty Level	14.6%	13.6%	14.1%

Data: U.S. Census, American Community Survey; U.S. Department of Commerce, Bureau of Economic Analysis

states—90.0% of the state's adult population has graduated from high school, compared to an 84.1% national average; 27.0% hold a bachelor degree or higher (national average is 27.0%); and 8.6% hold professional or graduate degrees compared to the national average of 10.1%.

Montana's total tax revenue was $3.0 billion for fiscal year 2005–6. The largest share of tax revenue in 2005–6 was generated from property taxes, followed by individual income taxes. On a per capita basis, residents of Montana paid taxes of $3,197, compared to the national average of $3,992 for 2005–6. In terms of business taxes, the state ranked fifty-first in a 2008 analysis by Anderson Economic Group. Forbes Magazine and the Tax Foundation ranked the state's business climate twenty-fourth and sixth, respectively.

Population Projections

Year	2010	2015	2020	2025
Total Population	968,598	999,489	1,022,735	1,037,387
Median Age	40.4	41.5	42.7	44.3
Population 18 Years of Age and Older	756,286	783,498	804,685	821,871
Population 65 Years of Age and Older	144,961	173,778	211,783	247,769

Data: U.S. Census Bureau

Workforce and Industry Profile

Workforce

	2000	2006	2007
Civilian Labor Force	468,865	493,842	502,031
Labor Force Participation Rate	68.2%	66.9%	67.1%
Unemployment Rate	4.8%	3.2%	3.4%
Average Wage Per Job (USD)	$24,274	$31,290	$32,640
Education Attainment (Population 25 Years and Older)	**(%)**	**(%)**	**(%)**
High School Graduate or Higher	87.2	90.1	90.0
Bachelors Degree or Higher	24.4	27.4	27.0
Graduate or Professional Degree	7.2	8.4	8.6

Data: U.S. Census Bureau, American Community Survey; U.S. Department of Commerce, Bureau of Economic Analysis; U.S. Department of Labor, Bureau of Labor Statistics

Industry Overview

	1998	2005	2006
Total Employees	277,144	326,887	342,526
Total Payroll ($1,000)	5,960,687	8,950,520	9,838,585
Total Establishments	30,957	35,736	36,649
Establishments with 1–19 Employees	28,134	32,411	33,184
Establishments with 20–49 Employees	2,000	2,376	2,441
Establishments with 50–249 Employees	767	872	942
Establishments with 250–999 Employees	51	70	75
Establishments with 1,000+ Employees	5	7	7

Data: U.S. Census Bureau, County Business Patterns

Major Industries (Ranked by 2006 Employment; Payroll in $1,000s)				
Industry	1998 Employment	2006 Employment	1998 Payroll	2006 Payroll
Retail Trade	48,285	57,949	771,476	1,261,262
Health Care and Social Assistance	45,242	57,188	1,067,519	1,806,169
Accommodation and Food Services	37,393	44,624	347,915	523,070
Construction	16,767	26,879	500,826	1,039,585
Professional, Scientific, Technical Services	12,362	22,677	352,733	816,215
Manufacturing	20,686	19,878	599,839	763,480
Finance and Insurance	12,780	16,993	403,122	664,170
Other Services (except Public Admin.)	13,315	14,786	201,904	294,101
Wholesale Trade	15,025	14,643	398,273	568,710
Admin., Support, Waste Mngt., Remediation Services	11,000	14,399	178,935	299,205

Data: U.S. Census Bureau, County Business Patterns

Taxes and Business Climate

State and Local Taxes		
Combined Revenues ($1,000)	2004–5	2005–6
Revenue from Property Taxes	997,447	1,058,805
Revenue from Sales and Gross Receipts Taxes	459,614	517,850
Revenue from Individual Income Taxes	713,390	768,911
Revenue from Corporate Income Taxes	98,214	153,675
Revenue from Other Taxes	454,037	520,434
Total Tax Revenue	2,722,702	3,019,675
Per Capita Taxes		
Property Tax Per Capita	1,066	1,121
Sales and Gross Receipts Tax Per Capita	491	548
Individual Income Tax Per Capita	762	814
Corporate Income Tax Per Capita	105	163
Other Taxes Per Capita	485	551
Total Taxes Per Capita	2,910	3,197

Data: U.S. Census Bureau; Anderson Economic Group, LLC

Business Climate Measures

Anderson Economic Group: 2008 Business Tax Ranking (1 is Best)	51
Forbes Magazine: 2008 Best States for Business Ranking (1 is Best)	24
Tax Foundation: 2009 Business Tax Climate Ranking (1 is Best)	6
2004–5 Employer Firm Births	3,641
2004–5 Employer Firm Terminations	2,904

Data: Anderson Economic Group; Tax Foundation; Forbes Magazine; U.S. Census, Statistics of U.S. Businesses

Voting Behavior and Elected Officials

Voter Registration and Turnout (%)

	1996	2000	2004	2008
Registered Voters Who Voted	68.9	58.9	70.6	73.5
Population Age 18+ Who Voted	62.1	61.1	64.2	66.6

Data: Dave Leip's Atlas of U.S. Presidential Elections

Presidential Election Results (Nationwide Winner Listed First)

2008	Popular Vote (%)	Electoral Votes
Barack Obama (Democrat)	47.2	0
John McCain (Republican)	49.4	3
Other	3.4	0
2004		
George W. Bush (Republican, Incumbent)	59.1	3
John Kerry (Democrat)	38.6	0
Other	2.4	0
2000		
George W. Bush (Republican)	58.4	3
Albert Gore (Democrat)	33.4	0
Ralph Nader (Green)	6.0	0
Other	2.3	0
1996		
William Clinton (Democrat, Incumbent)	41.2	0
Robert Dole (Republican)	44.1	3
H. Ross Perot (Reformist)	13.6	0
Other	1.1	0

Data: Dave Leip's Atlas of U.S. Presidential Elections

Governor and U.S. Congressional Seats

Governor	Party	Year Term Began	Term	Max. Consecutive Terms
Brian Schweitzer	D	2009	Second	2

U.S. Senators	Party	Year Elected	Term Expires	
Max Baucus	D	1978	2015	
Jon Tester	D	2006	2013	

U.S. Representatives		Republican	Democrat	Other
		1	0	0

Data: National Governors Association; U.S. Senate, Office of the Clerk; U.S. House of Representatives

Business and Economic Agencies

Agency	Website Address
Montana Chamber of Commerce	www.montanachamber.com
Montana Department of Commerce	www.commerce.state.mt.us
Montana Small Business Dev. Center	sbdc.mt.gov
Montana Secretary of State, Business Services Bureau	www.sos.state.mt.us/BSB

Data: Various agency websites

Nebraska

Nebraska is located in the West North Central region of the United States. Nebraska has a population of 1.8 million people, making it the thirteenth least populous state in 2007. The state's population increased by 63,308 people from 2000 to 2007, and is projected to increase to 1.8 million by 2025. This 0.1% projected annual growth rate is below the national average of 0.8%. From 2006 to 2007 the state's population grew by 0.4%. Per capita personal income in Nebraska was $36,189 in 2007, up from $34,383 in 2006. For 2007, this was $2,375 below the national average and the twenty-sixth lowest in the country. The state's per capita income grew at a compound annual rate of 3.9% from 2000 to 2007, compared to 3.7% nationally.

The state's workforce generally has less education than other states—27.5% hold a bachelor degree or higher (national average is 27.0%); and 8.8% hold professional or graduate degrees (national average is 10.1%); however, 89.6% of the state's adult population has graduated from high school,

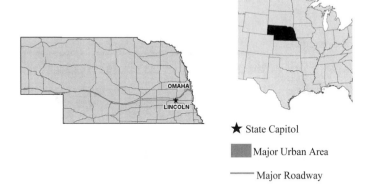

★ State Capitol

■ Major Urban Area

— Major Roadway

Demographic and Socioeconomic Profile

Demographics and Socioeconomic Figures			
Population and Households	**2000**	**2006**	**2007**
Total Population	1,711,263	1,768,331	1,774,571
Number of Households	666,184	700,888	699,728
Average Household Size	2.5	2.5	2.5
Age and Ethnicity			
Median Age	35.3	36.0	36.1
Population 18 Years of Age and Older	1,261,648	1,322,921	1,327,093
Population 65 Years of Age and Older	232,359	233,275	235,631
Caucasian Population	1,533,787	1,566,980	1,582,113
African-American Population	67,435	72,095	70,333
Hispanic Population	93,872	130,230	132,477
Asian Population	21,126	29,815	25,731
Foreign-Born Population (%)	4.4	5.6	5.6
Income			
Per Capita Personal Income (USD)	$27,625	$34,383	$36,189
Median Household Income (USD)	$39,250	$45,474	$47,085
Individuals below Poverty Level	9.7%	11.5%	11.2%

Data: U.S. Census, American Community Survey; U.S. Department of Commerce, Bureau of Economic Analysis

compared to an 84.1% national average. In 2006, the state's largest industry in terms of employment was retail trade, followed by manufacturing. The fastest growing industry was professional, scientific, and technical services, with 5.4% annual growth from 1998 to 2006.

In fiscal year 2005–6, Nebraska had total tax revenues of $6.9 billion. The largest share was generated from property taxes, followed by sales and gross receipts taxes. The per capita tax burden in Nebraska was $3,888 for 2005–6, some $104 below the national average, and a $133 increase from the 2004–5 per capita tax burden. In terms of business taxes, Nebraska ranked twenty-sixth in a 2008 report by Anderson Economic Group. The state's business climate was ranked tenth by Forbes Magazine and forty-second by the Tax Foundation.

Population Projections

Year	2010	2015	2020	2025
Total Population	1,768,997	1,788,508	1,802,678	1,812,787
Median Age	36.7	37.2	37.9	38.3
Population 18 Years of Age and Older	1,322,741	1,334,423	1,344,066	1,355,661
Population 65 Years of Age and Older	243,313	271,379	308,994	347,809

Data: U.S. Census Bureau

Workforce and Industry Profile

Workforce

	2000	2006	2007
Civilian Labor Force	949,762	974,476	984,665
Labor Force Participation Rate	74.0%	73.0%	73.3%
Unemployment Rate	2.8%	3.0%	2.9%
Average Wage Per Job (USD)	$27,692	$34,300	$35,270
Education Attainment (Population 25 Years and Older)	(%)	(%)	(%)
High School Graduate or Higher	86.6	89.5	89.6
Bachelors Degree or Higher	23.7	26.9	27.5
Graduate or Professional Degree	7.3	7.2	8.8

Data: U.S. Census Bureau, American Community Survey; U.S. Department of Commerce, Bureau of Economic Analysis; U.S. Department of Labor, Bureau of Labor Statistics

Industry Overview

	1998	2005	2006
Total Employees	720,252	773,082	789,231
Total Payroll ($1,000)	18,178,238	24,180,753	25,743,159
Total Establishments	48,655	51,440	51,906
Establishments with 1–19 Employees	42,487	44,698	44,978
Establishments with 20–49 Employees	3,813	4,237	4,389
Establishments with 50–249 Employees	2,050	2,170	2,193
Establishments with 250–999 Employees	258	284	297
Establishments with 1,000+ Employees	47	51	49

Data: U.S. Census Bureau, County Business Patterns

Major Industries (Ranked by 2006 Employment; Payroll in $1,000s)

Industry	1998 Employment	2006 Employment	1998 Payroll	2006 Payroll
Health Care and Social Assistance	95,015	112,008	2,487,228	3,883,371
Retail Trade	104,866	108,719	1,675,637	2,204,032
Manufacturing	109,645	105,416	3,255,216	3,789,275
Accommodation and Food Services	60,088	68,237	535,911	717,528
Admin., Support, Waste Mngt., Remediation Services	52,512	65,512	1,088,358	1,656,713
Finance and Insurance	47,979	59,095	1,710,584	2,859,987
Professional, Scientific, Technical Services	30,406	46,376	1,143,609	2,282,234
Construction	38,297	43,114	1,258,732	1,594,030
Wholesale Trade	40,357	37,859	1,255,481	1,690,629
Other Services (except Public Admin.)	33,786	36,797	530,062	731,682

Data: U.S. Census Bureau, County Business Patterns

Taxes and Business Climate

State and Local Taxes

Combined Revenues ($1,000)	2004–5	2005–6
Revenue from Property Taxes	2,101,827	2,234,031
Revenue from Sales and Gross Receipts Taxes	2,314,321	2,188,874
Revenue from Individual Income Taxes	1,393,897	1,545,024
Revenue from Corporate Income Taxes	198,380	262,296
Revenue from Other Taxes	577,813	644,349
Total Tax Revenue	6,586,238	6,874,574

Per Capita Taxes

	2004–5	2005–6
Property Tax Per Capita	1,198	1,263
Sales and Gross Receipts Tax Per Capita	1,319	1,238
Individual Income Tax Per Capita	795	874
Corporate Income Tax Per Capita	113	148
Other Taxes Per Capita	329	364
Total Taxes Per Capita	3,755	3,888

Data: U.S. Census Bureau; Anderson Economic Group, LLC

Business Climate Measures

Anderson Economic Group: 2008 Business Tax Ranking (1 is Best)	26
Forbes Magazine: 2008 Best States for Business Ranking (1 is Best)	10
Tax Foundation: 2009 Business Tax Climate Ranking (1 is Best)	42
2004–5 Employer Firm Births	4,356
2004–5 Employer Firm Terminations	3,938

Data: Anderson Economic Group; Tax Foundation; Forbes Magazine; U.S. Census, Statistics of U.S. Businesses

Voting Behavior and Elected Officials

Voter Registration and Turnout (%)

	1996	2000	2004	2008
Registered Voters Who Voted	66.7	64.2	67.1	69.2
Population Age 18+ Who Voted	55.9	55.2	60.0	60.4

Data: Dave Leip's Atlas of U.S. Presidential Elections

Presidential Election Results (Nationwide Winner Listed First)

2008	Popular Vote (%)	Electoral Votes
Barack Obama (Democrat)	41.6	1
John McCain (Republican)	56.5	4
Other	1.9	0
2004		
George W. Bush (Republican, Incumbent)	65.9	5
John Kerry (Democrat)	32.7	0
Other	1.4	0
2000		
George W. Bush (Republican)	62.3	5
Albert Gore (Democrat)	33.3	0
Ralph Nader (Green)	3.5	0
Other	1.0	0
1996		
William Clinton (Democrat, Incumbent)	35.0	0
Robert Dole (Republican)	53.7	5
H. Ross Perot (Reformist)	10.5	0
Other	0.9	0

Data: Dave Leip's Atlas of U.S. Presidential Elections

Governor and U.S. Congressional Seats				
Governor	**Party**	**Year Term Began**	**Term**	**Max. Consecutive Terms**
Dave Heineman	R	2007	Second	2
U.S. Senators	**Party**	**Year Elected**	**Term Expires**	
Mike Johanns	R	2008	2015	
Ben Nelson	D	2000	2013	
U.S. Representatives		**Republican**	**Democrat**	**Other**
		3	0	0

Data: National Governors Association; U.S. Senate, Office of the Clerk; U.S. House of Representatives

Business and Economic Agencies

Agency	Website Address
Nebraska Chamber of Commerce & Industry	www.nechamber.com
Nebraska Department of Economic Development	www.neded.org
Nebraska Small Business Dev. Center	nbdc.unomaha.edu
Nebraska Secretary of State, Corporations Division	www.sos.state.ne.us/business/corp_serv

Data: Various agency websites

Nevada

Nevada, located in the Mountain region of the United States, has a population of 2.6 million people, making it the sixteenth least populous state in 2007. The state's population increased by 567,125 people from 2000 to 2007, and is projected to increase to 3.9 million by 2025. This 2.3% projected annual growth rate compares to the projected national average of 0.8%. From 2006 to 2007 the state's population grew by 2.8%. Per capita personal income in Nevada was $39,649 in 2007, up from $39,015 in 2006. For 2007, this was seventeenth highest in the country and $1,085 above the national average. From 2000 to 2007 the per capita income in Nevada grew at a compound annual rate of 3.8%, compared to 3.7% nationally.

In 2006, the state's largest industry in terms of employment was accommodation and food services, followed by retail trade. The fastest growing industry was educational services with 11.3% annual growth from 1998 to 2006. The state's workforce is generally less educated than other states—83.7% of the state's adult population

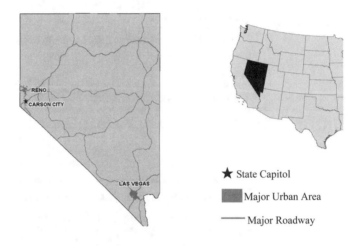

★ State Capitol

▇ Major Urban Area

── Major Roadway

Demographic and Socioeconomic Profile

Demographics and Socioeconomic Figures			
Population and Households	2000	2006	2007
Total Population	1,998,257	2,495,529	2,565,382
Number of Households	751,165	936,828	954,067
Average Household Size	2.6	2.6	2.7
Age and Ethnicity			
Median Age	35.0	35.6	35.7
Population 18 Years of Age and Older	1,488,526	1,861,082	1,901,032
Population 65 Years of Age and Older	218,497	275,026	284,768
Caucasian Population	1,503,083	1,837,860	1,897,158
African-American Population	132,490	183,064	190,238
Hispanic Population	393,539	610,051	644,485
Asian Population	89,121	147,363	155,603
Foreign-Born Population (%)	15.8	19.1	19.4
Income			
Per Capita Personal Income (USD)	$30,437	$39,015	$39,649
Median Household Income (USD)	$44,581	$52,998	$55,062
Individuals below Poverty Level	10.5%	10.3%	10.7%

Data: U.S. Census, American Community Survey; U.S. Department of Commerce, Bureau of Economic Analysis

has graduated from high school, compared to an 84.1% national average. Nationally, an average of 27.0% hold a bachelor degree or higher compared to 21.8% in Nevada; and 7.5% hold professional or graduate degrees (national average is 10.1%).

In fiscal year 2005–6, Nevada had total tax revenues of $9.8 billion. The largest share was generated from sales and gross receipts taxes, followed by property taxes. The per capita tax burden in Nevada was $3,913 for 2005–6, some $79 below the national average. In terms of business taxes, the state ranked thirty-seventh in a 2008 analysis by Anderson Economic Group. Forbes Magazine and the Tax Foundation ranked the state's business climate nineteenth and third, respectively.

Population Projections

Year	2010	2015	2020	2025
Total Population	2,690,531	3,058,190	3,452,283	3,863,298
Median Age	37.8	38.7	39.0	39.1
Population 18 Years of Age and Older	2,025,446	2,306,302	2,595,522	2,895,136
Population 65 Years of Age and Older	329,621	421,719	531,120	659,700

Data: U.S. Census Bureau

Workforce and Industry Profile

Workforce

	2000	2006	2007
Civilian Labor Force	1,062,845	1,295,085	1,322,643
Labor Force Participation Rate	69.8%	68.0%	68.5%
Unemployment Rate	4.5%	4.2%	4.7%
Average Wage Per Job (USD)	$32,276	$36,000	$37,440
Education Attainment (Population 25 Years and Older)	**(%)**	**(%)**	**(%)**
High School Graduate or Higher	80.7	83.9	83.7
Bachelors Degree or Higher	18.2	20.8	21.8
Graduate or Professional Degree	6.1	11.2	7.5

Data: U.S. Census Bureau, American Community Survey; U.S. Department of Commerce, Bureau of Economic Analysis; U.S. Department of Labor, Bureau of Labor Statistics

Industry Overview

	1998	2005	2006
Total Employees	800,861	1,089,422	1,165,375
Total Payroll ($1,000)	21,847,334	39,261,902	41,743,174
Total Establishments	44,613	58,561	61,164
Establishments with 1–19 Employees	38,274	49,794	51,833
Establishments with 20–49 Employees	3,946	5,296	5,599
Establishments with 50–249 Employees	2,041	2,976	3,201
Establishments with 250–999 Employees	263	397	418
Establishments with 1,000+ Employees	89	98	113

Data: U.S. Census Bureau, County Business Patterns

Major Industries (Ranked by 2006 Employment; Payroll in $1,000s)

Industry	1998 Employment	2006 Employment	1998 Payroll	2006 Payroll
Accommodation and Food Services	246,530	312,929	5,121,400	8,417,474
Retail Trade	95,507	142,965	2,038,341	3,804,955
Construction	77,682	139,482	2,705,048	5,880,538
Admin., Support, Waste Mngt., Remediation Services	53,102	102,249	1,172,519	2,705,583
Health Care and Social Assistance	60,524	90,231	1,938,561	3,965,055
Professional, Scientific, Technical Services	33,347	58,756	1,423,080	3,216,494
Manufacturing	39,029	46,747	1,298,552	2,075,064
Transportation and Warehousing	25,120	44,682	626,946	1,349,452
Finance and Insurance	27,360	40,161	1,012,252	2,069,353
Wholesale Trade	29,929	38,980	1,066,396	1,967,146

Data: U.S. Census Bureau, County Business Patterns

Taxes and Business Climate

State and Local Taxes

Combined Revenues ($1,000)	2004–5	2005–6
Revenue from Property Taxes	2,320,774	2,509,147
Revenue from Sales and Gross Receipts Taxes	5,333,746	5,746,729
Revenue from Individual Income Taxes	0	0
Revenue from Corporate Income Taxes	0	0
Revenue from Other Taxes	1,389,050	1,507,973
Total Tax Revenue	9,043,570	9,763,849

Per Capita Taxes

	2004–5	2005–6
Property Tax Per Capita	963	1,005
Sales and Gross Receipts Tax Per Capita	2,214	2,303
Individual Income Tax Per Capita	0	0
Corporate Income Tax Per Capita	0	0
Other Taxes Per Capita	577	604
Total Taxes Per Capita	3,754	3,913

Data: U.S. Census Bureau; Anderson Economic Group, LLC

Business Climate Measures

Anderson Economic Group: 2008 Business Tax Ranking (1 is Best)	37
Forbes Magazine: 2008 Best States for Business Ranking (1 is Best)	19
Tax Foundation: 2009 Business Tax Climate Ranking (1 is Best)	3
2004–5 Employer Firm Births	8,027
2004–5 Employer Firm Terminations	5,992

Data: Anderson Economic Group; Tax Foundation; Forbes Magazine; U.S. Census, Statistics of U.S. Businesses

Voting Behavior and Elected Officials

Voter Registration and Turnout (%)

	1996	2000	2004	2008
Registered Voters Who Voted	59.7	69.7	77.5	80.1
Population Age 18+ Who Voted	38.3	40.9	50.0	50.9

Data: Dave Leip's Atlas of U.S. Presidential Elections

Presidential Election Results (Nationwide Winner Listed First)

2008	Popular Vote (%)	Electoral Votes
Barack Obama (Democrat)	55.2	5
John McCain (Republican)	42.7	0
Other	2.2	0
2004		
George W. Bush (Republican, Incumbent)	50.5	5
John Kerry (Democrat)	47.9	0
Other	1.7	0
2000		
George W. Bush (Republican)	49.5	4
Albert Gore (Democrat)	46.0	0
Ralph Nader (Green)	2.5	0
Other	2.0	0
1996		
William Clinton (Democrat, Incumbent)	43.9	4
Robert Dole (Republican)	42.9	0
H. Ross Perot (Reformist)	9.5	0
Other	3.7	0

Data: Dave Leip's Atlas of U.S. Presidential Elections

Governor and U.S. Congressional Seats

Governor	Party	Year Term Began	Term	Max. Consecutive Terms
Jim Gibbons	R	2007	First	2

U.S. Senators	Party	Year Elected	Term Expires	
John Ensign	R	2000	2013	
Harry Reid	D	1986	2011	

U.S. Representatives	Republican	Democrat	Other
	1	2	0

Data: National Governors Association; U.S. Senate, Office of the Clerk; U.S. House of Representatives

Business and Economic Agencies

Agency	Website Address
Las Vegas Chamber of Commerce	www.lvchamber.com
Nevada Comission on Economic Development	www.expand2nevada.com
Nevada Small Business Dev. Center	www.nsbdc.org
Nevada Secretary of State, Commercial Recordings Division	www.sos.state.nv.us/comm_rec

Data: Various agency websites

New Hampshire

With a population of 1.3 million people, New Hampshire was the tenth least populous state in the United States in 2007. From 2000 to 2007 the state's population increased by 80,042 people, and is projected to increase to 1.6 million by 2025. This 1.0% projected annual growth rate compares to the projected national average of 0.8%. From 2006 to 2007 the state's population grew by 0.1%. The state's 2007 per capita personal income of $41,444 was higher compared to $39,655 in 2006 and the ninth highest in the United States, some $2,880 above the national average. Per capita income in New Hampshire grew at a compound annual rate of 3.1% from 2000 to 2007, compared to 3.7% nationally.

New Hampshire's largest industry in terms of 2006 employment was health care and social assistance. The fastest growing industry was arts, entertainment, and recreation, with 4.4% annual growth from 1998 to 2006. The second fastest growing industry was professional, scientific, and technical services. The state's workforce

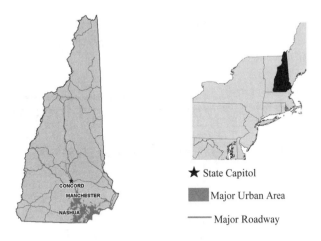

★ State Capitol

▨ Major Urban Area

— Major Roadway

Demographic and Socioeconomic Profile

Demographics and Socioeconomic Figures			
Population and Households	**2000**	**2006**	**2007**
Total Population	1,235,786	1,314,895	1,315,828
Number of Households	474,606	504,503	501,505
Average Household Size	2.5	2.5	2.5
Age and Ethnicity			
Median Age	37.1	39.3	39.8
Population 18 Years of Age and Older	926,885	1,017,217	1,017,230
Population 65 Years of Age and Older	148,039	161,836	165,668
Caucasian Population	1,186,448	1,250,231	1,247,023
African-American Population	8,984	13,842	12,546
Hispanic Population	19,910	29,721	32,621
Asian Population	15,422	26,136	26,790
Foreign-Born Population (%)	4.4	5.4	5.1
Income			
Per Capita Personal Income (USD)	$33,396	$39,655	$41,444
Median Household Income (USD)	$49,467	$59,683	$62,369
Individuals below Poverty Level	6.5%	8.0%	7.1%

Data: U.S. Census, American Community Survey; U.S. Department of Commerce, Bureau of Economic Analysis

is generally more educated than other states—90.5% of the state's adult population has graduated from high school, compared to an 84.1% national average; 32.5% hold a bachelor degree or higher (national average is 27.0%); and 11.5% hold professional or graduate degrees compared to the national average of 10.1%.

New Hampshire's total tax revenue was $4.5 billion for fiscal year 2005–6. The largest share of tax revenue in 2005–6 was generated from property taxes, followed by sales and gross receipts taxes. On a per capita basis, residents of New Hampshire paid taxes of $3,435, compared to the national average of $3,992 for 2005–6. In terms of business taxes, the state ranked forty-sixth in a 2008 analysis by Anderson Economic Group. Forbes Magazine and the Tax Foundation ranked the state's business climate twentieth and eighth, respectively.

Population Projections

Year	2010	2015	2020	2025
Total Population	1,385,560	1,456,679	1,524,751	1,586,348
Median Age	39.6	39.8	40.3	41.3
Population 18 Years of Age and Older	1,081,396	1,143,197	1,194,887	1,241,954
Population 65 Years of Age and Older	178,823	217,498	261,856	311,456

Data: U.S. Census Bureau

Workforce and Industry Profile

Workforce

	2000	2006	2007
Civilian Labor Force	694,254	736,780	738,212
Labor Force Participation Rate	73.1%	71.2%	71.1%
Unemployment Rate	2.7%	3.4%	3.5%
Average Wage Per Job (USD)	$34,738	$39,250	$40,780
Education Attainment (Population 25 Years and Older)	(%)	(%)	(%)
High School Graduate or Higher	87.4	89.9	90.5
Bachelors Degree or Higher	28.7	31.9	32.5
Graduate or Professional Degree	10.0	12.4	11.5

Data: U.S. Census Bureau, American Community Survey; U.S. Department of Commerce, Bureau of Economic Analysis; U.S. Department of Labor, Bureau of Labor Statistics

Industry Overview

	1998	2005	2006
Total Employees	518,526	562,398	577,415
Total Payroll ($1,000)	14,863,829	21,026,773	21,897,917
Total Establishments	36,842	39,224	39,376
Establishments with 1–19 Employees	32,118	33,999	33,939
Establishments with 20–49 Employees	2,969	3,290	3,429
Establishments with 50–249 Employees	1,526	1,712	1,800
Establishments with 250–999 Employees	211	199	186
Establishments with 1,000+ Employees	18	24	22

Data: U.S. Census Bureau, County Business Patterns

Major Industries (Ranked by 2006 Employment; Payroll in $1,000s)

Industry	1998 Employment	2006 Employment	1998 Payroll	2006 Payroll
Retail Trade	85,811	100,490	1,621,626	2,412,271
Health Care and Social Assistance	68,223	82,414	1,853,351	3,155,449
Manufacturing	101,513	76,358	3,540,699	3,745,751
Accommodation and Food Services	46,138	55,682	530,934	829,914
Admin., Support, Waste Mngt., Remediation Services	30,307	41,132	750,584	1,472,713
Professional, Scientific, Technical Services	22,048	30,165	904,628	1,756,175
Construction	22,749	29,085	831,245	1,386,356
Finance and Insurance	24,936	29,013	958,836	1,687,499
Educational Services	20,869	27,508	411,916	681,908
Wholesale Trade	22,912	24,880	946,987	1,414,229

Data: U.S. Census Bureau, County Business Patterns

Taxes and Business Climate

State and Local Taxes		
Combined Revenues ($1,000)	**2004–5**	**2005–6**
Revenue from Property Taxes	2,650,326	2,780,460
Revenue from Sales and Gross Receipts Taxes	705,116	707,927
Revenue from Individual Income Taxes	67,686	80,931
Revenue from Corporate Income Taxes	476,489	542,644
Revenue from Other Taxes	420,160	405,055
Total Tax Revenue	4,319,777	4,517,017
Per Capita Taxes		
Property Tax Per Capita	2,034	2,115
Sales and Gross Receipts Tax Per Capita	541	538
Individual Income Tax Per Capita	52	62
Corporate Income Tax Per Capita	366	413
Other Taxes Per Capita	322	308
Total Taxes Per Capita	3,315	3,435

Data: U.S. Census Bureau; Anderson Economic Group, LLC

Business Climate Measures

Anderson Economic Group: 2008 Business Tax Ranking (1 is Best)	46
Forbes Magazine: 2008 Best States for Business Ranking (1 is Best)	20
Tax Foundation: 2009 Business Tax Climate Ranking (1 is Best)	8
2004–5 Employer Firm Births	3,730
2004–5 Employer Firm Terminations	3,314

Data: Anderson Economic Group; Tax Foundation; Forbes Magazine; U.S. Census, Statistics of U.S. Businesses

Voting Behavior and Elected Officials

Voter Registration and Turnout (%)

	1996	2000	2004	2008
Registered Voters Who Voted	66.1	66.6	79.2	NaN
Population Age 18+ Who Voted	57.3	61.4	69.1	69.9

Data: Dave Leip's Atlas of U.S. Presidential Elections

Presidential Election Results (Nationwide Winner Listed First)

2008	Popular Vote (%)	Electoral Votes
Barack Obama (Democrat)	54.1	4
John McCain (Republican)	44.5	0
Other	1.4	0
2004		
George W. Bush (Republican, Incumbent)	48.9	0
John Kerry (Democrat)	50.3	4
Other	0.9	0
2000		
George W. Bush (Republican)	48.1	4
Albert Gore (Democrat)	46.8	0
Ralph Nader (Green)	3.9	0
Other	1.2	0
1996		
William Clinton (Democrat, Incumbent)	49.3	4
Robert Dole (Republican)	39.4	0
H. Ross Perot (Reformist)	9.7	0
Other	1.6	0

Data: Dave Leip's Atlas of U.S. Presidential Elections

Governor and U.S. Congressional Seats

Governor	Party	Year Term Began	Term	Max. Consecutive Terms
John Lynch	D	2009	Third	No limit

U.S. Senators	Party	Year Elected	Term Expires	
Jeanne Shaheen	D	2008	2015	
Judd Gregg	R	1992	2011	

U.S. Representatives		Republican	Democrat	Other
		0	2	0

Data: National Governors Association; U.S. Senate, Office of the Clerk; U.S. House of Representatives

Business and Economic Agencies

Agency	Website Address
Business and Industry Association of New Hampshire	www.nhbia.org
State of New Hampshire Economic Development	www.nheconomy.com
New Hampshire Small Business Dev. Center	www.nhsbdc.org
New Hampshire Secretary of State, Corporate Division	www.sos.nh.gov/corporate

Data: Various agency websites

New Jersey

New Jersey is located in the Middle Atlantic region of the United States. New Jersey has a population of 8.7 million people, making it the eleventh most populous state in 2007. The state's population increased by 271,570 people from 2000 to 2007, and is projected to increase to 9.6 million by 2025. This 0.6% projected annual growth rate is below the national average of 0.8%. From 2006 to 2007 the state's population declined by 0.4%. Per capita personal income in New Jersey was $49,238 in 2007, up from $46,328 in 2006. For 2007, this was $10,674 above the national average and the second highest in the country. The state's per capita income grew at a compound annual rate of 3.6% from 2000 to 2007, compared to 3.7% nationally.

The state's workforce generally has more education than other states—87.0% of the state's adult population has graduated from high school, compared to an 84.1% national average; 33.9% hold a bachelor degree or higher (national average is 27.0%); and 12.7% hold professional or graduate degrees (national average is 10.1%).

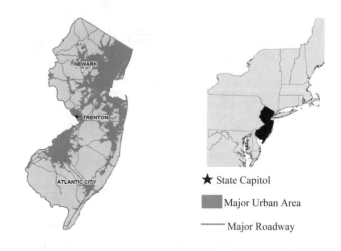

★ State Capitol

▮ Major Urban Area

— Major Roadway

Demographic and Socioeconomic Profile

Demographics and Socioeconomic Figures			
Population and Households	**2000**	**2006**	**2007**
Total Population	8,414,350	8,724,560	8,685,920
Number of Households	3,064,645	3,135,490	3,149,910
Average Household Size	2.7	2.7	2.7
Age and Ethnicity			
Median Age	36.7	38.2	38.4
Population 18 Years of Age and Older	6,332,876	6,634,907	6,623,152
Population 65 Years of Age and Older	1,113,035	1,125,605	1,134,691
Caucasian Population	6,099,439	6,073,160	6,037,580
African-American Population	1,127,266	1,187,161	1,185,829
Hispanic Population	1,116,149	1,364,699	1,382,029
Asian Population	481,794	652,378	648,484
Foreign-Born Population (%)	17.5	20.1	19.9
Income			
Per Capita Personal Income (USD)	$38,364	$46,328	$49,238
Median Household Income (USD)	$55,146	$64,470	$67,035
Individuals below Poverty Level	8.5%	8.7%	8.6%

Data: U.S. Census, American Community Survey; U.S. Department of Commerce, Bureau of Economic Analysis

In 2006, the state's largest industry in terms of employment was health care and social assistance, followed by retail trade. The fastest growing industry was forestry, fishing, hunting, and agricultural support, with 4.1% annual growth from 1998 to 2006.

In fiscal year 2005–6, New Jersey had total tax revenues of $47.3 billion. The largest share was generated from property taxes, followed by sales and gross receipts taxes. The per capita tax burden in New Jersey was $5,422 for 2005–6, some $1,430 above the national average, and a $506 increase from the 2004–5 per capita tax burden. In terms of business taxes, New Jersey ranked thirty-ninth in a 2008 report by Anderson Economic Group. The state's business climate was ranked thirty-fourth by Forbes Magazine and fiftieth by the Tax Foundation.

Population Projections

Year	2010	2015	2020	2025
Total Population	9,018,231	9,255,769	9,461,635	9,636,644
Median Age	38.9	39.3	39.6	40.2
Population 18 Years of Age and Older	6,930,007	7,151,894	7,323,271	7,477,125
Population 65 Years of Age and Older	1,231,585	1,385,167	1,552,544	1,762,460

Data: U.S. Census Bureau

Workforce and Industry Profile

Workforce

	2000	2006	2007
Civilian Labor Force	4,287,783	4,518,035	4,462,253
Labor Force Participation Rate	66.6%	66.9%	66.4%
Unemployment Rate	3.7%	4.6%	4.3%
Average Wage Per Job (USD)	$43,676	$45,450	$47,100
Education Attainment (Population 25 Years and Older)	(%)	(%)	(%)
High School Graduate or Higher	82.1	86.1	87.0
Bachelors Degree or Higher	29.8	33.5	33.9
Graduate or Professional Degree	11.0	10.9	12.7

Data: U.S. Census Bureau, American Community Survey; U.S. Department of Commerce, Bureau of Economic Analysis; U.S. Department of Labor, Bureau of Labor Statistics

Industry Overview

	1998	2005	2006
Total Employees	3,368,365	3,594,862	3,645,381
Total Payroll ($1,000)	125,787,145	166,018,238	175,501,555
Total Establishments	230,860	242,128	243,055
Establishments with 1–19 Employees	202,389	211,588	211,870
Establishments with 20–49 Employees	17,103	18,585	18,924
Establishments with 50–249 Employees	9,826	10,365	10,706
Establishments with 250–999 Employees	1,318	1,345	1,306
Establishments with 1,000+ Employees	224	245	249

Data: U.S. Census Bureau, County Business Patterns

Major Industries (Ranked by 2006 Employment; Payroll in $1,000s)				
Industry	1998 Employment	2006 Employment	1998 Payroll	2006 Payroll
Health Care and Social Assistance	405,935	494,382	13,192,467	20,462,346
Retail Trade	417,791	461,645	8,693,222	11,840,330
Admin., Support, Waste Mngt., Remediation Services	247,799	306,226	5,702,383	9,226,539
Manufacturing	405,275	297,021	16,756,666	15,590,977
Professional, Scientific, Technical Services	234,816	295,055	12,782,239	20,759,533
Accommodation and Food Services	249,836	284,905	3,897,674	5,386,628
Wholesale Trade	275,717	271,190	13,355,315	17,776,046
Finance and Insurance	200,646	227,612	11,166,663	18,393,147
Construction	143,243	181,404	5,828,494	9,887,851
Transportation and Warehousing	151,493	170,735	4,941,082	6,920,582

Data: U.S. Census Bureau, County Business Patterns

Taxes and Business Climate

State and Local Taxes		
Combined Revenues ($1,000)	2004–5	2005–6
Revenue from Property Taxes	19,196,599	20,549,427
Revenue from Sales and Gross Receipts Taxes	10,238,453	10,608,212
Revenue from Individual Income Taxes	8,224,290	10,506,565
Revenue from Corporate Income Taxes	2,224,633	2,508,428
Revenue from Other Taxes	2,673,379	3,135,045
Total Tax Revenue	42,557,354	47,307,677
Per Capita Taxes		
Property Tax Per Capita	2,217	2,355
Sales and Gross Receipts Tax Per Capita	1,183	1,216
Individual Income Tax Per Capita	950	1,204
Corporate Income Tax Per Capita	257	288
Other Taxes Per Capita	309	359
Total Taxes Per Capita	4,916	5,422

Data: U.S. Census Bureau; Anderson Economic Group, LLC

Business Climate Measures

Anderson Economic Group: 2008 Business Tax Ranking (1 is Best)	39
Forbes Magazine: 2008 Best States for Business Ranking (1 is Best)	34
Tax Foundation: 2009 Business Tax Climate Ranking (1 is Best)	50
2004–5 Employer Firm Births	25,059
2004–5 Employer Firm Terminations	23,108

Data: Anderson Economic Group; Tax Foundation; Forbes Magazine; U.S. Census, Statistics of U.S. Businesses

Voting Behavior and Elected Officials

Voter Registration and Turnout (%)

	1996	2000	2004	2008
Registered Voters Who Voted	71.4	67.7	72.1	72.4
Population Age 18+ Who Voted	51.0	50.3	55.5	58.5

Data: Dave Leip's Atlas of U.S. Presidential Elections

Presidential Election Results (Nationwide Winner Listed First)

2008	Popular Vote (%)	Electoral Votes
Barack Obama (Democrat)	57.2	15
John McCain (Republican)	41.6	0
Other	1.2	0
2004		
George W. Bush (Republican, Incumbent)	46.2	0
John Kerry (Democrat)	52.9	15
Other	0.8	0
2000		
George W. Bush (Republican)	40.3	0
Albert Gore (Democrat)	56.1	15
Ralph Nader (Green)	3.0	0
Other	0.6	0
1996		
William Clinton (Democrat, Incumbent)	53.7	15
Robert Dole (Republican)	35.9	0
H. Ross Perot (Reformist)	8.5	0
Other	1.9	0

Data: Dave Leip's Atlas of U.S. Presidential Elections

Governor and U.S. Congressional Seats

Governor	Party	Year Term Began	Term	Max. Consecutive Terms
Jon Corzine	D	2006	First	2

U.S. Senators	Party	Year Elected	Term Expires	
Frank R. Lautenberg	D	1982	2015	
Robert Menendez	D	2006	2013	

U.S. Representatives	Republican	Democrat	Other
	5	8	0

Data: National Governors Association; U.S. Senate, Office of the Clerk; U.S. House of Representatives

Business and Economic Agencies

Agency	Website Address
New Jersey State Chamber of Commerce	www.njchamber.com
New Jersey Economic Development Authority	www.njeda.com
New Jersey Small Business Dev. Center	www.njsbdc.com
New Jersey Department of State, Business and Corporate Information	www.state.nj.us/state/business

Data: Various agency websites

New Mexico

New Mexico, located in the Mountain region of the United States, has a population of 2.0 million people, making it the fifteenth least populous state in 2007. The state's population increased by 150,869 people from 2000 to 2007, and is projected to increase to 2.1 million by 2025. This 0.4% projected annual growth rate compares to the projected national average of 0.8%. From 2006 to 2007 the state's population grew by 0.8%. Per capita personal income in New Mexico was $30,604 in 2007, up from $29,725 in 2006. For 2007, this was fifth lowest in the country and $7,960 below the national average. From 2000 to 2007 the per capita income in New Mexico grew at a compound annual rate of 4.7%, compared to 3.7% nationally.

In 2006, the state's largest industry in terms of employment was health care and social assistance, followed by accommodation and food services. The fastest growing industry was management of companies and enterprises with 7.1% annual growth from 1998 to 2006. The state's workforce is generally less educated than other

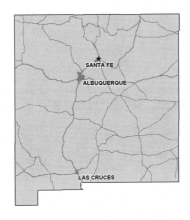

★ State Capitol

Major Urban Area

Major Roadway

Demographic and Socioeconomic Profile

Demographics and Socioeconomic Figures			
Population and Households	**2000**	**2006**	**2007**
Total Population	1,819,046	1,954,599	1,969,915
Number of Households	677,971	726,033	734,847
Average Household Size	2.6	2.6	2.6
Age and Ethnicity			
Median Age	34.6	35.2	36.0
Population 18 Years of Age and Older	1,311,478	1,444,249	1,473,150
Population 65 Years of Age and Older	212,490	241,279	252,570
Caucasian Population	1,214,680	1,325,762	1,360,378
African-American Population	33,513	39,654	44,646
Hispanic Population	765,610	860,687	874,685
Asian Population	18,286	25,983	27,006
Foreign-Born Population (%)	8.2	10.1	9.3
Income			
Per Capita Personal Income (USD)	$22,135	$29,725	$30,604
Median Household Income (USD)	$34,133	$40,629	$41,452
Individuals below Poverty Level	18.4%	18.5%	18.1%

Data: U.S. Census, American Community Survey; U.S. Department of Commerce, Bureau of Economic Analysis

states—82.3% of the state's adult population has graduated from high school, compared to an 84.1% national average. Nationally, an average of 27.0% hold a bachelor degree or higher compared to 24.8% in New Mexico; and 10.2% hold professional or graduate degrees (national average is 10.1%).

In fiscal year 2005–6, New Mexico had total tax revenues of $7.0 billion. The largest share was generated from sales and gross receipts taxes, followed by individual income taxes. The per capita tax burden in New Mexico was $3,568 for 2005–6, some $424 below the national average. In terms of business taxes, the state ranked fifteenth in a 2008 analysis by Anderson Economic Group. Forbes Magazine and the Tax Foundation ranked the state's business climate fifteenth and twenty-sixth, respectively.

Population Projections

Year	2010	2015	2020	2025
Total Population	1,980,225	2,041,539	2,084,341	2,106,584
Median Age	38.3	39.7	41.2	42.9
Population 18 Years of Age and Older	1,500,820	1,556,822	1,595,626	1,628,082
Population 65 Years of Age and Older	278,967	343,622	419,690	497,357

Data: U.S. Census Bureau

Workforce and Industry Profile

Workforce

	2000	2006	2007
Civilian Labor Force	852,293	935,350	945,700
Labor Force Participation Rate	63.5%	63.9%	63.6%
Unemployment Rate	5.0%	4.2%	3.5%
Average Wage Per Job (USD)	$27,497	$33,980	$35,790
Education Attainment (Population 25 Years and Older)	(%)	(%)	(%)
High School Graduate or Higher	78.9	81.5	82.3
Bachelors Degree or Higher	23.5	25.3	24.8
Graduate or Professional Degree	9.8	13.3	10.2

Data: U.S. Census Bureau, American Community Survey; U.S. Department of Commerce, Bureau of Economic Analysis; U.S. Department of Labor, Bureau of Labor Statistics

Industry Overview

	1998	2005	2006
Total Employees	540,186	595,249	628,681
Total Payroll ($1,000)	13,133,707	18,171,120	19,844,355
Total Establishments	42,608	45,006	45,940
Establishments with 1–19 Employees	37,254	39,033	39,642
Establishments with 20–49 Employees	3,544	3,906	4,132
Establishments with 50–249 Employees	1,618	1,847	1,927
Establishments with 250–999 Employees	173	204	223
Establishments with 1,000+ Employees	19	16	16

Data: U.S. Census Bureau, County Business Patterns

Major Industries (Ranked by 2006 Employment; Payroll in $1,000s)

Industry	1998 Employment	2006 Employment	1998 Payroll	2006 Payroll
Retail Trade	89,883	100,362	1,569,283	2,271,555
Health Care and Social Assistance	76,641	97,771	1,995,230	3,508,609
Accommodation and Food Services	65,149	80,849	672,950	1,041,546
Construction	42,164	56,900	1,061,850	1,917,739
Admin., Support, Waste Mngt., Remediation Services	32,347	44,961	669,284	1,073,144
Professional, Scientific, Technical Services	35,771	38,700	1,514,635	1,902,813
Manufacturing	40,561	35,250	1,216,861	1,446,298
Other Services (except Public Admin.)	26,279	27,072	418,964	589,811
Finance and Insurance	21,847	25,441	679,563	1,117,696
Wholesale Trade	21,672	21,844	652,200	876,064

Data: U.S. Census Bureau, County Business Patterns

Taxes and Business Climate

State and Local Taxes

Combined Revenues ($1,000)	2004–5	2005–6
Revenue from Property Taxes	863,071	954,082
Revenue from Sales and Gross Receipts Taxes	2,854,345	3,208,198
Revenue from Individual Income Taxes	1,086,015	1,123,954
Revenue from Corporate Income Taxes	242,462	377,185
Revenue from Other Taxes	1,023,435	1,311,037
Total Tax Revenue	6,069,328	6,974,456
Per Capita Taxes		
Property Tax Per Capita	450	488
Sales and Gross Receipts Tax Per Capita	1,489	1,641
Individual Income Tax Per Capita	567	575
Corporate Income Tax Per Capita	127	193
Other Taxes Per Capita	534	671
Total Taxes Per Capita	3,167	3,568

Data: U.S. Census Bureau; Anderson Economic Group, LLC

Business Climate Measures

Anderson Economic Group: 2008 Business Tax Ranking (1 is Best)	15
Forbes Magazine: 2008 Best States for Business Ranking (1 is Best)	15
Tax Foundation: 2009 Business Tax Climate Ranking (1 is Best)	26
2004–5 Employer Firm Births	4,545
2004–5 Employer Firm Terminations	3,925

Data: Anderson Economic Group; Tax Foundation; Forbes Magazine; U.S. Census, Statistics of U.S. Businesses

Voting Behavior and Elected Officials

Voter Registration and Turnout (%)

	1996	2000	2004	2008
Registered Voters Who Voted	66.4	61.5	68.4	69.6
Population Age 18+ Who Voted	45.4	45.6	55.1	56.4

Data: Dave Leip's Atlas of U.S. Presidential Elections

Presidential Election Results (Nationwide Winner Listed First)

2008	Popular Vote (%)	Electoral Votes
Barack Obama (Democrat)	56.9	5
John McCain (Republican)	41.8	0
Other	1.3	0
2004		
George W. Bush (Republican, Incumbent)	49.8	5
John Kerry (Democrat)	49.1	0
Other	1.1	0
2000		
George W. Bush (Republican)	47.9	0
Albert Gore (Democrat)	47.9	5
Ralph Nader (Green)	3.6	0
Other	0.7	0
1996		
William Clinton (Democrat, Incumbent)	49.2	5
Robert Dole (Republican)	41.9	0
H. Ross Perot (Reformist)	5.8	0
Other	3.2	0

Data: Dave Leip's Atlas of U.S. Presidential Elections

Governor and U.S. Congressional Seats

Governor	Party	Year Term Began	Term	Max. Consecutive Terms
Bill Richardson	D	2007	Second	2

U.S. Senators	Party	Year Elected	Term Expires	
Tom Udall	D	2008	2015	
Jeff Bingaman	D	1982	2013	

U.S. Representatives	Republican	Democrat	Other
	0	3	0

Data: National Governors Association; U.S. Senate, Office of the Clerk; U.S. House of Representatives

Business and Economic Agencies

Agency	Website Address
Association of Commerce and Industry of New Mexico	www.aci.nm.org
New Mexico Economic Development Department	www.edd.state.nm.us
New Mexico Small Business Dev. Center	www.nmsbdc.org
New Mexico, Public Regulation Commission	www.nmprc.state.nm.us/cb.htm

Data: Various agency websites

New York

With a population of 19.3 million people, New York was the third most populous state in the United States in 2007. From 2000 to 2007 the state's population increased by 321,272 people, and is projected to increase to 19.5 million by 2025. This 0.1% projected annual growth rate compares to the projected national average of 0.8%. From 2006 to 2007 the state's population showed a slight decline. The state's 2007 per capita personal income of $46,664 was higher compared to $43,962 in 2006 and the fifth highest in the United States, some $8,100 above the national average. Per capita income in New York grew at a compound annual rate of 4.2% from 2000 to 2007, compared to 3.7% nationally.

New York's largest industry in terms of 2006 employment was health care and social assistance. The fastest growing industry was arts, entertainment, and recreation, with 3.2% annual growth from 1998 to 2006. The second fastest growing industry was professional, scientific, and technical services. The state's workforce is generally more educated

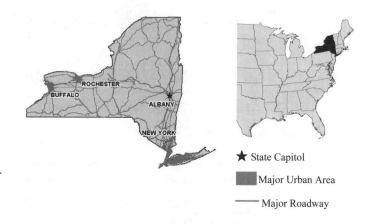

★ State Capitol

▮ Major Urban Area

── Major Roadway

Demographic and Socioeconomic Profile

Demographics and Socioeconomic Figures			
Population and Households	**2000**	**2006**	**2007**
Total Population	18,976,457	19,306,183	19,297,729
Number of Households	7,056,860	7,088,376	7,099,940
Average Household Size	2.6	2.6	2.6
Age and Ethnicity			
Median Age	35.9	37.4	37.7
Population 18 Years of Age and Older	14,302,266	14,792,694	14,881,415
Population 65 Years of Age and Older	2,450,697	2,520,888	2,543,787
Caucasian Population	12,891,118	12,816,272	12,742,889
African-American Population	2,986,242	2,990,260	3,010,970
Hispanic Population	2,865,016	3,139,590	3,159,732
Asian Population	1,044,423	1,322,971	1,328,767
Foreign-Born Population (%)	20.4	21.6	21.8
Income			
Per Capita Personal Income (USD)	$34,897	$43,962	$46,664
Median Household Income (USD)	$43,393	$51,384	$53,514
Individuals below Poverty Level	14.6%	14.2%	13.7%

Data: U.S. Census, American Community Survey; U.S. Department of Commerce, Bureau of Economic Analysis

than other states—84.1% of the state's adult population has graduated from high school, equal to the national average; 31.7% hold a bachelor degree or higher (national average is 27.0%); and 13.5% hold professional or graduate degrees compared to the national average of 10.1%.

New York's total tax revenue was $123.7 billion for fiscal year 2005–6, up from the 2004–5 total revenue of $111.1 billion. The largest share of tax revenue in 2005–6 was generated from individual income taxes, followed by property taxes. On a per capita basis, residents of New York paid taxes of $6,405, compared to the national average of $3,992 for 2005–6. In terms of business taxes, the state ranked thirty-second in a 2008 analysis by Anderson Economic Group. Forbes Magazine and the Tax Foundation ranked the state's business climate thirty-eighth and forty-ninth, respectively.

Population Projections

Year	2010	2015	2020	2025
Total Population	19,443,672	19,546,699	19,576,920	19,540,179
Median Age	37.9	38.1	38.6	39.1
Population 18 Years of Age and Older	15,022,796	15,193,695	15,201,880	15,171,558
Population 65 Years of Age and Older	2,651,655	2,943,496	3,250,020	3,606,687

Data: U.S. Census Bureau

Workforce and Industry Profile

Workforce			
	2000	2006	2007
Civilian Labor Force	9,166,972	9,498,563	9,574,776
Labor Force Participation Rate	63.0%	62.9%	62.7%
Unemployment Rate	4.5%	4.5%	4.5%
Average Wage Per Job (USD)	$45,357	$45,820	$47,610
Education Attainment (Population 25 Years and Older)	(%)	(%)	(%)
High School Graduate or Higher	79.1	84.1	84.1
Bachelors Degree or Higher	27.4	31.2	31.7
Graduate or Professional Degree	11.8	8.3	13.5

Data: U.S. Census Bureau, American Community Survey; U.S. Department of Commerce, Bureau of Economic Analysis; U.S. Department of Labor, Bureau of Labor Statistics

Industry Overview			
	1998	2005	2006
Total Employees	6,993,814	7,417,463	7,532,764
Total Payroll ($1,000)	274,634,982	370,842,630	398,192,315
Total Establishments	481,962	514,265	515,950
Establishments with 1–19 Employees	425,442	453,790	454,386
Establishments with 20–49 Employees	34,883	37,290	38,041
Establishments with 50–249 Employees	18,351	19,752	20,049
Establishments with 250–999 Employees	2,737	2,859	2,912
Establishments with 1,000+ Employees	549	574	562

Data: U.S. Census Bureau, County Business Patterns

Major Industries (Ranked by 2006 Employment; Payroll in $1,000s)

Industry	1998 Employment	2006 Employment	1998 Payroll	2006 Payroll
Health Care and Social Assistance	1,134,481	1,318,154	35,796,990	52,593,486
Retail Trade	800,566	901,418	15,427,452	22,552,518
Professional, Scientific, Technical Services	485,199	599,549	26,435,717	42,983,090
Finance and Insurance	587,464	577,925	56,877,864	93,112,281
Accommodation and Food Services	479,455	568,869	6,912,726	10,751,249
Manufacturing	752,511	551,471	27,017,165	24,831,985
Admin., Support, Waste Mngt., Remediation Services	449,222	513,029	11,375,703	18,572,388
Wholesale Trade	410,877	405,236	18,116,101	23,057,749
Other Services (except Public Admin.)	325,885	358,714	7,337,514	10,460,785
Educational Services	283,373	343,791	7,158,767	11,570,614

Data: U.S. Census Bureau, County Business Patterns

Taxes and Business Climate

State and Local Taxes

Combined Revenues ($1,000)	2004–5	2005–6
Revenue from Property Taxes	34,149,967	36,438,151
Revenue from Sales and Gross Receipts Taxes	27,975,721	31,601,085
Revenue from Individual Income Taxes	34,843,704	38,611,920
Revenue from Corporate Income Taxes	6,994,100	9,046,281
Revenue from Other Taxes	7,144,127	7,963,497
Total Tax Revenue	111,107,619	123,660,934
Per Capita Taxes		
Property Tax Per Capita	1,773	1,887
Sales and Gross Receipts Tax Per Capita	1,452	1,637
Individual Income Tax Per Capita	1,809	2,000
Corporate Income Tax Per Capita	363	469
Other Taxes Per Capita	371	412
Total Taxes Per Capita	5,768	6,405

Data: U.S. Census Bureau; Anderson Economic Group, LLC

Business Climate Measures

Anderson Economic Group: 2008 Business Tax Ranking (1 is Best)	32
Forbes Magazine: 2008 Best States for Business Ranking (1 is Best)	38
Tax Foundation: 2009 Business Tax Climate Ranking (1 is Best)	49
2004–5 Employer Firm Births	51,159
2004–5 Employer Firm Terminations	48,265

Data: Anderson Economic Group; Tax Foundation; Forbes Magazine; U.S. Census, Statistics of U.S. Businesses

Voting Behavior and Elected Officials

Voter Registration and Turnout (%)

	1996	2000	2004	2008
Registered Voters Who Voted	62.2	60.6	62.4	70.2
Population Age 18+ Who Voted	46.6	47.7	50.4	51.0

Data: Dave Leip's Atlas of U.S. Presidential Elections

Presidential Election Results (Nationwide Winner Listed First)

2008	Popular Vote (%)	Electoral Votes
Barack Obama (Democrat)	62.8	31
John McCain (Republican)	36.1	0
Other	1.1	0
2004		
George W. Bush (Republican, Incumbent)	40.1	0
John Kerry (Democrat)	58.4	31
Other	1.6	0
2000		
George W. Bush (Republican)	35.2	0
Albert Gore (Democrat)	60.2	33
Ralph Nader (Green)	3.6	0
Other	1.0	0
1996		
William Clinton (Democrat, Incumbent)	59.5	33
Robert Dole (Republican)	30.6	0
H. Ross Perot (Reformist)	8.0	0
Other	2.0	0

Data: Dave Leip's Atlas of U.S. Presidential Elections

Governor and U.S. Congressional Seats				
Governor	Party	Year Term Began	Term	Max. Consecutive Terms
David Paterson	D	2008	First	No limit
U.S. Senators	**Party**	**Year Elected**	**Term Expires**	
Kirsten Gillibrand	D	2009	2015	
Charles "Chuck" E. Schumer	D	1998	2011	
U.S. Representatives		**Republican**	**Democrat**	**Other**
		3	25	1

Data: National Governors Association; U.S. Senate, Office of the Clerk; U.S. House of Representatives

Business and Economic Agencies

Agency	Website Address
Business Council of New York State, Inc.	www.bcnys.org
Empire State Development	www.nylovesbiz.com/default.asp
New York State Small Business Dev. Center	www.nyssbdc.org
New York Department of State	www.dos.state.ny.us

Data: Various agency websites

North Carolina

North Carolina is located in the South Atlantic region of the United States. North Carolina has a population of 9.1 million people, making it the tenth most populous state in 2007. The state's population increased by 1,011,719 people from 2000 to 2007, and is projected to increase to 11.5 million by 2025. This 1.3% projected annual growth rate is above the national average of 0.8%. From 2006 to 2007 the state's population grew by 2.3%. Per capita personal income in North Carolina was $33,663 in 2007, up from $32,338 in 2006. For 2007, this was $4,901 below the national average and the fifteenth lowest in the country. The state's per capita income grew at a compound annual rate of 3.2% from 2000 to 2007, compared to 3.7% nationally.

The state's workforce generally has less education than other states—83.0% of the state's adult population has graduated from high school, compared to an 84.1% national average; 25.6% hold a bachelor degree or higher (national average is 27.0%); and 8.6% hold professional or graduate degrees

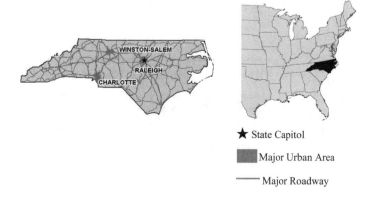

★ State Capitol

Major Urban Area

Major Roadway

Demographic and Socioeconomic Profile

Demographics and Socioeconomic Figures			
Population and Households	**2000**	**2006**	**2007**
Total Population	8,049,313	8,856,505	9,061,032
Number of Households	3,132,013	3,454,068	3,540,875
Average Household Size	2.5	2.5	2.5
Age and Ethnicity			
Median Age	35.3	36.6	36.8
Population 18 Years of Age and Older	6,087,996	6,701,486	6,848,148
Population 65 Years of Age and Older	969,822	1,071,799	1,103,036
Caucasian Population	5,802,165	6,224,663	6,340,312
African-American Population	1,734,154	1,892,469	1,928,080
Hispanic Population	372,964	597,382	639,623
Asian Population	111,292	162,578	163,503
Foreign-Born Population (%)	5.3	6.9	7.0
Income			
Per Capita Personal Income (USD)	$27,068	$32,338	$33,663
Median Household Income (USD)	$39,184	$42,625	$44,670
Individuals below Poverty Level	12.3%	14.7%	14.3%

Data: U.S. Census, American Community Survey; U.S. Department of Commerce, Bureau of Economic Analysis

(national average is 10.1%). In 2006, the state's largest industry in terms of employment was health care and social assistance, followed by retail trade. The fastest growing industry was professional, scientific, and technical services, with 5.6% annual growth from 1998 to 2006.

In fiscal year 2005–6, North Carolina had total tax revenues of $30 billion for fiscal year 2005–6, up from the 2004–5 total revenue of $27.3 billion. The largest share was generated from sales and gross receipts taxes, followed by individual income taxes. The per capita tax burden in North Carolina was $3,389 for 2005–6, some $603 below the national average, and a $243 increase from the 2004–5 per capita tax burden. In terms of business taxes, North Carolina ranked first in a 2008 report by Anderson Economic Group. The state's business climate was ranked forth by Forbes Magazine and thirty-ninth by the Tax Foundation.

Population Projections

Year	2010	2015	2020	2025
Total Population	9,345,823	10,010,770	10,709,289	11,449,153
Median Age	36.9	37.3	37.2	36.8
Population 18 Years of Age and Older	7,076,985	7,572,393	8,083,886	8,609,911
Population 65 Years of Age and Older	1,161,164	1,374,754	1,618,578	1,897,902

Data: U.S. Census Bureau

Workforce and Industry Profile

Workforce

	2000	2006	2007
Civilian Labor Force	4,123,812	4,464,875	4,506,144
Labor Force Participation Rate	67.4%	66.2%	65.5%
Unemployment Rate	3.7%	4.8%	4.7%
Average Wage Per Job (USD)	$31,068	$35,520	$36,900
Education Attainment (Population 25 Years and Older)	**(%)**	**(%)**	**(%)**
High School Graduate or Higher	78.1	82.0	83.0
Bachelors Degree or Higher	22.5	24.8	25.6
Graduate or Professional Degree	7.2	6.5	8.6

Data: U.S. Census Bureau, American Community Survey; U.S. Department of Commerce, Bureau of Economic Analysis; U.S. Department of Labor, Bureau of Labor Statistics

Industry Overview

	1998	2005	2006
Total Employees	3,223,178	3,409,968	3,524,814
Total Payroll ($1,000)	86,780,877	115,740,410	124,107,206
Total Establishments	198,690	216,994	222,431
Establishments with 1–19 Employees	170,676	185,763	189,886
Establishments with 20–49 Employees	17,002	19,642	20,511
Establishments with 50–249 Employees	9,411	10,101	10,515
Establishments with 250–999 Employees	1,426	1,293	1,321
Establishments with 1,000+ Employees	175	195	198

Data: U.S. Census Bureau, County Business Patterns

Major Industries (Ranked by 2006 Employment; Payroll in $1,000s)				
Industry	1998 Employment	2006 Employment	1998 Payroll	2006 Payroll
Manufacturing	771,282	535,689	22,452,407	20,683,093
Health Care and Social Assistance	375,399	487,956	10,495,546	17,327,701
Retail Trade	430,667	467,113	7,424,839	10,292,217
Accommodation and Food Services	260,453	331,448	2,668,813	4,214,617
Admin., Support, Waste Mngt., Remediation Services	188,349	278,485	3,608,799	6,966,210
Construction	205,750	242,148	5,926,419	9,061,401
Professional, Scientific, Technical Services	126,888	196,323	5,000,972	11,047,021
Finance and Insurance	133,120	185,335	5,316,012	11,805,931
Wholesale Trade	161,459	170,298	6,121,068	8,431,335
Other Services (except Public Admin.)	134,043	151,606	2,313,119	3,175,071

Data: U.S. Census Bureau, County Business Patterns

Taxes and Business Climate

State and Local Taxes		
Combined Revenues ($1,000)	2004–5	2005–6
Revenue from Property Taxes	6,449,622	6,985,360
Revenue from Sales and Gross Receipts Taxes	9,423,309	10,320,076
Revenue from Individual Income Taxes	8,427,553	9,467,278
Revenue from Corporate Income Taxes	1,271,985	1,308,022
Revenue from Other Taxes	1,734,639	1,932,028
Total Tax Revenue	27,307,108	30,012,764
Per Capita Taxes		
Property Tax Per Capita	743	789
Sales and Gross Receipts Tax Per Capita	1,086	1,165
Individual Income Tax Per Capita	971	1,069
Corporate Income Tax Per Capita	147	148
Other Taxes Per Capita	200	218
Total Taxes Per Capita	3,146	3,389

Data: U.S. Census Bureau; Anderson Economic Group, LLC

Business Climate Measures

Anderson Economic Group: 2008 Business Tax Ranking (1 is Best)	1
Forbes Magazine: 2008 Best States for Business Ranking (1 is Best)	4
Tax Foundation: 2009 Business Tax Climate Ranking (1 is Best)	39
2004–5 Employer Firm Births	22,335
2004–5 Employer Firm Terminations	19,032

Data: Anderson Economic Group; Tax Foundation; Forbes Magazine; U.S. Census, Statistics of U.S. Businesses

Voting Behavior and Elected Officials

Voter Registration and Turnout (%)

	1996	2000	2004	2008
Registered Voters Who Voted	58.3	56.8	64.0	68.9
Population Age 18+ Who Voted	45.6	47.8	55.4	63.0

Data: Dave Leip's Atlas of U.S. Presidential Elections

Presidential Election Results (Nationwide Winner Listed First)

2008	Popular Vote (%)	Electoral Votes
Barack Obama (Democrat)	49.7	15
John McCain (Republican)	49.4	0
Other	0.9	0
2004		
George W. Bush (Republican, Incumbent)	56.0	15
John Kerry (Democrat)	43.6	0
Other	0.4	0
2000		
George W. Bush (Republican)	56.0	14
Albert Gore (Democrat)	43.2	0
Ralph Nader (Green)	.0	0
Other	0.8	0
1996		
William Clinton (Democrat, Incumbent)	44.0	0
Robert Dole (Republican)	48.7	14
H. Ross Perot (Reformist)	6.7	0
Other	0.6	0

Data: Dave Leip's Atlas of U.S. Presidential Elections

Governor and U.S. Congressional Seats

Governor	Party	Year Term Began	Term	Max. Consecutive Terms
Beverly Perdue	D	2009	First	2

U.S. Senators	Party	Year Elected	Term Expires	
Kay Hagan	D	2008	2015	
Richard Burr	R	2004	2011	

U.S. Representatives		Republican	Democrat	Other
		5	8	0

Data: National Governors Association; U.S. Senate, Office of the Clerk; U.S. House of Representatives

Business and Economic Agencies

Agency	Website Address
North Carolina Citizens For Business & Industry	www.nccbi.org
North Carolina Department of Commerce	www.commerce.state.nc.us
North Carolina Small Business & Tech Dev. Center	www.sbtdc.org
Employment Security Comission	www.ncesc.com

Data: Various agency websites

North Dakota

North Dakota, located in the West North Central region of the United States, has a population of 639,715 people, making it the third least populous state in 2007. The state's population decreased by 2,485 people from 2000 to 2007, and is projected to decrease to 620,777 people by 2025. This –0.2% projected annual growth rate compares to the projected national average of 0.8%. From 2006 to 2007 the state's population grew by 0.6%. Per capita personal income in North Dakota was $35,955 in 2007, up from $33,034 in 2006. For 2007, this was twenty-fifth lowest in the country and $2,609 below the national average. From 2000 to 2007 the per capita income in North Dakota grew at a compound annual rate of 5.3%, compared to 3.7% nationally.

In 2006, the state's largest industry in terms of employment was health care and social assistance, followed by retail trade. The fastest growing industry was professional, scientific, and technical services, with 5.9% annual growth from 1998 to 2006. The state's workforce is generally less educated than

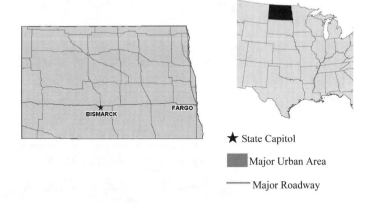

★ State Capitol

Major Urban Area

—— Major Roadway

Demographic and Socioeconomic Profile

Demographics and Socioeconomic Figures			
Population and Households	**2000**	**2006**	**2007**
Total Population	642,200	635,867	639,715
Number of Households	257,152	272,352	271,724
Average Household Size	2.4	2.2	2.3
Age and Ethnicity			
Median Age	36.2	37.1	37.1
Population 18 Years of Age and Older	481,301	492,255	496,634
Population 65 Years of Age and Older	94,597	92,829	92,373
Caucasian Population	593,785	578,919	580,333
African-American Population	3,673	5,999	5,301
Hispanic Population	7,568	9,332	9,704
Asian Population	3,342	4,348	6,708
Foreign-Born Population (%)	1.9	2.1	2.4
Income			
Per Capita Personal Income (USD)	$25,106	$33,034	$35,955
Median Household Income (USD)	$34,604	$41,919	$43,753
Individuals below Poverty Level	11.9%	11.4%	12.1%

Data: U.S. Census, American Community Survey; U.S. Department of Commerce, Bureau of Economic Analysis

other states—nationally, an average of 27.0% hold a bachelor degree or higher compared to 25.7% in North Dakota; and 6.4% hold professional or graduate degrees (national average is 10.1%); however, 89.0% of the state's adult population has graduated from high school, compared to an 84.1% national average.

In fiscal year 2005–6, North Dakota had total tax revenues of $2.4 billion. The largest share was generated from sales and gross receipts taxes, followed by property taxes. The per capita tax burden in North Dakota was $3,724 for 2005–6, some $268 below the national average. In terms of business taxes, the state ranked forty-second in a 2008 analysis by Anderson Economic Group. Forbes Magazine and the Tax Foundation ranked the state's business climate thirteenth and thirtieth, respectively.

Population Projections

Year	2010	2015	2020	2025
Total Population	636,623	635,133	630,112	620,777
Median Age	38.4	39.3	40.6	41.9
Population 18 Years of Age and Older	494,659	496,436	492,483	486,949
Population 65 Years of Age and Older	97,108	107,900	125,023	142,195

Data: U.S. Census Bureau

Workforce and Industry Profile

Workforce

	2000	2006	2007
Civilian Labor Force	345,881	357,960	366,042
Labor Force Participation Rate	71.3%	73.2%	73.9%
Unemployment Rate	2.9%	3.2%	3.1%
Average Wage Per Job (USD)	$24,683	$32,440	$33,650
Education Attainment (Population 25 Years and Older)	(%)	(%)	(%)
High School Graduate or Higher	83.9	88.1	89.0
Bachelors Degree or Higher	22.0	25.6	25.7
Graduate or Professional Degree	5.5	8.3	6.4

Data: U.S. Census Bureau, American Community Survey; U.S. Department of Commerce, Bureau of Economic Analysis; U.S. Department of Labor, Bureau of Labor Statistics

Industry Overview

	1998	2005	2006
Total Employees	249,476	270,479	278,423
Total Payroll ($1,000)	5,533,810	7,779,322	8,399,587
Total Establishments	20,288	21,061	21,332
Establishments with 1–19 Employees	17,815	18,384	18,570
Establishments with 20–49 Employees	1,618	1,727	1,768
Establishments with 50–249 Employees	774	849	889
Establishments with 250–999 Employees	72	93	95
Establishments with 1,000+ Employees	9	8	10

Data: U.S. Census Bureau, County Business Patterns

Major Industries (Ranked by 2006 Employment; Payroll in $1,000s)				
Industry	1998 Employment	2006 Employment	1998 Payroll	2006 Payroll
Health Care and Social Assistance	45,894	51,191	1,089,193	1,674,602
Retail Trade	41,402	44,748	655,415	914,057
Accommodation and Food Services	25,850	29,104	208,591	313,826
Manufacturing	23,209	25,584	670,183	916,398
Wholesale Trade	17,000	17,171	476,356	687,656
Construction	13,980	16,395	451,087	710,327
Finance and Insurance	12,526	15,261	371,331	608,321
Other Services (except Public Admin.)	13,819	13,514	184,901	240,679
Admin., Support, Waste Mngt., Remediation Services	10,953	12,081	177,802	248,931
Professional, Scientific, Technical Services	7,596	11,972	233,272	464,942

Data: U.S. Census Bureau, County Business Patterns

Taxes and Business Climate

State and Local Taxes		
Combined Revenues ($1,000)	2004–5	2005–6
Revenue from Property Taxes	619,912	634,373
Revenue from Sales and Gross Receipts Taxes	791,296	835,820
Revenue from Individual Income Taxes	242,008	275,630
Revenue from Corporate Income Taxes	75,838	120,115
Revenue from Other Taxes	392,334	501,713
Total Tax Revenue	2,121,388	2,367,651
Per Capita Taxes		
Property Tax Per Capita	975	998
Sales and Gross Receipts Tax Per Capita	1,244	1,314
Individual Income Tax Per Capita	381	433
Corporate Income Tax Per Capita	119	189
Other Taxes Per Capita	617	789
Total Taxes Per Capita	3,336	3,724

Data: U.S. Census Bureau; Anderson Economic Group, LLC

Business Climate Measures

Anderson Economic Group: 2008 Business Tax Ranking (1 is Best)	42
Forbes Magazine: 2008 Best States for Business Ranking (1 is Best)	13
Tax Foundation: 2009 Business Tax Climate Ranking (1 is Best)	30
2004–5 Employer Firm Births	1,718
2004–5 Employer Firm Terminations	1,514

Data: Anderson Economic Group; Tax Foundation; Forbes Magazine; U.S. Census, Statistics of U.S. Businesses

Voting Behavior and Elected Officials

Voter Registration and Turnout (%)

	1996	2000	2004	2008
Registered Voters Who Voted	.0	.0	.0	NaN
Population Age 18+ Who Voted	56.0	59.9	64.2	64.0

Data: Dave Leip's Atlas of U.S. Presidential Elections

Presidential Election Results (Nationwide Winner Listed First)

2008	Popular Vote (%)	Electoral Votes
Barack Obama (Democrat)	44.5	0
John McCain (Republican)	53.1	3
Other	2.5	0
2004		
George W. Bush (Republican, Incumbent)	62.9	3
John Kerry (Democrat)	35.5	0
Other	1.6	0
2000		
George W. Bush (Republican)	60.7	3
Albert Gore (Democrat)	33.1	0
Ralph Nader (Green)	3.3	0
Other	3.0	0
1996		
William Clinton (Democrat, Incumbent)	40.1	0
Robert Dole (Republican)	46.9	3
H. Ross Perot (Reformist)	12.2	0
Other	0.7	0

Data: Dave Leip's Atlas of U.S. Presidential Elections

Governor and U.S. Congressional Seats

Governor	Party	Year Term Began	Term	Max. Consecutive Terms
John Hoeven	R	2008	Third	No limit
U.S. Senators	**Party**	**Year Elected**	**Term Expires**	
Kent Conrad	D	1986	2013	
Byron L. Dorgan	D	1992	2011	
U.S. Representatives		**Republican**	**Democrat**	**Other**
		0	1	0

Data: National Governors Association; U.S. Senate, Office of the Clerk; U.S. House of Representatives

Business and Economic Agencies

Agency	Website Address
Greater North Dakota Chamber of Commerce	www.gnda.com
North Dakota Department of Commerce	www.growingnd.com
North Dakota Small Business Dev. Center	www.ndsbdc.org
North Dakota Secretary of State	www.nd.gov/sos/businessserv

Data: Various agency websites

Ohio

With a population of 11.5 million people, Ohio was the seventh most populous state in the United States in 2007. From 2000 to 2007 the state's population increased by 113,777 people, and is projected to increase to 11.6 million by 2025. This 0.1% projected annual growth rate compares to the projected national average of 0.8%. From 2006 to 2007 the state's population declined by 0.1%. The state's 2007 per capita personal income of $34,509 was higher compared to $33,217 in 2006 and the nineteenth lowest in the United States, some $4,055 below the national average. Per capita income in Ohio grew at a compound annual rate of 2.9% from 2000 to 2007, compared to 3.7% nationally.

Ohio's largest industry in terms of 2006 employment was health care and social assistance. The fastest growing industry was transportation and warehousing with 3.89% annual growth from 1998 to 2006. The second fastest growing industry was professional, scientific, and technical services. The state's workforce is generally less educated than

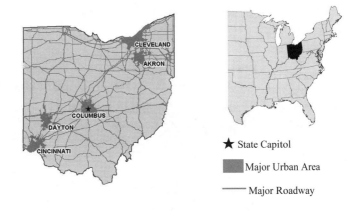

★ State Capitol

▨ Major Urban Area

── Major Roadway

Demographic and Socioeconomic Profile

Demographics and Socioeconomic Figures			
Population and Households	**2000**	**2006**	**2007**
Total Population	11,353,140	11,478,006	11,466,917
Number of Households	4,445,773	4,499,506	4,505,995
Average Household Size	2.5	2.5	2.5
Age and Ethnicity			
Median Age	36.2	37.6	37.8
Population 18 Years of Age and Older	8,467,999	8,705,230	8,711,989
Population 65 Years of Age and Older	1,508,095	1,528,079	1,546,539
Caucasian Population	9,640,523	9,645,844	9,629,758
African-American Population	1,288,359	1,357,343	1,344,674
Hispanic Population	213,889	265,762	281,940
Asian Population	132,131	175,000	177,947
Foreign-Born Population (%)	3.0	3.6	3.7
Income			
Per Capita Personal Income (USD)	$28,207	$33,217	$34,509
Median Household Income (USD)	$40,956	$44,532	$46,597
Individuals below Poverty Level	10.6%	13.3%	13.1%

Data: U.S. Census, American Community Survey; U.S. Department of Commerce, Bureau of Economic Analysis

other states—24.1% hold a bachelor degree or higher (national average is 27.0%); and 8.8% hold professional or graduate degrees compared to the national average of 10.1%; however, 87.1% of the state's adult population has graduated from high school, compared to an 84.1% national average.

Ohio's total tax revenue was $43.2 for fiscal year 2005–6, up from the 2004–5 total revenue of $41.7 billion. The largest share of tax revenue in 2005–6 was generated from individual income taxes, followed by sales and gross receipts taxes. On a per capita basis, residents of Ohio paid taxes of $3,768, compared to the national average of $3,992 for 2005–6. In terms of business taxes, the state ranked fourth in a 2008 analysis by Anderson Economic Group. Forbes Magazine and the Tax Foundation ranked the state's business climate thirty-ninth and forty-seventh, respectively.

Population Projections

Year	2010	2015	2020	2025
Total Population	11,576,181	11,635,446	11,644,058	11,605,738
Median Age	38.1	38.3	39.0	39.7
Population 18 Years of Age and Older	8,831,750	8,912,543	8,940,542	8,932,576
Population 65 Years of Age and Older	1,586,981	1,766,239	1,978,464	2,206,698

Data: U.S. Census Bureau

Workforce and Industry Profile

Workforce

	2000	2006	2007
Civilian Labor Force	5,807,036	5,933,957	5,976,724
Labor Force Participation Rate	67.3%	67.2%	67.3%
Unemployment Rate	4.0%	5.5%	5.6%
Average Wage Per Job (USD)	$32,507	$37,360	$38,640
Education Attainment (Population 25 Years and Older)	(%)	(%)	(%)
High School Graduate or Higher	83.0	86.2	87.1
Bachelors Degree or Higher	21.1	23.0	24.1
Graduate or Professional Degree	7.4	7.2	8.8

Data: U.S. Census Bureau, American Community Survey; U.S. Department of Commerce, Bureau of Economic Analysis; U.S. Department of Labor, Bureau of Labor Statistics

Industry Overview

	1998	2005	2006
Total Employees	4,806,046	4,762,618	4,825,510
Total Payroll ($1,000)	140,265,358	168,350,499	176,074,839
Total Establishments	270,343	270,968	269,914
Establishments with 1–19 Employees	227,768	227,995	226,252
Establishments with 20–49 Employees	25,666	25,869	26,269
Establishments with 50–249 Employees	14,702	14,952	15,257
Establishments with 250–999 Employees	1,927	1,872	1,839
Establishments with 1,000+ Employees	280	280	297

Data: U.S. Census Bureau, County Business Patterns

Major Industries (Ranked by 2006 Employment; Payroll in $1,000s)				
Industry	1998 Employment	2006 Employment	1998 Payroll	2006 Payroll
Manufacturing	994,788	787,946	37,590,541	36,124,518
Health Care and Social Assistance	628,383	730,349	17,364,658	25,960,929
Retail Trade	632,285	608,800	10,789,385	12,795,239
Accommodation and Food Services	404,645	440,755	3,839,217	5,011,134
Admin., Support, Waste Mngt., Remediation Services	298,272	356,234	5,734,863	9,036,980
Finance and Insurance	246,164	270,251	9,522,859	14,781,851
Professional, Scientific, Technical Services	207,796	250,095	8,391,803	13,261,589
Wholesale Trade	254,997	238,386	9,446,007	11,618,041
Other Services (except Public Admin.)	228,028	226,375	3,907,272	4,872,496
Construction	222,637	218,662	7,898,182	9,584,447

Data: U.S. Census Bureau, County Business Patterns

Taxes and Business Climate

State and Local Taxes		
Combined Revenues ($1,000)	2004–5	2005–6
Revenue from Property Taxes	11,973,971	12,596,479
Revenue from Sales and Gross Receipts Taxes	12,743,328	12,980,059
Revenue from Individual Income Taxes	13,079,167	13,766,469
Revenue from Corporate Income Taxes	1,345,910	1,136,382
Revenue from Other Taxes	2,572,378	2,767,483
Total Tax Revenue	41,714,754	43,246,872
Per Capita Taxes		
Property Tax Per Capita	1,045	1,097
Sales and Gross Receipts Tax Per Capita	1,112	1,131
Individual Income Tax Per Capita	1,141	1,199
Corporate Income Tax Per Capita	117	99
Other Taxes Per Capita	224	241
Total Taxes Per Capita	3,640	3,768

Data: U.S. Census Bureau; Anderson Economic Group, LLC

Business Climate Measures

Anderson Economic Group: 2008 Business Tax Ranking (1 is Best)	4
Forbes Magazine: 2008 Best States for Business Ranking (1 is Best)	39
Tax Foundation: 2009 Business Tax Climate Ranking (1 is Best)	47
2004–5 Employer Firm Births	22,239
2004–5 Employer Firm Terminations	22,388

Data: Anderson Economic Group; Tax Foundation; Forbes Magazine; U.S. Census, Statistics of U.S. Businesses

Voting Behavior and Elected Officials

Voter Registration and Turnout (%)

	1996	2000	2004	2008
Registered Voters Who Voted	66.3	62.4	70.6	68.9
Population Age 18+ Who Voted	54.3	55.6	65.3	65.6

Data: Dave Leip's Atlas of U.S. Presidential Elections

Presidential Election Results (Nationwide Winner Listed First)

2008	Popular Vote (%)	Electoral Votes
Barack Obama (Democrat)	51.4	20
John McCain (Republican)	46.8	0
Other	1.8	0
2004		
George W. Bush (Republican, Incumbent)	50.8	20
John Kerry (Democrat)	48.7	0
Other	0.5	0
2000		
George W. Bush (Republican)	50.0	21
Albert Gore (Democrat)	46.5	0
Ralph Nader (Green)	2.5	0
Other	1.1	0
1996		
William Clinton (Democrat, Incumbent)	47.4	21
Robert Dole (Republican)	41.0	0
H. Ross Perot (Reformist)	10.7	0
Other	1.0	0

Data: Dave Leip's Atlas of U.S. Presidential Elections

Governor and U.S. Congressional Seats				
Governor	**Party**	**Year Term Began**	**Term**	**Max. Consecutive Terms**
Ted Strickland	D	2007	First	2
U.S. Senators	**Party**	**Year Elected**	**Term Expires**	
Sherrod Brown	D	2006	2013	
George V. Voinovich	R	1998	2011	
U.S. Representatives		**Republican**	**Democrat**	**Other**
		8	10	0

Data: National Governors Association; U.S. Senate, Office of the Clerk; U.S. House of Representatives

Business and Economic Agencies

Agency	Website Address
Ohio Chamber of Commerce	www.ohiochamber.com
Ohio Department of Development	www.odod.state.oh.us
Ohio Small Business Dev. Center	www.odod.state.oh.us/edd/osb/sbdc
Ohio Secretary of State	www.sos.state.oh.us

Data: Various agency websites

Oklahoma

Oklahoma is located in the West South Central region of the United States. Oklahoma has a population of 3.6 million people, making it the twenty-seventh most populous state in 2007. The state's population increased by 166,662 people from 2000 to 2007, and is projected to increase to 3.8 million by 2025. This 0.3% projected annual growth rate is below the national average of 0.8%. From 2006 to 2007 the state's population grew by 1.1%. Per capita personal income in Oklahoma was $34,910 in 2007, up from $32,398 in 2006. For 2007, this was $3,654 below the national average and the twenty-first lowest in the country. The state's per capita income grew at a compound annual rate of 5.2% from 2000 to 2007, compared to 3.7% nationally.

The state's workforce generally has less education than other states—22.8% hold a bachelor degree or higher (national average is 27.0%); and 7.6% hold professional or graduate degrees (national average is 10.1%); however, 84.8% of the state's adult population has graduated from high school,

★ State Capitol

▣ Major Urban Area

— Major Roadway

Demographic and Socioeconomic Profile

Demographics and Socioeconomic Figures			
Population and Households	**2000**	**2006**	**2007**
Total Population	3,450,654	3,579,212	3,617,316
Number of Households	1,342,293	1,385,300	1,399,932
Average Household Size	2.5	2.5	2.5
Age and Ethnicity			
Median Age	35.5	36.2	36.1
Population 18 Years of Age and Older	2,560,390	2,684,026	2,716,061
Population 65 Years of Age and Older	455,700	475,637	478,818
Caucasian Population	2,624,679	2,698,032	2,710,090
African-American Population	258,532	263,271	270,332
Hispanic Population	177,768	244,822	259,867
Asian Population	45,546	59,164	57,885
Foreign-Born Population (%)	3.8	4.9	5.0
Income			
Per Capita Personal Income (USD)	$24,407	$32,398	$34,910
Median Household Income (USD)	$33,400	$38,770	$41,567
Individuals below Poverty Level	14.7%	17.0%	15.9%

Data: U.S. Census, American Community Survey; U.S. Department of Commerce, Bureau of Economic Analysis

compared to an 84.1% national average. In 2006, the state's largest industry in terms of employment was health care and social assistance, followed by retail trade. The fastest growing industry was arts, entertainment, and recreation, with 5.7% annual growth from 1998 to 2006.

In fiscal year 2005–6, Oklahoma had total tax revenues of $11.3 billion. The largest share was generated from sales and gross receipts taxes, followed by individual income taxes. The per capita tax burden in Oklahoma was $3,145 for 2005–6, some $847 below the national average, and a $296 increase from the 2004–5 per capita tax burden. In terms of business taxes, Oklahoma ranked twelfth in a 2008 report by Anderson Economic Group. The state's business climate was ranked twenty-sixth by Forbes Magazine and eighteenth by the Tax Foundation.

Population Projections

Year	2010	2015	2020	2025
Total Population	3,591,516	3,661,694	3,735,690	3,820,994
Median Age	36.8	37.3	37.9	38.0
Population 18 Years of Age and Older	2,696,443	2,746,485	2,801,647	2,870,485
Population 65 Years of Age and Older	494,966	553,761	625,384	702,307

Data: U.S. Census Bureau

Workforce and Industry Profile

Workforce

	2000	2006	2007
Civilian Labor Force	1,661,045	1,719,628	1,738,010
Labor Force Participation Rate	64.4%	63.9%	63.9%
Unemployment Rate	3.1%	4.0%	4.1%
Average Wage Per Job (USD)	$26,988	$32,570	$33,720
Education Attainment (Population 25 Years and Older)	(%)	(%)	(%)
High School Graduate or Higher	80.6	84.3	84.8
Bachelors Degree or Higher	20.3	22.1	22.8
Graduate or Professional Degree	6.8	10.0	7.6

Data: U.S. Census Bureau, American Community Survey; U.S. Department of Commerce, Bureau of Economic Analysis; U.S. Department of Labor, Bureau of Labor Statistics

Industry Overview

	1998	2005	2006
Total Employees	1,167,709	1,220,285	1,276,921
Total Payroll ($1,000)	28,667,008	37,620,071	41,356,648
Total Establishments	84,881	88,548	89,628
Establishments with 1–19 Employees	73,827	76,986	77,464
Establishments with 20–49 Employees	7,124	7,462	7,821
Establishments with 50–249 Employees	3,453	3,587	3,796
Establishments with 250–999 Employees	420	445	483
Establishments with 1,000+ Employees	57	68	64

Data: U.S. Census Bureau, County Business Patterns

Major Industries (Ranked by 2006 Employment; Payroll in $1,000s)				
Industry	1998 Employment	2006 Employment	1998 Payroll	2006 Payroll
Health Care and Social Assistance	171,498	193,346	4,149,804	6,225,221
Retail Trade	165,852	175,630	2,605,428	3,595,127
Manufacturing	168,140	142,148	5,241,720	5,871,367
Accommodation and Food Services	104,489	127,600	956,839	1,376,747
Admin., Support, Waste Mngt., Remediation Services	79,011	100,479	1,404,856	2,339,507
Professional, Scientific, Technical Services	49,645	69,567	1,721,291	3,013,746
Construction	54,900	69,149	1,478,200	2,377,587
Other Services (except Public Admin.)	61,363	62,697	962,404	1,210,406
Finance and Insurance	57,364	61,083	1,825,437	2,495,149
Wholesale Trade	61,096	61,012	1,919,885	2,656,013

Data: U.S. Census Bureau, County Business Patterns

Taxes and Business Climate

State and Local Taxes		
Combined Revenues ($1,000)	2004–5	2005–6
Revenue from Property Taxes	1,718,634	1,802,461
Revenue from Sales and Gross Receipts Taxes	3,891,471	4,232,031
Revenue from Individual Income Taxes	2,468,609	2,755,776
Revenue from Corporate Income Taxes	168,890	304,381
Revenue from Other Taxes	1,825,498	2,162,621
Total Tax Revenue	10,073,102	11,257,270
Per Capita Taxes		
Property Tax Per Capita	486	504
Sales and Gross Receipts Tax Per Capita	1,101	1,182
Individual Income Tax Per Capita	698	770
Corporate Income Tax Per Capita	48	85
Other Taxes Per Capita	516	604
Total Taxes Per Capita	2,849	3,145

Data: U.S. Census Bureau; Anderson Economic Group, LLC

Business Climate Measures

Anderson Economic Group: 2008 Business Tax Ranking (1 is Best)	12
Forbes Magazine: 2008 Best States for Business Ranking (1 is Best)	26
Tax Foundation: 2009 Business Tax Climate Ranking (1 is Best)	18
2004–5 Employer Firm Births	8,692
2004–5 Employer Firm Terminations	7,734

Data: Anderson Economic Group; Tax Foundation; Forbes Magazine; U.S. Census, Statistics of U.S. Businesses

Voting Behavior and Elected Officials

Voter Registration and Turnout (%)

	1996	2000	2004	2008
Registered Voters Who Voted	61.0	55.3	68.3	67.0
Population Age 18+ Who Voted	49.7	48.2	55.6	53.9

Data: Dave Leip's Atlas of U.S. Presidential Elections

Presidential Election Results (Nationwide Winner Listed First)

2008	Popular Vote (%)	Electoral Votes
Barack Obama (Democrat)	34.4	0
John McCain (Republican)	65.7	7
Other	0.0	0
2004		
George W. Bush (Republican, Incumbent)	65.6	7
John Kerry (Democrat)	34.4	0
Other	0.0	0
2000		
George W. Bush (Republican)	60.3	8
Albert Gore (Democrat)	38.4	0
Ralph Nader (Green)	.0	0
Other	1.3	0
1996		
William Clinton (Democrat, Incumbent)	40.5	0
Robert Dole (Republican)	48.3	8
H. Ross Perot (Reformist)	10.8	0
Other	0.5	0

Data: Dave Leip's Atlas of U.S. Presidential Elections

Governor and U.S. Congressional Seats

Governor	Party	Year Term Began	Term	Max. Consecutive Terms
Brad Henry	D	2007	Second	2

U.S. Senators	Party	Year Elected	Term Expires
James M. Inhofe	R	1994	2015
Tom Coburn	R	2004	2011

U.S. Representatives	Republican	Democrat	Other
	4	1	0

Data: National Governors Association; U.S. Senate, Office of the Clerk; U.S. House of Representatives

Business and Economic Agencies

Agency	Website Address
The State Chamber	www.okstatechamber.com
Oklahoma Advantage, Oklahoma Department of Commerce	www.okcommerce.gov
Oklahoma Small Business Dev. Center	www.osbdc.org
Oklahoma Secretary of State	www.sos.state.ok.us/business/business_filing.htm

Data: Various agency websites

Oregon

Oregon, located in the Pacific region of the United States, has a population of 3.7 million people, making it the twenty-fourth least populous state in 2007. The state's population increased by 326,056 people from 2000 to 2007, and is projected to increase to 4.5 million by 2025. This 1.1% projected annual growth rate compares to the projected national average of 0.8%. From 2006 to 2007 the state's population grew by 1.3%. Per capita personal income in Oregon was $35,027 in 2007, up from $33,252 in 2006. For 2007, this was twenty-second lowest in the country and $3,537 below the national average. From 2000 to 2007 the per capita income in Oregon grew at a compound annual rate of 3.2%, compared to 3.7% nationally.

In 2006, the state's largest industry in terms of employment was health care and social assistance, followed by accommodation and food services. The fastest growing industry was educational services, with 4.2% annual growth from 1998 to 2006. The state's workforce is generally more educated than

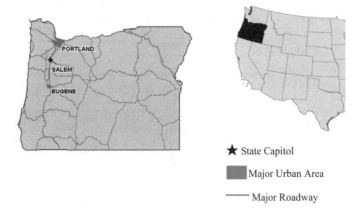

★ State Capitol

▓ Major Urban Area

— Major Roadway

Demographic and Socioeconomic Profile

Demographics and Socioeconomic Figures			
Population and Households	**2000**	**2006**	**2007**
Total Population	3,421,399	3,700,758	3,747,455
Number of Households	1,333,723	1,449,662	1,471,965
Average Household Size	2.5	2.5	2.5
Age and Ethnicity			
Median Age	36.3	37.6	37.9
Population 18 Years of Age and Older	2,577,129	2,843,141	2,882,701
Population 65 Years of Age and Older	437,887	476,865	487,669
Caucasian Population	2,957,510	3,186,177	3,216,232
African-American Population	53,032	63,631	62,852
Hispanic Population	273,938	379,034	396,145
Asian Population	99,136	135,746	134,150
Foreign-Born Population (%)	8.5	9.7	9.8
Income			
Per Capita Personal Income (USD)	$28,097	$33,252	$35,027
Median Household Income (USD)	$40,916	$46,230	$48,730
Individuals below Poverty Level	11.6%	13.3%	12.9%

Data: U.S. Census, American Community Survey; U.S. Department of Commerce, Bureau of Economic Analysis

other states—88.0% of the state's adult population has graduated from high school, compared to an 84.1% national average. Nationally, an average of 27.0% hold a bachelor degree or higher compared to 28.3% in Oregon; and 10.3% hold professional or graduate degrees (national average is 10.1%).

In fiscal year 2005–6, Oregon had total tax revenues of $12.4 billion. The largest share was generated from individual income taxes, followed by property taxes. The per capita tax burden in Oregon was $3,351 for 2005–6, some $641 below the national average. In terms of business taxes, the state ranked twenty-eighth in a 2008 analysis by Anderson Economic Group. Forbes Magazine and the Tax Foundation ranked the state's business climate sixteenth and ninth, respectively.

Population Projections

Year	2010	2015	2020	2025
Total Population	3,790,996	4,012,924	4,260,393	4,536,418
Median Age	37.6	37.9	38.5	38.9
Population 18 Years of Age and Older	2,927,830	3,097,346	3,279,891	3,483,880
Population 65 Years of Age and Older	494,328	590,784	704,866	805,717

Data: U.S. Census Bureau

Workforce and Industry Profile

Workforce

	2000	2006	2007
Civilian Labor Force	1,810,150	1,898,847	1,924,576
Labor Force Participation Rate	68.5%	65.8%	65.6%
Unemployment Rate	5.1%	5.4%	5.1%
Average Wage Per Job (USD)	$32,774	$38,570	$40,040
Education Attainment (Population 25 Years and Older)	(%)	(%)	(%)
High School Graduate or Higher	85.1	87.6	88.0
Bachelors Degree or Higher	25.1	27.6	28.3
Graduate or Professional Degree	8.7	9.6	10.3

Data: U.S. Census Bureau, American Community Survey; U.S. Department of Commerce, Bureau of Economic Analysis; U.S. Department of Labor, Bureau of Labor Statistics

Industry Overview

	1998	2005	2006
Total Employees	1,310,750	1,409,576	1,461,664
Total Payroll ($1,000)	37,722,920	50,019,294	53,563,190
Total Establishments	99,183	108,571	110,684
Establishments with 1–19 Employees	86,688	95,175	96,671
Establishments with 20–49 Employees	8,151	8,660	9,084
Establishments with 50–249 Employees	3,831	4,182	4,356
Establishments with 250–999 Employees	456	484	506
Establishments with 1,000+ Employees	57	70	67

Data: U.S. Census Bureau, County Business Patterns

Major Industries (Ranked by 2006 Employment; Payroll in $1,000s)				
Industry	1998 Employment	2006 Employment	1998 Payroll	2006 Payroll
Retail Trade	182,706	208,077	3,622,503	5,029,887
Manufacturing	211,636	188,896	7,624,969	8,368,306
Health Care and Social Assistance	150,105	186,663	4,199,706	7,387,890
Accommodation and Food Services	125,462	145,702	1,363,861	2,093,443
Construction	78,753	96,718	2,718,801	4,142,953
Admin., Support, Waste Mngt., Remediation Services	81,555	95,419	1,621,416	2,388,234
Professional, Scientific, Technical Services	62,828	79,754	2,380,263	4,023,807
Wholesale Trade	77,517	77,393	2,950,647	3,875,626
Finance and Insurance	59,843	68,502	2,501,220	3,712,668
Other Services (except Public Admin.)	57,303	63,346	1,028,385	1,493,030

Data: U.S. Census Bureau, County Business Patterns

Taxes and Business Climate

State and Local Taxes		
Combined Revenues ($1,000)	2004–5	2005–6
Revenue from Property Taxes	3,562,960	3,684,953
Revenue from Sales and Gross Receipts Taxes	971,506	1,079,102
Revenue from Individual Income Taxes	4,829,181	5,537,385
Revenue from Corporate Income Taxes	365,347	489,235
Revenue from Other Taxes	1,377,997	1,612,310
Total Tax Revenue	11,106,991	12,402,985
Per Capita Taxes		
Property Tax Per Capita	982	996
Sales and Gross Receipts Tax Per Capita	268	292
Individual Income Tax Per Capita	1,330	1,496
Corporate Income Tax Per Capita	101	132
Other Taxes Per Capita	380	436
Total Taxes Per Capita	3,060	3,351

Data: U.S. Census Bureau; Anderson Economic Group, LLC

Business Climate Measures

Anderson Economic Group: 2008 Business Tax Ranking (1 is Best)	28
Forbes Magazine: 2008 Best States for Business Ranking (1 is Best)	16
Tax Foundation: 2009 Business Tax Climate Ranking (1 is Best)	9
2004–5 Employer Firm Births	11,828
2004–5 Employer Firm Terminations	9,352

Data: Anderson Economic Group; Tax Foundation; Forbes Magazine; U.S. Census, Statistics of U.S. Businesses

Voting Behavior and Elected Officials

Voter Registration and Turnout (%)

	1996	2000	2004	2008
Registered Voters Who Voted	70.2	78.5	85.8	84.9
Population Age 18+ Who Voted	57.1	59.5	67.8	63.4

Data: Dave Leip's Atlas of U.S. Presidential Elections

Presidential Election Results (Nationwide Winner Listed First)

2008	Popular Vote (%)	Electoral Votes
Barack Obama (Democrat)	56.8	7
John McCain (Republican)	40.4	0
Other	2.9	0
2004		
George W. Bush (Republican, Incumbent)	47.2	0
John Kerry (Democrat)	51.4	7
Other	1.5	0
2000		
George W. Bush (Republican)	46.5	0
Albert Gore (Democrat)	47.0	7
Ralph Nader (Green)	5.0	0
Other	1.5	0
1996		
William Clinton (Democrat, Incumbent)	47.2	7
Robert Dole (Republican)	39.1	0
H. Ross Perot (Reformist)	8.8	0
Other	5.0	0

Data: Dave Leip's Atlas of U.S. Presidential Elections

Governor and U.S. Congressional Seats				
Governor	Party	Year Term Began	Term	Max. Consecutive Terms
Ted Kulongoski	D	2007	Second	2
U.S. Senators	Party	Year Elected	Term Expires	
Jeff Merkley	D	2009	2015	
Ron Wyden	D	1996	2011	
U.S. Representatives		Republican	Democrat	Other
		1	4	0

Data: National Governors Association; U.S. Senate, Office of the Clerk; U.S. House of Representatives

Business and Economic Agencies

Agency	Website Address
Associated Oregon Industries, Inc.	www.aoi.org
Oregon Economic and Community Development Department	econ.oregon.gov
Oregon Small Busines Development Center	www.bizcenter.org
Oregon Secretary of State, Corporation Division	www.filinginoregon.com

Data: Various agency websites

Pennsylvania

With a population of 12.4 million people, Pennsylvania was the sixth most populous state in the United States in 2007. From 2000 to 2007 the state's population increased by 151,738 people, and is projected to increase to 12.8 million by 2025. This 0.2% projected annual growth rate compares to the projected national average of 0.8%. From 2006 to 2007 the state's population declined by 0.1%. The state's 2007 per capita personal income of 38,740 was higher compared to $36,689 in 2006 and the nineteenth highest in the United States, some $176 above the national average. Per capita income in Pennsylvania grew at a compound annual rate of 3.9% from 2000 to 2007, compared to 3.7% nationally.

Pennsylvania's largest industry in terms of 2006 employment was health care and social assistance. The fastest growing industry was transportation and warehousing, with 4.2% annual growth from 1998 to 2006. The state's workforce is generally less educated than other states—25.8% hold a bachelor degree or higher (national average is 27.0%); and 9.9%

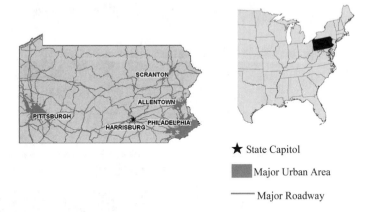

★ State Capitol

Major Urban Area

—— Major Roadway

Demographic and Socioeconomic Profile

Demographics and Socioeconomic Figures			
Population and Households	**2000**	**2006**	**2007**
Total Population	12,281,054	12,440,621	12,432,792
Number of Households	4,777,003	4,845,603	4,873,482
Average Household Size	2.5	2.5	2.5
Age and Ethnicity			
Median Age	38.0	39.6	39.7
Population 18 Years of Age and Older	9,362,066	9,633,087	9,646,036
Population 65 Years of Age and Older	1,920,257	1,883,234	1,887,376
Caucasian Population	10,486,177	10,429,732	10,408,647
African-American Population	1,211,669	1,289,799	1,289,389
Hispanic Population	392,121	527,142	554,348
Asian Population	216,631	289,289	294,314
Foreign-Born Population (%)	4.1	5.1	5.4
Income			
Per Capita Personal Income (USD)	$29,695	$36,689	$38,740
Median Household Income (USD)	$40,106	$46,259	$48,576
Individuals below Poverty Level	11.0%	12.1%	11.6%

Data: U.S. Census, American Community Survey; U.S. Department of Commerce, Bureau of Economic Analysis

hold professional or graduate degrees compared to the national average of 10.1%; however, 86.8% of the state's adult population has graduated from high school, compared to an 84.1% national average.

Pennsylvania's total tax revenue was $49.1 billion for fiscal year 2005–6, up from the 2004–5 total revenue of $46.0 billion. The largest share of tax revenue in 2005–6 was generated from sales and gross receipts taxes, followed by property taxes. On a per capita basis, residents of Pennsylvania paid taxes of $3,944, compared to the national average of $3,992 for 2005–6. In terms of business taxes, the state ranked twentieth in a 2008 analysis by Anderson Economic Group. Forbes Magazine and the Tax Foundation ranked the state's business climate forty-first and twenty-eighth, respectively.

Population Projections

Year	2010	2015	2020	2025
Total Population	12,584,487	12,710,938	12,787,354	12,801,945
Median Age	40.0	40.3	40.6	41.4
Population 18 Years of Age and Older	9,836,892	9,970,245	10,016,274	10,023,766
Population 65 Years of Age and Older	1,956,235	2,148,982	2,403,118	2,688,781

Data: U.S. Census Bureau

Workforce and Industry Profile

Workforce

	2000	2006	2007
Civilian Labor Force	6,085,833	6,306,050	6,297,105
Labor Force Participation Rate	64.2%	64.7%	64.5%
Unemployment Rate	4.2%	4.7%	4.4%
Average Wage Per Job (USD)	$34,015	$37,580	$38,960
Education Attainment (Population 25 Years and Older)	(%)	(%)	(%)
High School Graduate or Higher	81.9	86.2	86.8
Bachelors Degree or Higher	22.4	25.4	25.8
Graduate or Professional Degree	8.4	11.3	9.9

Data: U.S. Census Bureau, American Community Survey; U.S. Department of Commerce, Bureau of Economic Analysis; U.S. Department of Labor, Bureau of Labor Statistics

Industry Overview

	1998	2005	2006
Total Employees	4,906,190	5,082,630	5,189,949
Total Payroll ($1,000)	145,569,019	189,692,284	200,537,253
Total Establishments	292,659	303,333	304,058
Establishments with 1–19 Employees	250,822	258,823	258,205
Establishments with 20–49 Employees	25,263	26,891	27,974
Establishments with 50–249 Employees	14,282	15,284	15,507
Establishments with 250–999 Employees	1,971	2,025	2,065
Establishments with 1,000+ Employees	321	310	307

Data: U.S. Census Bureau, County Business Patterns

Major Industries (Ranked by 2006 Employment; Payroll in $1,000s)				
Industry	1998 Employment	2006 Employment	1998 Payroll	2006 Payroll
Health Care and Social Assistance	740,333	860,829	20,979,688	31,205,707
Retail Trade	645,472	679,188	11,092,400	14,873,208
Manufacturing	818,215	663,812	28,636,023	29,913,140
Accommodation and Food Services	364,480	411,031	3,736,716	5,419,937
Professional, Scientific, Technical Services	266,917	316,047	12,571,204	19,624,584
Finance and Insurance	272,427	306,427	11,510,271	18,997,048
Admin., Support, Waste Mngt., Remediation Services	278,403	306,181	5,632,982	8,205,328
Construction	225,797	257,300	8,279,710	12,214,188
Other Services (except Public Admin.)	239,673	248,483	4,148,515	5,511,081
Wholesale Trade	234,940	241,755	9,203,086	12,600,159

Data: U.S. Census Bureau, County Business Patterns

Taxes and Business Climate

State and Local Taxes		
Combined Revenues ($1,000)	2004–5	2005–6
Revenue from Property Taxes	13,390,534	14,214,051
Revenue from Sales and Gross Receipts Taxes	13,637,892	14,266,955
Revenue from Individual Income Taxes	11,461,650	12,326,373
Revenue from Corporate Income Taxes	1,703,295	2,116,954
Revenue from Other Taxes	5,825,887	6,138,302
Total Tax Revenue	46,019,258	49,062,635
Per Capita Taxes		
Property Tax Per Capita	1,083	1,143
Sales and Gross Receipts Tax Per Capita	1,103	1,147
Individual Income Tax Per Capita	927	991
Corporate Income Tax Per Capita	138	170
Other Taxes Per Capita	471	493
Total Taxes Per Capita	3,721	3,944

Data: U.S. Census Bureau; Anderson Economic Group, LLC

Business Climate Measures

Anderson Economic Group: 2008 Business Tax Ranking (1 is Best)	20
Forbes Magazine: 2008 Best States for Business Ranking (1 is Best)	41
Tax Foundation: 2009 Business Tax Climate Ranking (1 is Best)	28
2004–5 Employer Firm Births	26,417
2004–5 Employer Firm Terminations	24,596

Data: Anderson Economic Group; Tax Foundation; Forbes Magazine; U.S. Census, Statistics of U.S. Businesses

Voting Behavior and Elected Officials

Voter Registration and Turnout (%)

	1996	2000	2004	2008
Registered Voters Who Voted	66.2	63.1	69.0	NaN
Population Age 18+ Who Voted	49.0	52.5	60.5	62.3

Data: Dave Leip's Atlas of U.S. Presidential Elections

Presidential Election Results (Nationwide Winner Listed First)

2008	Popular Vote (%)	Electoral Votes
Barack Obama (Democrat)	54.5	21
John McCain (Republican)	44.2	0
Other	1.3	0
2004		
George W. Bush (Republican, Incumbent)	48.4	0
John Kerry (Democrat)	50.9	21
Other	0.7	0
2000		
George W. Bush (Republican)	46.4	0
Albert Gore (Democrat)	50.6	23
Ralph Nader (Green)	2.1	0
Other	0.9	0
1996		
William Clinton (Democrat, Incumbent)	49.2	23
Robert Dole (Republican)	40.0	0
H. Ross Perot (Reformist)	9.6	0
Other	1.3	0

Data: Dave Leip's Atlas of U.S. Presidential Elections

Governor and U.S. Congressional Seats

Governor	Party	Year Term Began	Term	Max. Consecutive Terms
Edward Rendell	D	2007	Second	2

U.S. Senators	Party	Year Elected	Term Expires	
Bob Casey, Jr.	D	2006	2013	
Arlen Specter	R	1980	2011	

U.S. Representatives		Republican	Democrat	Other
		7	12	0

Data: National Governors Association; U.S. Senate, Office of the Clerk; U.S. House of Representatives

Business and Economic Agencies

Agency	Website Address
Pennsylvania Chamber of Business & Industry	www.pachamber.org
Pennsylvania Department of Community and Economic Development	www.newpa.com
Pennsylvania Small Business Dev. Center	www.pasbdc.org
Pennsylvania Department of State	www.dos.state.pa.us/corps

Data: Various agency websites

Rhode Island

Rhode Island is located in the New England region of the United States. Rhode Island has a population of 1.1 million people, making it the eighth least populous state in 2007. The state's population increased by 9,513 people from 2000 to 2007, and is projected to increase to 1.2 million by 2025. This 0.5% projected annual growth rate is below the national average of 0.8%. From 2006 to 2007 the state's population declined by 0.9%. Per capita personal income in Rhode Island was $39,712 in 2007, up from $37,261 in 2006. For 2007, this was $1,148 above the national average and the sixteenth highest in the country. The state's per capita income grew at a compound annual rate of 4.5% from 2000 to 2007, compared to 3.7% nationally.

The state's workforce generally has more education than other states—29.8% hold a bachelor degree or higher (national average is 27.0%); and 11.8% hold professional or graduate degrees (national average is 10.1%); however, only 83.0% of the state's adult population has graduated from high school,

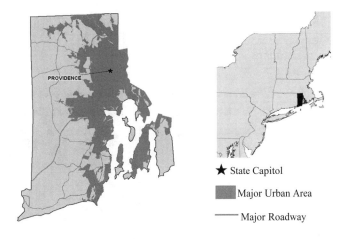

★ State Capitol

▆ Major Urban Area

—— Major Roadway

Demographic and Socioeconomic Profile

Demographics and Socioeconomic Figures			
Population and Households	**2000**	**2006**	**2007**
Total Population	1,048,319	1,067,610	1,057,832
Number of Households	408,424	405,627	402,538
Average Household Size	2.5	2.5	2.5
Age and Ethnicity			
Median Age	36.7	38.4	38.3
Population 18 Years of Age and Older	800,810	830,163	823,011
Population 65 Years of Age and Older	152,719	147,444	146,260
Caucasian Population	890,766	882,370	875,512
African-American Population	45,236	54,396	59,107
Hispanic Population	90,452	117,708	118,934
Asian Population	23,825	29,406	29,635
Foreign-Born Population (%)	11.4	12.6	12.7
Income			
Per Capita Personal Income (USD)	$29,214	$37,261	$39,712
Median Household Income (USD)	$42,090	$51,814	$53,568
Individuals below Poverty Level	11.9%	11.1%	12.0%

Data: U.S. Census, American Community Survey; U.S. Department of Commerce, Bureau of Economic Analysis

compared to an 84.1% national average. In 2006, the state's largest industry in terms of employment was retail trade, followed by manufacturing. The fastest growing industry was arts, entertainment, and recreation, with 5.8% annual growth from 1998 to 2006.

In fiscal year 2005–6, Rhode Island had total tax revenues of $4.7 billion. The largest share was generated from property taxes, followed by sales and gross receipts taxes. The per capita tax burden in Rhode Island was $4,384 for 2005–6, some $391 above the national average, and a $166 increase from the 2004–5 per capita tax burden. In terms of business taxes, Rhode Island ranked fortieth in a 2008 report by Anderson Economic Group. The state's business climate was ranked forty-fifth by Forbes Magazine and forty-sixth by the Tax Foundation.

Population Projections

Year	2010	2015	2020	2025
Total Population	1,116,652	1,139,543	1,154,230	1,157,855
Median Age	38.2	38.2	39.2	39.7
Population 18 Years of Age and Older	867,379	891,204	900,219	901,037
Population 65 Years of Age and Older	157,358	175,242	197,972	224,508

Data: U.S. Census Bureau

Workforce and Industry Profile

Workforce

	2000	2006	2007
Civilian Labor Force	543,404	577,338	572,483
Labor Force Participation Rate	66.8%	68.4%	68.6%
Unemployment Rate	4.2%	5.1%	5.2%
Average Wage Per Job (USD)	$32,615	$40,580	$42,210
Education Attainment (Population 25 Years and Older)	(%)	(%)	(%)
High School Graduate or Higher	78.0	82.4	83.0
Bachelors Degree or Higher	25.6	29.6	29.8
Graduate or Professional Degree	9.7	7.9	11.8

Data: U.S. Census Bureau, American Community Survey; U.S. Department of Commerce, Bureau of Economic Analysis; U.S. Department of Labor, Bureau of Labor Statistics

Industry Overview

	1998	2005	2006
Total Employees	402,485	442,291	440,797
Total Payroll ($1,000)	11,115,638	15,756,079	17,072,822
Total Establishments	28,245	30,331	30,398
Establishments with 1–19 Employees	24,651	26,255	26,288
Establishments with 20–49 Employees	2,242	2,546	2,560
Establishments with 50–249 Employees	1,165	1,366	1,395
Establishments with 250–999 Employees	162	137	131
Establishments with 1,000+ Employees	25	27	24

Data: U.S. Census Bureau, County Business Patterns

Major Industries (Ranked by 2006 Employment; Payroll in $1,000s)				
Industry	1998 Employment	2006 Employment	1998 Payroll	2006 Payroll
Health Care and Social Assistance	68,633	82,430	1,914,868	3,050,162
Retail Trade	46,781	56,145	834,011	1,486,712
Manufacturing	74,181	54,061	2,341,311	2,362,712
Accommodation and Food Services	33,837	41,924	384,469	626,213
Finance and Insurance	24,277	32,524	917,996	1,892,452
Admin., Support, Waste Mngt., Remediation Services	28,065	22,815	563,833	613,808
Educational Services	18,410	22,661	429,108	722,185
Professional, Scientific, Technical Services	15,973	21,987	632,606	1,150,889
Construction	16,290	21,915	614,594	1,103,537
Other Services (except Public Admin.)	16,913	19,302	314,071	477,429

Data: U.S. Census Bureau, County Business Patterns

Taxes and Business Climate

State and Local Taxes		
Combined Revenues ($1,000)	2004–5	2005–6
Revenue from Property Taxes	1,819,413	1,887,857
Revenue from Sales and Gross Receipts Taxes	1,386,537	1,405,205
Revenue from Individual Income Taxes	998,042	1,019,482
Revenue from Corporate Income Taxes	113,326	169,865
Revenue from Other Taxes	182,306	197,571
Total Tax Revenue	4,499,624	4,679,980
Per Capita Taxes		
Property Tax Per Capita	1,706	1,768
Sales and Gross Receipts Tax Per Capita	1,300	1,316
Individual Income Tax Per Capita	936	955
Corporate Income Tax Per Capita	106	159
Other Taxes Per Capita	171	185
Total Taxes Per Capita	4,218	4,384

Data: U.S. Census Bureau; Anderson Economic Group, LLC

Business Climate Measures	
Anderson Economic Group: 2008 Business Tax Ranking (1 is Best)	40
Forbes Magazine: 2008 Best States for Business Ranking (1 is Best)	45
Tax Foundation: 2009 Business Tax Climate Ranking (1 is Best)	46
2004–5 Employer Firm Births	2,727
2004–5 Employer Firm Terminations	2,534

Data: Anderson Economic Group; Tax Foundation; Forbes Magazine; U.S. Census, Statistics of U.S. Businesses

Voting Behavior and Elected Officials

Voter Registration and Turnout (%)	1996	2000	2004	2008
Registered Voters Who Voted	64.8	60.9	61.7	67.0
Population Age 18+ Who Voted	52.0	51.1	52.5	57.1

Data: Dave Leip's Atlas of U.S. Presidential Elections

Presidential Election Results (Nationwide Winner Listed First)		
2008	Popular Vote (%)	Electoral Votes
Barack Obama (Democrat)	63.1	4
John McCain (Republican)	35.2	0
Other	1.7	0
2004		
George W. Bush (Republican, Incumbent)	38.7	0
John Kerry (Democrat)	59.4	4
Other	1.9	0
2000		
George W. Bush (Republican)	31.9	0
Albert Gore (Democrat)	61.0	4
Ralph Nader (Green)	6.1	0
Other	1.0	0
1996		
William Clinton (Democrat, Incumbent)	59.7	4
Robert Dole (Republican)	26.8	0
H. Ross Perot (Reformist)	11.2	0
Other	2.3	0

Data: Dave Leip's Atlas of U.S. Presidential Elections

Governor and U.S. Congressional Seats				
Governor	Party	Year Term Began	Term	Max. Consecutive Terms
Don Carcieri	R	2007	Second	2
U.S. Senators	Party	Year Elected	Term Expires	
Jack Reed	D	1996	2015	
Sheldon Whitehouse	D	2006	2013	
U.S. Representatives		Republican	Democrat	Other
		0	2	0

Data: National Governors Association; U.S. Senate, Office of the Clerk; U.S. House of Representatives

Business and Economic Agencies

Agency	Website Address
Narragansett Rhode Island Chamber of Commerce	www.narragansettri.com/chamber/
Rhode Island Economic Development Corporation	www.riedc.com
Rhode Island Small Business Dev. Center	www.risbdc.org
Rhode Island Secretary of State	www.sec.state.ri.us/corps

Data: Various agency websites

South Carolina

South Carolina, located in the South Atlantic region of the United States, has a population of 4.4 million people, making it the twenty-fourth most populous state in 2007. The state's population increased by 395,697 people from 2000 to 2007, and is projected to increase to 5.0 million by 2025. This 0.7% projected annual growth rate compares to the projected national average of 0.8%. From 2006 to 2007 the state's population grew by 2.0%. Per capita personal income in South Carolina was $31,048 in 2007, up from $29,688 in 2006. For 2007, this was seventh lowest in the country and $7,516 below the national average. From 2000 to 2007 the per capita income in South Carolina grew at a compound annual rate of 3.5%, compared to 3.7% nationally.

In 2006, the state's largest industry in terms of employment was retail trade, followed by health care and social assistance. The fastest growing industry was transportation and warehousing with 5.6% annual growth from 1998 to 2006. The state's workforce is generally less educated than other

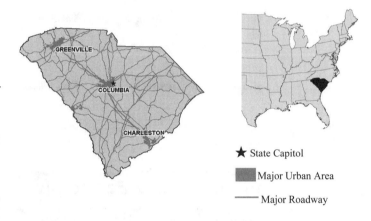

★ State Capitol

▮ Major Urban Area

— Major Roadway

Demographic and Socioeconomic Profile

Demographics and Socioeconomic Figures			
Population and Households	**2000**	**2006**	**2007**
Total Population	4,012,012	4,321,249	4,407,709
Number of Households	1,533,854	1,656,978	1,702,564
Average Household Size	2.5	2.5	2.5
Age and Ethnicity			
Median Age	35.4	37.1	37.4
Population 18 Years of Age and Older	3,002,919	3,282,383	3,350,053
Population 65 Years of Age and Older	485,845	553,855	572,382
Caucasian Population	2,695,678	2,908,324	2,968,269
African-American Population	1,182,727	1,237,900	1,253,575
Hispanic Population	92,828	148,632	165,921
Asian Population	36,505	46,939	54,720
Foreign-Born Population (%)	2.9	4.1	4.3
Income			
Per Capita Personal Income (USD)	$24,424	$29,688	$31,048
Median Household Income (USD)	$37,082	$41,100	$43,329
Individuals below Poverty Level	14.1%	15.7%	15.0%

Data: U.S. Census, American Community Survey; U.S. Department of Commerce, Bureau of Economic Analysis

states—82.1% of the state's adult population has graduated from high school, compared to an 84.1% national average. Nationally, an average of 27.0% hold a bachelor degree or higher compared to 23.5% in South Carolina; and 8.2% hold professional or graduate degrees (national average is 10.1%).

In fiscal year 2005–6, South Carolina had total tax revenues of $12.4 billion. The largest share was generated from sales and gross receipts taxes, followed by property taxes. The per capita tax burden in South Carolina was $2,880 for 2005–6, some $1,112 below the national average. In terms of business taxes, the state ranked twenty-ninth in a 2008 analysis by Anderson Economic Group. Forbes Magazine and the Tax Foundation ranked the state's business climate twenty-ninth and twenty-fifth, respectively.

Population Projections

Year	2010	2015	2020	2025
Total Population	4,446,704	4,642,137	4,822,577	4,989,550
Median Age	38.4	39.4	40.3	41.0
Population 18 Years of Age and Older	3,410,355	3,580,984	3,737,193	3,878,805
Population 65 Years of Age and Older	605,660	729,179	866,250	1,009,242

Data: U.S. Census Bureau

Workforce and Industry Profile

Workforce

	2000	2006	2007
Civilian Labor Force	1,972,850	2,126,439	2,125,073
Labor Force Participation Rate	65.7%	63.9%	63.1%
Unemployment Rate	3.6%	6.5%	5.6%
Average Wage Per Job (USD)	$28,179	$33,400	$34,650
Education Attainment (Population 25 Years and Older)	(%)	(%)	(%)
High School Graduate or Higher	76.3	81.3	82.1
Bachelors Degree or Higher	20.4	22.7	23.5
Graduate or Professional Degree	6.9	7.2	8.2

Data: U.S. Census Bureau, American Community Survey; U.S. Department of Commerce, Bureau of Economic Analysis; U.S. Department of Labor, Bureau of Labor Statistics

Industry Overview

	1998	2005	2006
Total Employees	1,526,106	1,584,914	1,633,441
Total Payroll ($1,000)	38,559,169	49,450,267	52,189,166
Total Establishments	94,985	103,416	105,296
Establishments with 1–19 Employees	82,048	88,962	90,204
Establishments with 20–49 Employees	7,980	9,158	9,533
Establishments with 50–249 Employees	4,195	4,595	4,818
Establishments with 250–999 Employees	670	614	648
Establishments with 1,000+ Employees	92	87	93

Data: U.S. Census Bureau, County Business Patterns

Major Industries (Ranked by 2006 Employment; Payroll in $1,000s)				
Industry	1998 Employment	2006 Employment	1998 Payroll	2006 Payroll
Manufacturing	343,295	263,605	10,898,250	10,950,338
Retail Trade	213,800	228,874	3,393,667	4,859,578
Health Care and Social Assistance	161,581	197,901	4,600,631	7,203,996
Accommodation and Food Services	145,493	181,191	1,490,773	2,297,369
Admin., Support, Waste Mngt., Remediation Services	122,913	140,155	2,183,375	3,184,641
Construction	111,427	118,318	2,973,943	4,023,389
Professional, Scientific, Technical Services	58,476	80,757	2,264,270	4,108,784
Other Services (except Public Admin.)	67,783	78,843	1,076,923	1,616,050
Finance and Insurance	58,771	69,745	1,972,715	2,974,811
Wholesale Trade	60,762	67,865	2,056,717	3,071,330

Data: U.S. Census Bureau, County Business Patterns

Taxes and Business Climate

State and Local Taxes		
Combined Revenues ($1,000)	2004–5	2005–6
Revenue from Property Taxes	3,738,818	3,960,046
Revenue from Sales and Gross Receipts Taxes	4,230,882	4,486,960
Revenue from Individual Income Taxes	2,691,473	2,727,251
Revenue from Corporate Income Taxes	246,935	296,753
Revenue from Other Taxes	892,532	973,142
Total Tax Revenue	11,800,640	12,444,152
Per Capita Taxes		
Property Tax Per Capita	879	916
Sales and Gross Receipts Tax Per Capita	994	1,038
Individual Income Tax Per Capita	633	631
Corporate Income Tax Per Capita	58	69
Other Taxes Per Capita	210	225
Total Taxes Per Capita	2,773	2,880

Data: U.S. Census Bureau; Anderson Economic Group, LLC

Business Climate Measures	
Anderson Economic Group: 2008 Business Tax Ranking (1 is Best)	29
Forbes Magazine: 2008 Best States for Business Ranking (1 is Best)	29
Tax Foundation: 2009 Business Tax Climate Ranking (1 is Best)	25
2004–5 Employer Firm Births	10,750
2004–5 Employer Firm Terminations	8,925

Data: Anderson Economic Group; Tax Foundation; Forbes Magazine; U.S. Census, Statistics of U.S. Businesses

Voting Behavior and Elected Officials

Voter Registration and Turnout (%)				
	1996	2000	2004	2008
Registered Voters Who Voted	63.3	61.1	69.9	74.5
Population Age 18+ Who Voted	41.5	46.1	51.8	57.3

Data: Dave Leip's Atlas of U.S. Presidential Elections

Presidential Election Results (Nationwide Winner Listed First)		
2008	Popular Vote (%)	Electoral Votes
Barack Obama (Democrat)	44.9	0
John McCain (Republican)	53.9	8
Other	1.2	0
2004		
George W. Bush (Republican, Incumbent)	58.0	8
John Kerry (Democrat)	40.9	0
Other	1.1	0
2000		
George W. Bush (Republican)	56.8	8
Albert Gore (Democrat)	40.9	0
Ralph Nader (Green)	1.5	0
Other	0.8	0
1996		
William Clinton (Democrat, Incumbent)	44.0	0
Robert Dole (Republican)	49.9	8
H. Ross Perot (Reformist)	5.6	0
Other	0.7	0

Data: Dave Leip's Atlas of U.S. Presidential Elections

Governor and U.S. Congressional Seats

Governor	Party	Year Term Began	Term	Max. Consecutive Terms
Mark Sanford	R	2007	Second	2

U.S. Senators	Party	Year Elected	Term Expires	
Lindsey Graham	R	2002	2015	
Jim DeMint	R	2004	2011	

U.S. Representatives		Republican	Democrat	Other
		4	2	0

Data: National Governors Association; U.S. Senate, Office of the Clerk; U.S. House of Representatives

Business and Economic Agencies

Agency	Website Address
South Carolina Chamber of Commerce	www.scchamber.net
South Carolina Economic Development Directory	www.sciway.net/econ
South Carolina Small Business Dev. Center	scsbdc.moore.sc.edu
South Carolina Secretary of State	www.scsos.com

Data: Various agency websites

South Dakota

With a population of 796,215 people, South Dakota was the fifth least populous state in the United States in 2007. From 2000 to 2007 the state's population increased by 41,371 people, and is projected to slightly increase to 801,845 people by 2025. From 2006 to 2007 the state's population grew 1.8%. The state's 2007 per capita personal income of $35,664 was higher compared to $32,405 in 2006 and twenty-third lowest in the United States, some $2,900 below the national average. Per capita income in South Dakota grew at a compound annual rate of 4.8% from 2000 to 2007, compared to 3.7% nationally.

South Dakota's largest industry in terms of 2006 employment was retail trade. The fastest growing industry was management of companies and enterprises, with 10.1% annual growth from 1998 to 2006. The second fastest growing industry was professional, scientific, and technical services. The state's workforce is generally less educated than other states—25.0% hold a bachelor degree or higher (national average is 27.0%); and 7.0%

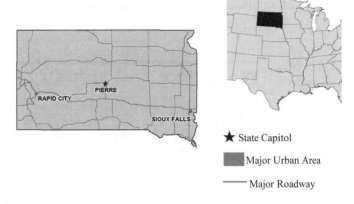

★ State Capitol

▮ Major Urban Area

── Major Roadway

Demographic and Socioeconomic Profile

Demographics and Socioeconomic Figures			
Population and Households	2000	2006	2007
Total Population	754,844	781,919	796,215
Number of Households	290,245	312,477	312,912
Average Household Size	2.5	2.4	2.5
Age and Ethnicity			
Median Age	35.6	37.3	37.1
Population 18 Years of Age and Older	552,118	587,942	600,012
Population 65 Years of Age and Older	108,116	111,639	113,804
Caucasian Population	669,477	681,785	695,699
African-American Population	4,518	5,262	8,679
Hispanic Population	10,386	15,544	16,532
Asian Population	4,729	7,064	6,665
Foreign-Born Population (%)	1.8	2.2	1.8
Income			
Per Capita Personal Income (USD)	$25,720	$32,405	$35,664
Median Household Income (USD)	$35,282	$42,791	$43,424
Individuals below Poverty Level	13.2%	13.6%	13.1%

Data: U.S. Census, American Community Survey; U.S. Department of Commerce, Bureau of Economic Analysis

hold professional or graduate degrees compared to the national average of 10.1%; however, 88.2% of the state's adult population has graduated from high school, compared to an 84.1% national average.

South Dakota's total tax revenue was $2.2 billion for fiscal year 2005–6, up from the 2004–5 total revenue of $2.1 billion. The largest share of tax revenue in 2005–6 was generated from sales and gross receipts taxes, followed by property taxes. On a per capita basis, residents of South Dakota paid taxes of $2,886, compared to the national average of $3,992 for 2005–6. In terms of business taxes, the state ranked ninth in a 2008 analysis by Anderson Economic Group. Forbes Magazine and the Tax Foundation ranked the state's business climate twenty-third and second, respectively.

Population Projections

Year	2010	2015	2020	2025
Total Population	786,399	796,954	801,939	801,845
Median Age	37.5	38.3	39.6	40.8
Population 18 Years of Age and Older	592,247	600,551	604,727	605,728
Population 65 Years of Age and Older	114,459	127,974	148,398	169,663

Data: U.S. Census Bureau

Workforce and Industry Profile

Workforce

	2000	2006	2007
Civilian Labor Force	408,685	430,992	442,085
Labor Force Participation Rate	72.8%	73.1%	73.2%
Unemployment Rate	2.7%	3.2%	2.9%
Average Wage Per Job (USD)	$24,802	$30,460	$31,540
Education Attainment (Population 25 Years and Older)	**(%)**	**(%)**	**(%)**
High School Graduate or Higher	84.6	88.3	88.2
Bachelors Degree or Higher	21.5	24.9	25.0
Graduate or Professional Degree	6.0	7.5	7.0

Data: U.S. Census Bureau, American Community Survey; U.S. Department of Commerce, Bureau of Economic Analysis; U.S. Department of Labor, Bureau of Labor Statistics

Industry Overview

	1998	2005	2006
Total Employees	289,422	310,802	325,105
Total Payroll ($1,000)	6,403,476	8,860,458	9,406,003
Total Establishments	23,521	25,205	25,482
Establishments with 1–19 Employees	20,842	22,276	22,409
Establishments with 20–49 Employees	1,762	1,903	1,992
Establishments with 50–249 Employees	815	915	955
Establishments with 250–999 Employees	93	102	117
Establishments with 1,000+ Employees	9	9	9

Data: U.S. Census Bureau, County Business Patterns

Major Industries (Ranked by 2006 Employment; Payroll in $1,000s)				
Industry	1998 Employment	2006 Employment	1998 Payroll	2006 Payroll
Health Care and Social Assistance	48,237	57,279	1,200,868	1,986,964
Retail Trade	47,784	51,499	771,746	1,053,274
Manufacturing	48,082	42,215	1,371,454	1,454,431
Accommodation and Food Services	29,168	36,108	254,740	414,298
Finance and Insurance	20,034	27,220	564,637	1,050,786
Construction	13,992	18,897	402,173	686,536
Wholesale Trade	16,089	14,712	431,329	552,325
Other Services (except Public Admin.)	12,924	14,281	186,226	264,445
Admin., Support, Waste Mngt., Remediation Services	8,289	10,854	134,475	228,193
Professional, Scientific, Technical Services	7,499	10,233	193,922	387,710

Data: U.S. Census Bureau, County Business Patterns

Taxes and Business Climate

State and Local Taxes		
Combined Revenues ($1,000)	2004–5	2005–6
Revenue from Property Taxes	730,122	767,181
Revenue from Sales and Gross Receipts Taxes	1,123,745	1,216,007
Revenue from Individual Income Taxes	0	0
Revenue from Corporate Income Taxes	49,142	61,865
Revenue from Other Taxes	200,811	195,723
Total Tax Revenue	2,103,820	2,240,776
Per Capita Taxes		
Property Tax Per Capita	936	981
Sales and Gross Receipts Tax Per Capita	1,441	1,555
Individual Income Tax Per Capita	0	0
Corporate Income Tax Per Capita	63	79
Other Taxes Per Capita	257	250
Total Taxes Per Capita	2,697	2,866

Data: U.S. Census Bureau; Anderson Economic Group, LLC

Business Climate Measures

Anderson Economic Group: 2008 Business Tax Ranking (1 is Best)	9
Forbes Magazine: 2008 Best States for Business Ranking (1 is Best)	23
Tax Foundation: 2009 Business Tax Climate Ranking (1 is Best)	2
2004–5 Employer Firm Births	2,207
2004–5 Employer Firm Terminations	1,947

Data: Anderson Economic Group; Tax Foundation; Forbes Magazine; U.S. Census, Statistics of U.S. Businesses

Voting Behavior and Elected Officials

Voter Registration and Turnout (%)

	1996	2000	2004	2008
Registered Voters Who Voted	70.4	67.1	77.3	72.0
Population Age 18+ Who Voted	60.5	57.3	68.2	63.7

Data: Dave Leip's Atlas of U.S. Presidential Elections

Presidential Election Results (Nationwide Winner Listed First)

2008	Popular Vote (%)	Electoral Votes
Barack Obama (Democrat)	44.8	0
John McCain (Republican)	53.2	3
Other	2.1	0
2004		
George W. Bush (Republican, Incumbent)	59.9	3
John Kerry (Democrat)	38.4	0
Other	1.7	0
2000		
George W. Bush (Republican)	60.3	3
Albert Gore (Democrat)	37.6	0
Ralph Nader (Green)	.0	0
Other	2.1	0
1996		
William Clinton (Democrat, Incumbent)	43.0	0
Robert Dole (Republican)	46.5	3
H. Ross Perot (Reformist)	9.7	0
Other	0.8	0

Data: Dave Leip's Atlas of U.S. Presidential Elections

Governor and U.S. Congressional Seats

Governor	Party	Year Term Began	Term	Max. Consecutive Terms
Michael Rounds	R	2007	Second	2
U.S. Senators	**Party**	**Year Elected**	**Term Expires**	
Tim Johnson	D	1996	2015	
John Thune	R	2004	2011	
U.S. Representatives		**Republican**	**Democrat**	**Other**
		0	1	0

Data: National Governors Association; U.S. Senate, Office of the Clerk; U.S. House of Representatives

Business and Economic Agencies

Agency	Website Address
South Dakota Chamber of Commerce & Industry	www.sdchamber.biz
South Dakota's Governor's Office of Economic Development	www.sdreadytowork.com
South Dakota Small Business Dev. Center	www.sdsbdc.org
South Dakota Secretary of State	www.sdsos.gov/busineservices/ busineservices_overview.shtm

Data: Various agency websites

Tennessee

Tennessee is located in the East South Central region of the United States. Tennessee has a population of 6.1 million people, making it the seventeenth most populous state in 2007. The state's population increased by 467,436 people from 2000 to 2007, and is projected to increase to 7.1 million by 2025. This 0.8% projected annual growth rate is equal to the national average. From 2006 to 2007 the state's population grew by 2.0%. Per capita personal income in Tennessee was $33,373 in 2007, up from $32,305 in 2006. For 2007, this was $5,191 below the national average and the thirteenth lowest in the country. The state's per capita income grew at a compound annual rate of 3.6% from 2000 to 2007, compared to 3.7% nationally.

The state's workforce generally has less education than other states—81.4% of the state's adult population has graduated from high school, compared to an 84.1% national average; 21.8% hold a bachelor degree or higher (national average is 27.0%); and 7.6% hold professional or graduate degrees

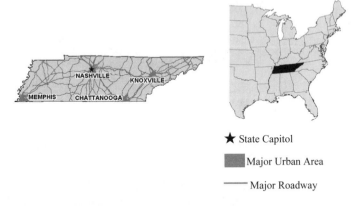

★ State Capitol

Major Urban Area

—— Major Roadway

Demographic and Socioeconomic Profile

Demographics and Socioeconomic Figures			
Population and Households	**2000**	**2006**	**2007**
Total Population	5,689,283	6,038,803	6,156,719
Number of Households	2,232,905	2,375,123	2,407,765
Average Household Size	2.5	2.5	2.5
Age and Ethnicity			
Median Age	35.9	37.2	37.5
Population 18 Years of Age and Older	4,292,047	4,591,753	4,685,625
Population 65 Years of Age and Older	702,839	767,093	790,563
Caucasian Population	4,562,454	4,781,578	4,868,752
African-American Population	929,864	1,011,726	1,029,129
Hispanic Population	119,425	187,747	211,552
Asian Population	54,132	76,208	79,214
Foreign-Born Population (%)	2.8	3.9	4.1
Income			
Per Capita Personal Income (USD)	$26,097	$32,305	$33,373
Median Household Income (USD)	$36,360	$40,315	$42,367
Individuals below Poverty Level	13.5%	16.2%	15.9%

Data: U.S. Census, American Community Survey; U.S. Department of Commerce, Bureau of Economic Analysis

(national average is 10.1%). In 2006, the state's largest industry in terms of employment was health care and social assistance, followed by retail trade. The fastest growing industry was professional, scientific, and technical services, with 4.9% annual growth from 1998 to 2006.

In fiscal year 2005–6, Tennessee had total tax revenues of $17.2 billion. The largest share was generated from sales and gross receipts taxes, followed by property taxes. The per capita tax burden in Tennessee was $2,855 for 2005–6, some $1,137 below the national average, but a $185 increase from the 2004–5 per capita tax burden. In terms of business taxes, Tennessee ranked third in a 2008 report by Anderson Economic Group. The state's business climate was ranked seventeenth by Forbes Magazine and the Tax Foundation.

Population Projections

Year	2010	2015	2020	2025
Total Population	6,230,852	6,502,017	6,780,670	7,073,125
Median Age	37.9	38.2	38.6	38.5
Population 18 Years of Age and Older	4,751,937	4,963,306	5,173,458	5,383,849
Population 65 Years of Age and Older	829,023	968,919	1,121,063	1,279,981

Data: U.S. Census Bureau

Workforce and Industry Profile

Workforce

	2000	2006	2007
Civilian Labor Force	2,871,539	2,990,152	3,013,380
Labor Force Participation Rate	65.9%	64.1%	63.5%
Unemployment Rate	4.0%	5.2%	4.8%
Average Wage Per Job (USD)	$30,554	$34,240	$35,380
Education Attainment (Population 25 Years and Older)	(%)	(%)	(%)
High School Graduate or Higher	75.9	80.9	81.4
Bachelors Degree or Higher	19.6	21.7	21.8
Graduate or Professional Degree	6.8	8.0	7.6

Data: U.S. Census Bureau, American Community Survey; U.S. Department of Commerce, Bureau of Economic Analysis; U.S. Department of Labor, Bureau of Labor Statistics

Industry Overview

	1998	2005	2006
Total Employees	2,299,348	2,378,754	2,473,352
Total Payroll ($1,000)	62,441,176	80,959,818	86,500,766
Total Establishments	131,110	133,098	135,074
Establishments with 1–19 Employees	111,021	111,913	113,031
Establishments with 20–49 Employees	12,072	12,992	13,492
Establishments with 50–249 Employees	6,894	7,050	7,371
Establishments with 250–999 Employees	992	995	1,029
Establishments with 1,000+ Employees	131	148	151

Data: U.S. Census Bureau, County Business Patterns

Major Industries (Ranked by 2006 Employment; Payroll in $1,000s)				
Industry	1998 Employment	2006 Employment	1998 Payroll	2006 Payroll
Manufacturing	482,811	393,385	15,020,254	16,003,944
Health Care and Social Assistance	281,083	344,315	8,307,173	13,313,830
Retail Trade	311,720	332,982	5,322,361	7,267,020
Accommodation and Food Services	189,001	231,986	2,078,502	2,963,595
Admin., Support, Waste Mngt., Remediation Services	157,976	196,949	3,011,742	4,894,836
Professional, Scientific, Technical Services	86,439	126,735	3,301,052	6,054,825
Construction	120,575	123,659	3,762,360	4,894,200
Wholesale Trade	125,204	120,649	4,390,902	5,887,558
Transportation and Warehousing	86,518	120,491	2,745,830	4,558,242
Finance and Insurance	101,293	117,865	4,003,336	6,498,389

Data: U.S. Census Bureau, County Business Patterns

Taxes and Business Climate

State and Local Taxes		
Combined Revenues ($1,000)	2004–5	2005–6
Revenue from Property Taxes	3,894,418	4,125,714
Revenue from Sales and Gross Receipts Taxes	9,381,111	10,093,787
Revenue from Individual Income Taxes	155,333	192,764
Revenue from Corporate Income Taxes	805,601	928,349
Revenue from Other Taxes	1,756,673	1,899,705
Total Tax Revenue	15,993,136	17,240,319
Per Capita Taxes		
Property Tax Per Capita	650	683
Sales and Gross Receipts Tax Per Capita	1,566	1,671
Individual Income Tax Per Capita	26	32
Corporate Income Tax Per Capita	135	154
Other Taxes Per Capita	293	315
Total Taxes Per Capita	2,670	2,855

Data: U.S. Census Bureau; Anderson Economic Group, LLC

Business Climate Measures

Anderson Economic Group: 2008 Business Tax Ranking (1 is Best)	3
Forbes Magazine: 2008 Best States for Business Ranking (1 is Best)	17
Tax Foundation: 2009 Business Tax Climate Ranking (1 is Best)	17
2004–5 Employer Firm Births	13,007
2004–5 Employer Firm Terminations	11,996

Data: Anderson Economic Group; Tax Foundation; Forbes Magazine; U.S. Census, Statistics of U.S. Businesses

Voting Behavior and Elected Officials

Voter Registration and Turnout (%)

	1996	2000	2004	2008
Registered Voters Who Voted	66.5	65.3	73.1	71.8
Population Age 18+ Who Voted	46.9	48.4	54.8	55.5

Data: Dave Leip's Atlas of U.S. Presidential Elections

Presidential Election Results (Nationwide Winner Listed First)

2008	Popular Vote (%)	Electoral Votes
Barack Obama (Democrat)	41.8	0
John McCain (Republican)	56.9	11
Other	1.3	0
2004		
George W. Bush (Republican, Incumbent)	56.8	11
John Kerry (Democrat)	42.5	0
Other	0.7	0
2000		
George W. Bush (Republican)	51.2	11
Albert Gore (Democrat)	47.3	0
Ralph Nader (Green)	1.0	0
Other	0.6	0
1996		
William Clinton (Democrat, Incumbent)	48.0	11
Robert Dole (Republican)	45.6	0
H. Ross Perot (Reformist)	5.6	0
Other	0.8	0

Data: Dave Leip's Atlas of U.S. Presidential Elections

Governor and U.S. Congressional Seats

Governor	Party	Year Term Began	Term	Max. Consecutive Terms
Phil Bredesen	D	2007	Second	2

U.S. Senators	Party	Year Elected	Term Expires	
Lamar Alexandar	R	2002	2015	
Bob Corker	R	2006	2013	

U.S. Representatives		Republican	Democrat	Other
		4	5	0

Data: National Governors Association; U.S. Senate, Office of the Clerk; U.S. House of Representatives

Business and Economic Agencies

Agency	Website Address
Tennessee Chamber of Commerce & Industry	www.tnchamber.org
Tennessee Department of Economic and Community Development	www.state.tn.us/ecd
Tennessee Small Business Development Centers	www.tsbdc.org
Tennessee Department of State, Division of Business Services	www.state.tn.us/sos/bus_svc

Data: Various agency websites

Texas

Texas, located in the West South Central region of the United States, has a population of 23.9 million people, making it the second most populous state in 2007. The state's population increased by 3.1 million people from 2000 to 2007, and is projected to increase to 30.9 million by 2025. This 1.4% projected annual growth rate compares to the projected national average of 0.8%. From 2006 to 2007 the state's population grew by 1.7%. Per capita personal income in Texas was $37,006 in 2007, up from $35,058 in 2006. For 2007, this was twenty-ninth lowest in the country and $1,558 below the national average. From 2000 to 2007 the per capita income in Texas grew at a compound annual rate of 3.9%, compared to 3.7% nationally.

In 2006, the state's largest industry in terms of employment was retail trade, followed by health care and social assistance. The fastest growing industry was educational services, with 3.9% annual growth from 1998 to 2006. The state's workforce is generally less educated than other states—79.1% of the state's adult population

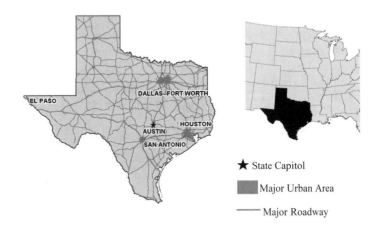

★ State Capitol

▓ Major Urban Area

——— Major Roadway

Demographic and Socioeconomic Profile

Demographics and Socioeconomic Figures			
Population and Households	**2000**	**2006**	**2007**
Total Population	20,851,820	23,507,783	23,904,380
Number of Households	7,393,354	8,109,388	8,244,022
Average Household Size	2.7	2.8	2.8
Age and Ethnicity			
Median Age	32.3	33.1	33.2
Population 18 Years of Age and Older	14,977,890	17,004,929	17,274,933
Population 65 Years of Age and Older	2,067,467	2,329,442	2,389,802
Caucasian Population	14,797,985	16,405,937	16,804,155
African-American Population	2,385,554	2,718,515	2,757,554
Hispanic Population	6,670,122	8,385,118	8,600,385
Asian Population	555,928	787,208	806,844
Foreign-Born Population (%)	13.9	15.9	16.0
Income			
Per Capita Personal Income (USD)	$28,313	$35,058	$37,006
Median Household Income (USD)	$39,927	$44,922	$47,548
Individuals below Poverty Level	15.4%	16.9%	16.3%

Data: U.S. Census, American Community Survey; U.S. Department of Commerce, Bureau of Economic Analysis

has graduated from high school, compared to an 84.1% national average. Nationally, an average of 27.0% hold a bachelor degree or higher compared to 25.2% in Texas; and 8.2% hold professional or graduate degrees (national average is 10.1%).

In fiscal year 2005–6, Texas had total tax revenues of $75.7 billion. The largest share was generated from sales and gross receipts taxes, followed by property taxes. The per capita tax burden in Texas was $3,222 for 2005–6, some $771 below the national average. In terms of business taxes, the state ranked twenty-fourth in a 2008 analysis by Anderson Economic Group. Forbes Magazine and the Tax Foundation ranked the state's business climate ninth and seventh, respectively.

Population Projections

Year	2010	2015	2020	2025
Total Population	24,648,888	26,585,801	28,634,896	30,865,134
Median Age	33.4	33.8	34.3	34.6
Population 18 Years of Age and Older	17,863,480	19,209,583	20,666,629	22,405,639
Population 65 Years of Age and Older	2,587,383	3,112,883	3,755,814	4,500,152

Data: U.S. Census Bureau

Workforce and Industry Profile

Workforce

	2000	2006	2007
Civilian Labor Force	10,347,847	11,487,496	11,474,987
Labor Force Participation Rate	68.1%	66.5%	65.8%
Unemployment Rate	4.4%	4.9%	4.4%
Average Wage Per Job (USD)	$34,941	$36,410	$37,880
Education Attainment (Population 25 Years and Older)	(%)	(%)	(%)
High School Graduate or Higher	75.7	78.6	79.1
Bachelors Degree or Higher	23.2	24.7	25.2
Graduate or Professional Degree	7.6	9.4	8.2

Data: U.S. Census Bureau, American Community Survey; U.S. Department of Commerce, Bureau of Economic Analysis; U.S. Department of Labor, Bureau of Labor Statistics

Industry Overview

	1998	2005	2006
Total Employees	7,570,820	8,305,102	8,711,476
Total Payroll ($1,000)	229,185,833	315,809,126	347,735,827
Total Establishments	462,875	497,458	509,080
Establishments with 1–19 Employees	395,406	423,838	431,361
Establishments with 20–49 Employees	41,631	45,386	47,674
Establishments with 50–249 Employees	22,411	24,822	26,061
Establishments with 250–999 Employees	2,981	3,229	3,472
Establishments with 1,000+ Employees	446	483	512

Data: U.S. Census Bureau, County Business Patterns

Major Industries (Ranked by 2006 Employment; Payroll in $1,000s)				
Industry	1998 Employment	2006 Employment	1998 Payroll	2006 Payroll
Retail Trade	977,678	1,128,050	18,492,576	26,068,384
Health Care and Social Assistance	911,042	1,126,394	24,604,759	40,360,460
Admin., Support, Waste Mngt., Remediation Services	678,374	868,646	14,845,110	23,979,444
Accommodation and Food Services	661,430	850,618	7,361,124	11,408,301
Manufacturing	986,892	846,465	36,331,404	40,922,070
Construction	457,076	553,834	14,281,869	23,593,142
Professional, Scientific, Technical Services	413,798	551,673	19,768,171	35,551,169
Wholesale Trade	436,035	463,522	17,141,752	26,082,170
Finance and Insurance	360,254	453,185	15,639,191	26,356,497
Other Services (except Public Admin.)	373,791	406,636	6,532,243	9,472,365

Data: U.S. Census Bureau, County Business Patterns

Taxes and Business Climate

State and Local Taxes		
Combined Revenues ($1,000)	2004–5	2005–6
Revenue from Property Taxes	30,275,679	32,486,125
Revenue from Sales and Gross Receipts Taxes	31,110,381	34,103,814
Revenue from Individual Income Taxes	0	0
Revenue from Corporate Income Taxes	1	1
Revenue from Other Taxes	7,747,801	9,142,110
Total Tax Revenue	69,133,862	75,732,050
Per Capita Taxes		
Property Tax Per Capita	1,325	1,382
Sales and Gross Receipts Tax Per Capita	1,362	1,451
Individual Income Tax Per Capita	0	0
Corporate Income Tax Per Capita	0	0
Other Taxes Per Capita	339	389
Total Taxes Per Capita	3,026	3,222

Data: U.S. Census Bureau; Anderson Economic Group, LLC

Business Climate Measures

Anderson Economic Group: 2008 Business Tax Ranking (1 is Best)	24
Forbes Magazine: 2008 Best States for Business Ranking (1 is Best)	9
Tax Foundation: 2009 Business Tax Climate Ranking (1 is Best)	7
2004–5 Employer Firm Births	53,502
2004–5 Employer Firm Terminations	47,223

Data: Anderson Economic Group; Tax Foundation; Forbes Magazine; U.S. Census, Statistics of U.S. Businesses

Voting Behavior and Elected Officials

Voter Registration and Turnout (%)

	1996	2000	2004	2008
Registered Voters Who Voted	58.8	62.4	67.4	69.3
Population Age 18+ Who Voted	41.3	42.8	46.7	46.8

Data: Dave Leip's Atlas of U.S. Presidential Elections

Presidential Election Results (Nationwide Winner Listed First)

2008	Popular Vote (%)	Electoral Votes
Barack Obama (Democrat)	43.6	0
John McCain (Republican)	55.4	34
Other	1.0	0
2004		
George W. Bush (Republican, Incumbent)	61.1	34
John Kerry (Democrat)	38.2	0
Other	0.7	0
2000		
George W. Bush (Republican)	59.3	32
Albert Gore (Democrat)	38.0	0
Ralph Nader (Green)	2.2	0
Other	0.6	0
1996		
William Clinton (Democrat, Incumbent)	43.8	0
Robert Dole (Republican)	48.8	32
H. Ross Perot (Reformist)	6.8	0
Other	0.7	0

Data: Dave Leip's Atlas of U.S. Presidential Elections

Governor and U.S. Congressional Seats				
Governor	**Party**	**Year Term Began**	**Term**	**Max. Consecutive Terms**
Rick Perry	R	2007	Second	No limit
U.S. Senators	**Party**	**Year Elected**	**Term Expires**	
John Cornyn	R	2002	2015	
Kay Bailey Hutchison	R	1993	2013	
U.S. Representatives		**Republican**	**Democrat**	**Other**
		20	12	0

Data: National Governors Association; U.S. Senate, Office of the Clerk; U.S. House of Representatives

Business and Economic Agencies

Agency	Website Address
Texas Association of Business	www.txbiz.org
Office of the Governor, Economic Development Office and Tourism	www.governor.state.tx.us/ecodevo
Texas Small Business Development Center	www.business.txstate.edu/sbdc
Texas Secretary of State, Corporations Section	www.sos.state.tx.us/corp

Data: Various agency websites

Utah

With a population of 2.6 million people, Utah was the seventeenth least populous state in the United States in 2007. From 2000 to 2007 the state's population increased by 412,161 people, and is projected to increase to 3.2 million by 2025. This 1.1% projected annual growth rate compares to the projected national average of 0.8%. From 2006 to 2007 the state's population grew by 3.7%. The state's 2007 per capita personal income of $30,090 was higher compared to $29,769 in 2006 but the third lowest in the United States, some $8,474 below the national average. Per capita income in Utah grew at a compound annual rate of 3.4% from 2000 to 2007, compared to 3.7% nationally.

Utah's largest industry in terms of 2006 employment was manufacturing. The fastest growing industry was professional, scientific, and technical services, with 6.4% annual growth from 1998 to 2006. The second fastest growing industry was arts, entertainment, and recreation. The state's workforce is generally more educated than other states—90.2% of the

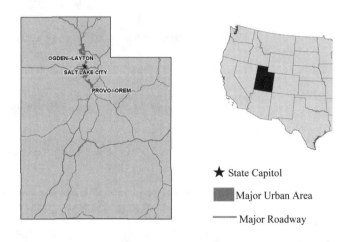

★ State Capitol

▉ Major Urban Area

— Major Roadway

Demographic and Socioeconomic Profile

Demographics and Socioeconomic Figures			
Population and Households	**2000**	**2006**	**2007**
Total Population	2,233,169	2,550,063	2,645,330
Number of Households	701,281	814,028	835,320
Average Household Size	3.1	3.1	3.1
Age and Ethnicity			
Median Age	27.1	28.4	28.4
Population 18 Years of Age and Older	1,516,338	1,757,891	1,826,942
Population 65 Years of Age and Older	190,531	223,960	232,044
Caucasian Population	1,991,560	2,271,604	2,381,687
African-American Population	16,150	22,742	25,465
Hispanic Population	200,005	286,113	306,514
Asian Population	36,878	49,079	52,107
Foreign-Born Population (%)	7.1	8.3	8.2
Income			
Per Capita Personal Income (USD)	$23,878	$29,769	$30,090
Median Household Income (USD)	$45,726	$51,309	$55,109
Individuals below Poverty Level	9.4%	10.6%	9.7%

Data: U.S. Census, American Community Survey; U.S. Department of Commerce, Bureau of Economic Analysis

state's adult population has graduated from high school, compared to an 84.1% national average; 28.7% hold a bachelor degree or higher (national average is 27.0%); and 9.1% hold professional or graduate degrees compared to the national average of 10.1%.

Utah's total tax revenue was $8.3 billion for fiscal year 2005–6, up from the 2004–5 total revenue of $7.3 billion. The largest share of tax revenue in 2005–6 was generated from sales and gross receipts taxes, followed by individual income taxes. On a per capita basis, residents of Utah paid taxes of $3,248, compared to the national average of $3,992 for 2005–6. In terms of business taxes, the state ranked fourteenth in a 2008 analysis by Anderson Economic Group. Forbes Magazine and the Tax Foundation ranked the state's business climate second and eleventh, respectively.

Population Projections

Year	2010	2015	2020	2025
Total Population	2,595,013	2,783,040	2,990,094	3,225,680
Median Age	29.5	30.1	30.3	30.4
Population 18 Years of Age and Older	1,776,028	1,910,568	2,069,975	2,244,888
Population 65 Years of Age and Older	234,798	280,969	341,095	405,543

Data: U.S. Census Bureau

Workforce and Industry Profile

Workforce

	2000	2006	2007
Civilian Labor Force	1,136,036	1,311,073	1,356,550
Labor Force Participation Rate	71.8%	71.8%	71.5%
Unemployment Rate	3.4%	2.9%	2.7%
Average Wage Per Job (USD)	$29,229	$35,540	$37,080
Education Attainment (Population 25 Years and Older)	**(%)**	**(%)**	**(%)**
High School Graduate or Higher	87.7	90.2	90.2
Bachelors Degree or Higher	26.1	28.6	28.7
Graduate or Professional Degree	8.3	12.8	9.1

Data: U.S. Census Bureau, American Community Survey; U.S. Department of Commerce, Bureau of Economic Analysis; U.S. Department of Labor, Bureau of Labor Statistics

Industry Overview

	1998	2005	2006
Total Employees	866,146	974,686	1,039,095
Total Payroll ($1,000)	22,199,933	30,970,696	35,175,397
Total Establishments	52,025	65,549	68,754
Establishments with 1–19 Employees	44,560	57,040	59,718
Establishments with 20–49 Employees	4,716	5,326	5,555
Establishments with 50–249 Employees	2,355	2,778	3,029
Establishments with 250–999 Employees	341	350	390
Establishments with 1,000+ Employees	53	55	62

Data: U.S. Census Bureau, County Business Patterns

Major Industries (Ranked by 2006 Employment; Payroll in $1,000s)

Industry	1998 Employment	2006 Employment	1998 Payroll	2006 Payroll
Retail Trade	117,336	139,157	2,014,702	3,149,078
Manufacturing	124,504	118,492	3,923,759	4,960,143
Health Care and Social Assistance	83,229	113,344	2,278,267	3,820,811
Admin., Support, Waste Mngt., Remediation Services	78,929	100,999	1,437,965	2,757,847
Accommodation and Food Services	76,781	91,313	736,994	1,115,339
Construction	58,005	81,656	1,732,765	3,080,814
Professional, Scientific, Technical Services	43,350	71,274	1,618,657	3,291,185
Finance and Insurance	40,957	52,205	1,385,462	2,415,841
Wholesale Trade	44,727	47,566	1,515,979	2,193,807
Other Services (except Public Admin.)	45,158	46,316	936,360	1,211,315

Data: U.S. Census Bureau, County Business Patterns

Taxes and Business Climate

State and Local Taxes		
Combined Revenues ($1,000)	2004–5	2005–6
Revenue from Property Taxes	1,792,451	1,876,730
Revenue from Sales and Gross Receipts Taxes	3,017,459	3,315,036
Revenue from Individual Income Taxes	1,926,697	2,277,478
Revenue from Corporate Income Taxes	188,845	348,129
Revenue from Other Taxes	378,512	465,780
Total Tax Revenue	7,303,964	8,283,153
Per Capita Taxes		
Property Tax Per Capita	716	736
Sales and Gross Receipts Tax Per Capita	1,205	1,300
Individual Income Tax Per Capita	769	893
Corporate Income Tax Per Capita	75	137
Other Taxes Per Capita	151	183
Total Taxes Per Capita	2,916	3,248

Data: U.S. Census Bureau; Anderson Economic Group, LLC

Business Climate Measures

Anderson Economic Group: 2008 Business Tax Ranking (1 is Best)	14
Forbes Magazine: 2008 Best States for Business Ranking (1 is Best)	2
Tax Foundation: 2009 Business Tax Climate Ranking (1 is Best)	11
2004–5 Employer Firm Births	8,290
2004–5 Employer Firm Terminations	6,331

Data: Anderson Economic Group; Tax Foundation; Forbes Magazine; U.S. Census, Statistics of U.S. Businesses

Voting Behavior and Elected Officials

Voter Registration and Turnout (%)

	1996	2000	2004	2008
Registered Voters Who Voted	63.4	68.6	72.6	66.7
Population Age 18+ Who Voted	49.9	50.8	57.7	52.3

Data: Dave Leip's Atlas of U.S. Presidential Elections

Presidential Election Results (Nationwide Winner Listed First)

2008	Popular Vote (%)	Electoral Votes
Barack Obama (Democrat)	34.3	0
John McCain (Republican)	62.3	5
Other	3.4	0
2004		
George W. Bush (Republican, Incumbent)	71.5	5
John Kerry (Democrat)	26.0	0
Other	2.5	0
2000		
George W. Bush (Republican)	66.8	5
Albert Gore (Democrat)	26.3	0
Ralph Nader (Green)	4.7	0
Other	2.2	0
1996		
William Clinton (Democrat, Incumbent)	33.3	0
Robert Dole (Republican)	54.4	5
H. Ross Perot (Reformist)	10.0	0
Other	2.4	0

Data: Dave Leip's Atlas of U.S. Presidential Elections

Governor and U.S. Congressional Seats				
Governor	Party	Year Term Began	Term	Max. Consecutive Terms
Jon Huntsman	R	2005	First	3
U.S. Senators	**Party**	**Year Elected**	**Term Expires**	
Robert Bennett	R	1992	2011	
Orrin Hatch	R	1976	2013	
U.S. Representatives		**Republican**	**Democrat**	**Other**
		2	1	0

Data: National Governors Association; U.S. Senate, Office of the Clerk; U.S. House of Representatives

Business and Economic Agencies

Agency	Website Address
n/a	n/a
Utah Governor's Office of Economic Development	goed.utah.gov
Utah Small Business Dev. Center	www.utahsbdc.org
Utah Department of Commerce	www.commerce.utah.gov

Data: Various agency websites

Vermont

Vermont is located in the New England region of the United States. Vermont has a population of 621,254 people, making it the second least populous state in 2007. The state's population increased by 12,427 people from 2000 to 2007, and is projected to increase to 703,288 people by 2025. This 0.7% projected annual growth rate is below the national average of 0.8%. From 2006 to 2007 the state's population declined by 0.4%. Per capita personal income in Vermont was $37,446 in 2007, up from $34,623 in 2006. For 2007, this was $1,118 below the national average and the twenty-first highest in the country. The state's per capita income grew at a compound annual rate of 4.4% from 2000 to 2007, compared to 3.7% nationally.

The state's workforce generally has more education than other states—90.3% of the state's adult population has graduated from high school, compared to an 84.1% national average; 33.6% hold a bachelor degree or higher (national average is 27.0%); and 12.9% hold professional or graduate degrees

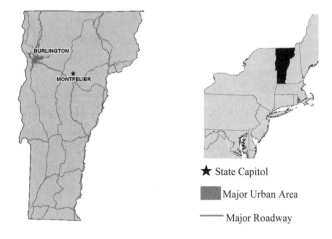

★ State Capitol

▨ Major Urban Area

— Major Roadway

Demographic and Socioeconomic Profile

Demographics and Socioeconomic Figures			
Population and Households	**2000**	**2006**	**2007**
Total Population	608,827	623,908	621,254
Number of Households	240,634	253,808	252,580
Average Household Size	2.4	2.4	2.4
Age and Ethnicity			
Median Age	37.7	40.6	40.6
Population 18 Years of Age and Older	461,248	490,004	489,562
Population 65 Years of Age and Older	77,295	82,945	84,085
Caucasian Population	588,836	600,529	597,245
African-American Population	2,981	5,167	3,873
Hispanic Population	5,316	6,644	8,061
Asian Population	4,851	5,693	6,951
Foreign-Born Population (%)	3.8	3.9	3.4
Income			
Per Capita Personal Income (USD)	$27,680	$34,623	$37,446
Median Household Income (USD)	$40,856	$47,665	$49,907
Individuals below Poverty Level	9.4%	10.3%	10.1%

Data: U.S. Census, American Community Survey; U.S. Department of Commerce, Bureau of Economic Analysis

(national average is 10.1%). In 2006, the state's largest industry in terms of employment was health care and social assistance, followed by manufacturing. The fastest growing industry was management of companies and enterprises, with 8.2% annual growth from 1998 to 2006.

In fiscal year 2005–6, Vermont had total tax revenues of $2.8 billion. The largest share was generated from property taxes, followed by sales and gross receipts taxes. The per capita tax burden in Vermont was $4,413 for 2005–6, some $420 above the national average, and a $258 increase from the 2004–5 per capita tax burden. In terms of business taxes, Vermont ranked forty-ninth in a 2008 report by Anderson Economic Group. The state's business climate was ranked thirty-sixth by Forbes Magazine and forty-third by the Tax Foundation.

Population Projections

Year	2010	2015	2020	2025
Total Population	652,512	673,169	690,686	703,288
Median Age	40.6	41.1	41.5	42.8
Population 18 Years of Age and Older	520,140	541,204	554,847	563,723
Population 65 Years of Age and Older	93,442	113,487	136,449	158,159

Data: U.S. Census Bureau

Workforce and Industry Profile

Workforce

	2000	2006	2007
Civilian Labor Force	335,798	361,044	353,992
Labor Force Participation Rate	70.8%	71.3%	70.6%
Unemployment Rate	2.7%	3.6%	4.0%
Average Wage Per Job (USD)	$28,914	$36,350	$38,060
Education Attainment (Population 25 Years and Older)	**(%)**	**(%)**	**(%)**
High School Graduate or Higher	86.4	89.8	90.3
Bachelors Degree or Higher	29.4	32.4	33.6
Graduate or Professional Degree	11.1	13.2	12.9

Data: U.S. Census Bureau, American Community Survey; U.S. Department of Commerce, Bureau of Economic Analysis; U.S. Department of Labor, Bureau of Labor Statistics

Industry Overview

	1998	2005	2006
Total Employees	239,034	261,656	263,838
Total Payroll ($1,000)	5,907,989	8,284,548	8,566,778
Total Establishments	21,261	22,273	22,317
Establishments with 1–19 Employees	19,113	19,914	19,910
Establishments with 20–49 Employees	1,406	1,570	1,622
Establishments with 50–249 Employees	657	690	696
Establishments with 250–999 Employees	75	87	77
Establishments with 1,000+ Employees	10	12	12

Data: U.S. Census Bureau, County Business Patterns

Major Industries (Ranked by 2006 Employment; Payroll in $1,000s)

Industry	1998 Employment	2006 Employment	1998 Payroll	2006 Payroll
Retail Trade	37,212	41,072	645,573	950,704
Health Care and Social Assistance	32,784	39,844	819,150	1,354,974
Manufacturing	44,836	36,964	1,495,644	1,663,607
Accommodation and Food Services	27,550	29,408	298,343	418,753
Professional, Scientific, Technical Services	9,228	17,025	353,212	660,387
Construction	12,699	16,308	385,573	689,310
Educational Services	12,254	13,802	217,795	341,643
Wholesale Trade	10,792	10,677	348,198	441,280
Finance and Insurance	9,370	9,785	355,166	512,828
Other Services (except Public Admin.)	8,675	9,481	153,936	218,237

Data: U.S. Census Bureau, County Business Patterns

Taxes and Business Climate

State and Local Taxes

Combined Revenues ($1,000)	2004–5	2005–6
Revenue from Property Taxes	1,056,355	1,148,328
Revenue from Sales and Gross Receipts Taxes	787,102	810,900
Revenue from Individual Income Taxes	500,464	542,012
Revenue from Corporate Income Taxes	68,962	86,083
Revenue from Other Taxes	161,878	165,674
Total Tax Revenue	2,574,761	2,752,997

Per Capita Taxes

	2004–5	2005–6
Property Tax Per Capita	1,705	1,841
Sales and Gross Receipts Tax Per Capita	1,270	1,300
Individual Income Tax Per Capita	808	869
Corporate Income Tax Per Capita	111	138
Other Taxes Per Capita	261	266
Total Taxes Per Capita	4,155	4,412

Data: U.S. Census Bureau; Anderson Economic Group, LLC

Business Climate Measures

Anderson Economic Group: 2008 Business Tax Ranking (1 is Best)	49
Forbes Magazine: 2008 Best States for Business Ranking (1 is Best)	36

Business Climate Measures	
Tax Foundation: 2009 Business Tax Climate Ranking (1 is Best)	43
2004–5 Employer Firm Births	1,832
2004–5 Employer Firm Terminations	1,721

Data: Anderson Economic Group; Tax Foundation; Forbes Magazine; U.S. Census, Statistics of U.S. Businesses

Voting Behavior and Elected Officials

Voter Registration and Turnout (%)				
	1996	2000	2004	2008
Registered Voters Who Voted	67.1	68.9	70.3	71.5
Population Age 18+ Who Voted	58.1	63.8	64.8	66.4

Data: Dave Leip's Atlas of U.S. Presidential Elections

Presidential Election Results (Nationwide Winner Listed First)		
2008	Popular Vote (%)	Electoral Votes
Barack Obama (Democrat)	67.5	3
John McCain (Republican)	30.5	0
Other	2.1	0
2004		
George W. Bush (Republican, Incumbent)	38.8	0
John Kerry (Democrat)	58.9	3
Other	2.3	0
2000		
George W. Bush (Republican)	40.7	0
Albert Gore (Democrat)	50.6	3
Ralph Nader (Green)	6.9	0
Other	1.8	0
1996		
William Clinton (Democrat, Incumbent)	53.4	3
Robert Dole (Republican)	31.1	0
H. Ross Perot (Reformist)	12.0	0
Other	3.6	0

Data: Dave Leip's Atlas of U.S. Presidential Elections

Governor and U.S. Congressional Seats				
Governor	Party	Year Term Began	Term	Max. Consecutive Terms
Jim Douglas	R	2007	Second	No limit
U.S. Senators	Party	Year Elected	Term Expires	
Bernie Sanders	I	2006	2013	
Patrick Leahy	D	1974	2011	
U.S. Representatives		Republican	Democrat	Other
		0	1	0

Data: National Governors Association; U.S. Senate, Office of the Clerk; U.S. House of Representatives

Business and Economic Agencies

Agency	Website Address
Vermont Chamber of Commerce	www.vtchamber.com
Vermont Department of Economic Development	www.thinkvermont.com
Vermont Small Business Dev. Center	www.vtsbdc.org
Vermont Secretary of State, Corporations	www.sec.state.vt.us/corps

Data: Various agency websites

Virginia

Virginia, located in the South Atlantic region of the United States, has a population of 7.7 million people, making it the twelfth most populous state in 2007. The state's population increased by 633,576 people from 2000 to 2007, and is projected to increase to 9.4 million by 2025. This 1.1% projected annual growth rate compares to the projected national average of 0.8%. From 2006 to 2007 the state's population grew by 0.9%. Per capita personal income in Virginia was $41,561 in 2007, up from $39,564 in 2006. For 2007, this was eighth highest in the country and $2,997 above the national average. From 2000 to 2007 the per capita income in Virginia grew at a compound annual rate of 4.2%, compared to 3.7% nationally.

In 2006, the state's largest industry in terms of employment was professional, scientific, and technical services, followed by health care and social assistance. The fastest growing industry was professional, scientific, and technical services, with 5.0% annual growth from 1998 to 2006. The state's workforce is generally more educated than other states—85.9% of

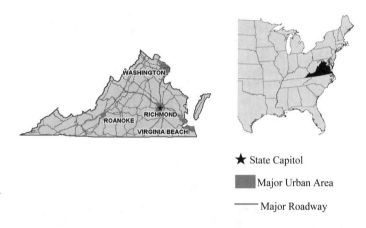

★ State Capitol

Major Urban Area

Major Roadway

Demographic and Socioeconomic Profile

Demographics and Socioeconomic Figures			
Population and Households	**2000**	**2006**	**2007**
Total Population	7,078,515	7,642,884	7,712,091
Number of Households	2,699,173	2,905,071	2,932,234
Average Household Size	2.5	2.6	2.6
Age and Ethnicity			
Median Age	35.7	36.9	37.0
Population 18 Years of Age and Older	5,342,691	5,837,331	5,888,856
Population 65 Years of Age and Older	790,567	886,014	905,831
Caucasian Population	5,116,929	5,413,295	5,429,003
African-American Population	1,384,008	1,496,076	1,509,278
Hispanic Population	327,273	470,871	500,707
Asian Population	256,355	365,515	373,305
Foreign-Born Population (%)	8.1	10.1	10.3
Income			
Per Capita Personal Income (USD)	$31,087	$39,564	$41,561
Median Household Income (USD)	$46,677	$56,277	$59,562
Individuals below Poverty Level	9.6%	9.6%	9.9%

Data: U.S. Census, American Community Survey; U.S. Department of Commerce, Bureau of Economic Analysis

the state's adult population has graduated from high school, compared to an 84.1% national average. Nationally, an average of 27.0% hold a bachelor degree or higher compared to 33.6% in Virginia; and 13.7% hold professional or graduate degrees (national average is 10.1%).

In fiscal year 2005–6, Virginia had total tax revenues of $30.1 billion. The largest share was generated from property taxes, followed by individual income taxes. The per capita tax burden in Virginia was $3,933 for 2005–6, some $59 below the national average. In terms of business taxes, the state ranked twenty-seventh in a 2008 analysis by Anderson Economic Group. Forbes Magazine and the Tax Foundation ranked the state's business climate first and fifteenth, respectively.

Population Projections

Year	2010	2015	2020	2025
Total Population	8,010,245	8,466,864	8,917,395	9,364,304
Median Age	37.2	37.2	37.3	37.5
Population 18 Years of Age and Older	6,130,061	6,484,801	6,817,484	7,155,835
Population 65 Years of Age and Older	994,359	1,193,453	1,404,580	1,634,012

Data: U.S. Census Bureau

Workforce and Industry Profile

Workforce

	2000	2006	2007
Civilian Labor Force	3,584,037	3,998,569	4,067,520
Labor Force Participation Rate	67.6%	69.3%	69.4%
Unemployment Rate	2.3%	3.0%	3.0%
Average Wage Per Job (USD)	$35,172	$41,450	$42,880
Education Attainment (Population 25 Years and Older)	(%)	(%)	(%)
High School Graduate or Higher	81.5	85.4	85.9
Bachelors Degree or Higher	29.5	32.8	33.6
Graduate or Professional Degree	11.6	10.7	13.7

Data: U.S. Census Bureau, American Community Survey; U.S. Department of Commerce, Bureau of Economic Analysis; U.S. Department of Labor, Bureau of Labor Statistics

Industry Overview

	1998	2005	2006
Total Employees	2,700,589	3,060,127	3,174,363
Total Payroll ($1,000)	81,261,075	121,801,479	128,998,539
Total Establishments	172,182	193,067	197,263
Establishments with 1–19 Employees	147,954	164,708	167,460
Establishments with 20–49 Employees	15,065	17,796	18,631
Establishments with 50–249 Employees	7,933	9,150	9,733
Establishments with 250–999 Employees	1,080	1,239	1,264
Establishments with 1,000+ Employees	150	174	175

Data: U.S. Census Bureau, County Business Patterns

Major Industries (Ranked by 2006 Employment; Payroll in $1,000s)

Industry	1998 Employment	2006 Employment	1998 Payroll	2006 Payroll
Retail Trade	381,550	441,222	6,814,272	10,073,738
Professional, Scientific, Technical Services	252,923	373,145	12,668,638	26,053,639
Health Care and Social Assistance	293,642	362,262	8,276,316	14,057,038
Accommodation and Food Services	234,205	298,742	2,583,716	4,238,643
Manufacturing	368,397	289,176	12,148,259	12,377,621
Construction	178,057	241,953	5,235,341	9,678,298
Admin., Support, Waste Mngt., Remediation Services	193,746	239,077	3,863,555	7,434,191
Finance and Insurance	131,159	170,248	5,444,898	10,673,403
Other Services (except Public Admin.)	141,679	165,329	3,105,675	4,821,649
Wholesale Trade	106,663	121,244	4,036,250	6,060,906

Data: U.S. Census Bureau, County Business Patterns

Taxes and Business Climate

State and Local Taxes

Combined Revenues ($1,000)	2004–5	2005–6
Revenue from Property Taxes	8,390,045	9,233,053
Revenue from Sales and Gross Receipts Taxes	7,640,559	8,090,645
Revenue from Individual Income Taxes	8,352,366	9,073,077
Revenue from Corporate Income Taxes	605,959	863,320
Revenue from Other Taxes	2,670,257	2,798,725
Total Tax Revenue	27,659,186	30,058,820
Per Capita Taxes		
Property Tax Per Capita	1,110	1,208
Sales and Gross Receipts Tax Per Capita	1,011	1,059
Individual Income Tax Per Capita	1,105	1,187
Corporate Income Tax Per Capita	80	113
Other Taxes Per Capita	353	366
Total Taxes Per Capita	3,660	3,933

Data: U.S. Census Bureau; Anderson Economic Group, LLC

Business Climate Measures

Anderson Economic Group: 2008 Business Tax Ranking (1 is Best)	27
Forbes Magazine: 2008 Best States for Business Ranking (1 is Best)	1
Tax Foundation: 2009 Business Tax Climate Ranking (1 is Best)	15
2004–5 Employer Firm Births	19,817
2004–5 Employer Firm Terminations	16,545

Data: Anderson Economic Group; Tax Foundation; Forbes Magazine; U.S. Census, Statistics of U.S. Businesses

Voting Behavior and Elected Officials

Voter Registration and Turnout (%)

	1996	2000	2004	2008
Registered Voters Who Voted	72.7	72.6	76.5	75.8
Population Age 18+ Who Voted	47.5	51.3	57.2	63.2

Data: Dave Leip's Atlas of U.S. Presidential Elections

Presidential Election Results (Nationwide Winner Listed First)

2008	Popular Vote (%)	Electoral Votes
Barack Obama (Democrat)	52.6	13
John McCain (Republican)	46.3	0
Other	1.0	0
2004		
George W. Bush (Republican, Incumbent)	53.7	13
John Kerry (Democrat)	45.5	0
Other	0.8	0
2000		
George W. Bush (Republican)	52.5	13
Albert Gore (Democrat)	44.4	0
Ralph Nader (Green)	2.2	0
Other	0.9	0
1996		
William Clinton (Democrat, Incumbent)	45.2	0
Robert Dole (Republican)	47.1	13
H. Ross Perot (Reformist)	6.6	0
Other	1.1	0

Data: Dave Leip's Atlas of U.S. Presidential Elections

Governor and U.S. Congressional Seats				
Governor	**Party**	**Year Term Began**	**Term**	**Max. Consecutive Terms**
Timothy Kaine	D	2006	First	1
U.S. Senators	**Party**	**Year Elected**	**Term Expires**	
Mark R. Warner	D	2008	2015	
Jim Webb	D	2006	2013	
U.S. Representatives		**Republican**	**Democrat**	**Other**
		5	6	0

Data: National Governors Association; U.S. Senate, Office of the Clerk; U.S. House of Representatives

Business and Economic Agencies

Agency	Website Address
Virginia Chamber of Commerce	www.vachamber.com
Virginia Economic Development Partnership	www.yesvirginia.org
Virginia Small Business Dev. Center	www.virginiasbdc.com
Virginia State Corporation Commission	www.scc.virginia.gov/division/clk

Data: Various agency websites

Washington

With a population of 6.5 million people, Washington was the thirteenth least populous state in the United States in 2007. From 2000 to 2007 the state's population increased by 574,303 people, and is projected to increase to 8.0 million by 2025. This 1.2% projected annual growth rate compares to the projected national average of 0.8%. From 2006 to 2007 the state's population grew by 1.1%. The state's 2007 per capita personal income of $41,062 was higher compared to $38,067 in 2006 and the tenth highest in the United States, some $2,498 above the national average. Per capita income in Washington grew at a compound annual rate of 3.7% from 2000 to 2007, matching 3.7% nationally.

Washington's largest industry in terms of 2006 employment was retail trade. The fastest growing industry was information, with 6.3% annual growth from 1998 to 2006. The second fastest growing industry was arts, entertainment, and recreation. The state's workforce is generally more educated than other states—89.3% of the

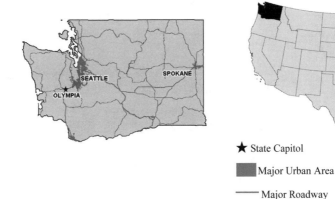

★ State Capitol

▪ Major Urban Area

— Major Roadway

Demographic and Socioeconomic Profile

Demographics and Socioeconomic Figures			
Population and Households	**2000**	**2006**	**2007**
Total Population	5,894,121	6,395,798	6,468,424
Number of Households	2,271,398	2,471,912	2,501,509
Average Household Size	2.5	2.5	2.5
Age and Ethnicity			
Median Age	35.3	36.7	37.1
Population 18 Years of Age and Older	4,384,341	4,867,922	4,931,615
Population 65 Years of Age and Older	662,162	736,716	756,683
Caucasian Population	4,815,072	5,148,130	5,219,137
African-American Population	185,052	217,868	217,876
Hispanic Population	439,841	580,027	610,006
Asian Population	320,979	423,976	429,406
Foreign-Born Population (%)	10.4	12.4	12.3
Income			
Per Capita Personal Income (USD)	$31,779	$38,067	$41,062
Median Household Income (USD)	$45,776	$52,583	$55,591
Individuals below Poverty Level	10.6%	11.8%	11.4%

Data: U.S. Census, American Community Survey; U.S. Department of Commerce, Bureau of Economic Analysis

state's adult population has graduated from high school, compared to an 84.1% national average; 30.3% hold a bachelor degree or higher (national average is 27.0%); and 10.8% hold professional or graduate degrees compared to the national average of 10.1%.

Washington's total tax revenue was $25.2 billion for fiscal year 2005–6, up from the 2004–5 total revenue of $23.0 billion. The largest share of tax revenue in 2005–6 was generated from sales and gross receipts taxes, followed by property taxes. On a per capita basis, residents of Washington paid taxes of $3,935, compared to the national average of $3,992 for 2005–6. In terms of business taxes, the state ranked eighteenth in a 2008 analysis by Anderson Economic Group. Forbes Magazine and the Tax Foundation ranked the state's business climate third and twelfth, respectively.

Population Projections

Year	2010	2015	2020	2025
Total Population	6,541,963	6,950,610	7,432,136	7,996,400
Median Age	37.3	37.3	37.7	38.1
Population 18 Years of Age and Older	5,053,540	5,389,525	5,748,788	6,164,834
Population 65 Years of Age and Older	795,528	965,506	1,168,199	1,380,872

Data: U.S. Census Bureau

Workforce and Industry Profile

Workforce

	2000	2006	2007
Civilian Labor Force	3,050,021	3,326,524	3,391,248
Labor Force Participation Rate	68.3%	67.6%	67.8%
Unemployment Rate	5.0%	5.0%	4.5%
Average Wage Per Job (USD)	$37,090	$42,910	$44,710
Education Attainment (Population 25 Years and Older)	(%)	(%)	(%)
High School Graduate or Higher	87.1	89.0	89.3
Bachelors Degree or Higher	27.7	30.5	30.3
Graduate or Professional Degree	9.3	6.6	10.8

Data: U.S. Census Bureau, American Community Survey; U.S. Department of Commerce, Bureau of Economic Analysis; U.S. Department of Labor, Bureau of Labor Statistics

Industry Overview

	1998	2005	2006
Total Employees	2,134,598	2,316,296	2,421,269
Total Payroll ($1,000)	73,268,188	94,928,122	104,191,371
Total Establishments	161,473	175,658	179,908
Establishments with 1–19 Employees	142,096	154,332	157,568
Establishments with 20–49 Employees	12,485	13,633	14,187
Establishments with 50–249 Employees	6,136	6,847	7,255
Establishments with 250–999 Employees	667	745	794
Establishments with 1,000+ Employees	89	101	104

Data: U.S. Census Bureau, County Business Patterns

Major Industries (Ranked by 2006 Employment; Payroll in $1,000s)				
Industry	1998 Employment	2006 Employment	1998 Payroll	2006 Payroll
Health Care and Social Assistance	269,465	329,463	7,767,349	13,446,556
Retail Trade	288,387	328,899	6,107,356	8,570,108
Manufacturing	335,467	257,611	13,655,822	13,202,734
Accommodation and Food Services	195,249	225,923	2,165,493	3,498,605
Construction	143,168	184,453	5,224,593	8,653,717
Professional, Scientific, Technical Services	117,463	157,086	5,122,866	9,800,402
Admin., Support, Waste Mngt., Remediation Services	116,150	141,043	2,992,866	4,800,519
Wholesale Trade	120,196	130,164	4,704,938	6,698,084
Finance and Insurance	96,128	123,316	4,272,989	7,733,124
Information	67,312	109,936	4,514,573	9,952,881

Data: U.S. Census Bureau, County Business Patterns

Taxes and Business Climate

State and Local Taxes		
Combined Revenues ($1,000)	2004–5	2005–6
Revenue from Property Taxes	6,637,299	6,910,760
Revenue from Sales and Gross Receipts Taxes	13,825,212	15,413,133
Revenue from Individual Income Taxes	0	0
Revenue from Corporate Income Taxes	4	5
Revenue from Other Taxes	2,511,527	2,844,909
Total Tax Revenue	22,974,042	25,168,807
Per Capita Taxes		
Property Tax Per Capita	1,058	1,081
Sales and Gross Receipts Tax Per Capita	2,205	2,410
Individual Income Tax Per Capita	0	0
Corporate Income Tax Per Capita	0	0
Other Taxes Per Capita	401	445
Total Taxes Per Capita	3,664	3,935

Data: U.S. Census Bureau; Anderson Economic Group, LLC

Business Climate Measures

Anderson Economic Group: 2008 Business Tax Ranking (1 is Best)	18
Forbes Magazine: 2008 Best States for Business Ranking (1 is Best)	3
Tax Foundation: 2009 Business Tax Climate Ranking (1 is Best)	12
2004–5 Employer Firm Births	19,695
2004–5 Employer Firm Terminations	16,113

Data: Anderson Economic Group; Tax Foundation; Forbes Magazine; U.S. Census, Statistics of U.S. Businesses

Voting Behavior and Elected Officials

Voter Registration and Turnout (%)

	1996	2000	2004	2008
Registered Voters Who Voted	73.2	74.6	81.5	84.0
Population Age 18+ Who Voted	54.8	56.8	61.7	61.8

Data: Dave Leip's Atlas of U.S. Presidential Elections

Presidential Election Results (Nationwide Winner Listed First)

2008	Popular Vote (%)	Electoral Votes
Barack Obama (Democrat)	57.4	11
John McCain (Republican)	40.3	0
Other	2.3	0
2004		
George W. Bush (Republican, Incumbent)	45.6	0
John Kerry (Democrat)	52.8	11
Other	1.6	0
2000		
George W. Bush (Republican)	44.6	0
Albert Gore (Democrat)	50.2	11
Ralph Nader (Green)	4.1	0
Other	1.1	0
1996		
William Clinton (Democrat, Incumbent)	49.8	11
Robert Dole (Republican)	37.3	0
H. Ross Perot (Reformist)	8.9	0
Other	3.9	0

Data: Dave Leip's Atlas of U.S. Presidential Elections

Governor and U.S. Congressional Seats				
Governor	**Party**	**Year Term Began**	**Term**	**Max. Consecutive Terms**
Christine Gregoire	D	2009	Second	No limit
U.S. Senators	**Party**	**Year Elected**	**Term Expires**	
Maria Cantwell	D	2000	2013	
Patty Murray	D	1992	2011	
U.S. Representatives		**Republican**	**Democrat**	**Other**
		3	6	0

Data: National Governors Association; U.S. Senate, Office of the Clerk; U.S. House of Representatives

Business and Economic Agencies

Agency	Website Address
Association of Washington Business	www.awb.org
Department of Community, Trade, and Economic Development	www.cted.wa.gov
Washington Small Business Dev. Center	www.wsbdc.org
Washington Secretary of State	www.secstate.wa.gov

Data: Various agency websites

West Virginia

West Virginia is located in the South Atlantic region of the United States. West Virginia has a population of 1.8 million people, making it the fourteenth least populous state in 2007. The state's population increased by 3,691 people from 2000 to 2007, but is projected to decrease slightly by 2025. This –0.1% projected annual growth rate is below the national average of 0.8%. From 2006 to 2007 the state's population declined by 0.4%. Per capita personal income in West Virginia was $29,293 in 2007, up from $28,073 in 2006. For 2007, this was $9,271 below the national average and the second lowest in the country. The state's per capita income grew at a compound annual rate of 4.2% from 2000 to 2007, compared to 3.7% nationally.

The state's workforce generally has less education than other states—81.2% of the state's adult population has graduated from high school, compared to an 84.1% national average; 17.3% hold a bachelor degree or higher (national average is 27.0%); and 6.6% hold professional or graduate degrees (national average is 10.1%).

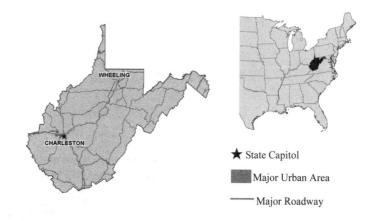

★ State Capitol

Major Urban Area

Major Roadway

Demographic and Socioeconomic Profile

Demographics and Socioeconomic Figures			
Population and Households	2000	2006	2007
Total Population	1,808,344	1,818,470	1,812,035
Number of Households	736,481	743,064	733,849
Average Household Size	2.4	2.4	2.4
Age and Ethnicity			
Median Age	38.9	40.7	40.4
Population 18 Years of Age and Older	1,406,569	1,428,249	1,424,576
Population 65 Years of Age and Older	276,826	279,117	280,657
Caucasian Population	1,717,482	1,721,098	1,710,622
African-American Population	55,999	58,693	62,397
Hispanic Population	11,774	14,383	19,200
Asian Population	9,445	10,479	10,126
Foreign-Born Population (%)	1.1	1.2	1.3
Income			
Per Capita Personal Income (USD)	$21,899	$28,067	$29,293
Median Household Income (USD)	$29,696	$35,059	$37,060
Individuals below Poverty Level	17.9%	17.3%	16.9%

Data: U.S. Census, American Community Survey; U.S. Department of Commerce, Bureau of Economic Analysis

In 2006, the state's largest industry in terms of employment was health care and social assistance, followed by retail trade. The fastest growing industry was arts, entertainment, and recreation, with 6.9% annual growth from 1998 to 2006.

In fiscal year 2005–6, West Virginia had total tax revenues of $5.9 billion. The largest share was generated from sales and gross receipts taxes, followed by individual income taxes. The per capita tax burden in West Virginia was $3,235 for 2005–6, some $757 below the national average, and a $161 increase from the 2004–5 per capita tax burden. In terms of business taxes, West Virginia ranked forty-third in a 2008 report by Anderson Economic Group. The state's business climate was ranked fiftieth by Forbes Magazine and thirty-sixth by the Tax Foundation.

Population Projections

Year	2010	2015	2020	2025
Total Population	1,829,141	1,822,758	1,801,112	1,766,435
Median Age	41.4	42.7	43.9	45.4
Population 18 Years of Age and Older	1,446,830	1,450,163	1,443,442	1,428,017
Population 65 Years of Age and Older	292,402	329,775	372,024	408,533

Data: U.S. Census Bureau

Workforce and Industry Profile

Workforce

	2000	2006	2007
Civilian Labor Force	808,861	806,996	813,195
Labor Force Participation Rate	56.5%	56.2%	56.3%
Unemployment Rate	5.5%	4.9%	4.3%
Average Wage Per Job (USD)	$26,887	$31,440	$32,310
Education Attainment (Population 25 Years and Older)	(%)	(%)	(%)
High School Graduate or Higher	75.2	81.0	81.2
Bachelors Degree or Higher	14.8	16.5	17.3
Graduate or Professional Degree	5.9	8.4	6.6

Data: U.S. Census Bureau, American Community Survey; U.S. Department of Commerce, Bureau of Economic Analysis; U.S. Department of Labor, Bureau of Labor Statistics

Industry Overview

	1998	2005	2006
Total Employees	547,234	565,499	583,196
Total Payroll ($1,000)	13,278,895	16,323,457	17,262,957
Total Establishments	41,703	40,735	40,566
Establishments with 1–19 Employees	36,537	35,419	35,083
Establishments with 20–49 Employees	3,330	3,425	3,496
Establishments with 50–249 Employees	1,628	1,667	1,760
Establishments with 250–999 Employees	184	199	197
Establishments with 1,000+ Employees	24	25	30

Data: U.S. Census Bureau, County Business Patterns

Major Industries (Ranked by 2006 Employment; Payroll in $1,000s)				
Industry	1998 Employment	2006 Employment	1998 Payroll	2006 Payroll
Health Care and Social Assistance	99,695	113,497	2,520,213	3,604,938
Retail Trade	89,474	95,522	1,348,903	1,777,447
Manufacturing	74,424	63,832	2,595,303	2,667,964
Accommodation and Food Services	52,369	60,338	514,087	689,124
Admin., Support, Waste Mngt., Remediation Services	23,736	33,157	441,041	678,441
Construction	29,587	32,918	785,188	1,263,262
Other Services (except Public Admin.)	26,797	26,821	398,111	503,983
Mining	21,325	24,572	997,383	1,456,719
Professional, Scientific, Technical Services	18,472	24,536	487,462	890,824
Finance and Insurance	21,212	21,921	573,186	734,114

Data: U.S. Census Bureau, County Business Patterns

Taxes and Business Climate

State and Local Taxes		
Combined Revenues ($1,000)	2004–5	2005–6
Revenue from Property Taxes	1,008,409	1,059,060
Revenue from Sales and Gross Receipts Taxes	2,211,808	2,245,736
Revenue from Individual Income Taxes	1,171,987	1,297,720
Revenue from Corporate Income Taxes	463,249	533,027
Revenue from Other Taxes	695,293	746,899
Total Tax Revenue	5,550,746	5,882,442
Per Capita Taxes		
Property Tax Per Capita	558	582
Sales and Gross Receipts Tax Per Capita	1,225	1,235
Individual Income Tax Per Capita	649	714
Corporate Income Tax Per Capita	257	293
Other Taxes Per Capita	385	411
Total Taxes Per Capita	3,074	3,235

Data: U.S. Census Bureau; Anderson Economic Group, LLC

Business Climate Measures

Anderson Economic Group: 2008 Business Tax Ranking (1 is Best)	43
Forbes Magazine: 2008 Best States for Business Ranking (1 is Best)	50
Tax Foundation: 2009 Business Tax Climate Ranking (1 is Best)	36
2004–5 Employer Firm Births	3,594
2004–5 Employer Firm Terminations	3,536

Data: Anderson Economic Group; Tax Foundation; Forbes Magazine; U.S. Census, Statistics of U.S. Businesses

Voting Behavior and Elected Officials

Voter Registration and Turnout (%)

	1996	2000	2004	2008
Registered Voters Who Voted	65.6	60.8	64.7	58.9
Population Age 18+ Who Voted	44.9	46.1	53.3	50.1

Data: Dave Leip's Atlas of U.S. Presidential Elections

Presidential Election Results (Nationwide Winner Listed First)

2008	Popular Vote (%)	Electoral Votes
Barack Obama (Democrat)	42.6	0
John McCain (Republican)	55.7	5
Other	1.8	0
2004		
George W. Bush (Republican, Incumbent)	56.1	5
John Kerry (Democrat)	43.2	0
Other	0.7	0
2000		
George W. Bush (Republican)	51.9	5
Albert Gore (Democrat)	45.6	0
Ralph Nader (Green)	1.7	0
Other	0.8	0
1996		
William Clinton (Democrat, Incumbent)	51.5	5
Robert Dole (Republican)	36.8	0
H. Ross Perot (Reformist)	11.3	0
Other	0.5	0

Data: Dave Leip's Atlas of U.S. Presidential Elections

Governor and U.S. Congressional Seats				
Governor	Party	Year Term Began	Term	Max. Consecutive Terms
Joe Manchin	D	2005	First	2
U.S. Senators	Party	Year Elected	Term Expires	
Jay Rockefeller	D	1984	2015	
Robert C. Byrd	D	1958	2013	
U.S. Representatives		Republican	Democrat	Other
		1	2	0

Data: National Governors Association; U.S. Senate, Office of the Clerk; U.S. House of Representatives

Business and Economic Agencies

Agency	Website Address
West Virginia Chamber of Commerce	www.wvchamber.com
West Virginia Development Office	www.wvdo.org
West Virginia Small Business Dev. Center	www.sbdcwv.org
West Virginia Secretary of State	www.wv.gov/sec.aspx?pgID=1

Data: Various agency websites

Wisconsin

Wisconsin, located in the East North Central region of the United States, has a population of 5.6 million people, making it the twentieth most populous state in 2007. The state's population increased by 237,965 people from 2000 to 2007, and is projected to increase to 6.1 million by 2025. This 0.5% projected annual growth rate compares to the projected national average of 0.8%. From 2006 to 2007 the state's population grew by 0.8%. Per capita personal income in Wisconsin was $36,241 in 2007, up from $34,476 in 2006. For 2007, this was twenty-seventh lowest in the country and $2,323 below the national average. From 2000 to 2007 the per capita income in Wisconsin grew at a compound annual rate of 3.5%, compared to 3.7% nationally.

In 2006, the state's largest industry in terms of employment was health care and social assistance, followed by retail trade. The fastest growing industry was mining, with 7.3% annual growth from 1998 to 2006. The state's workforce is generally less educated than other states—nationally, an average of 27.0% hold

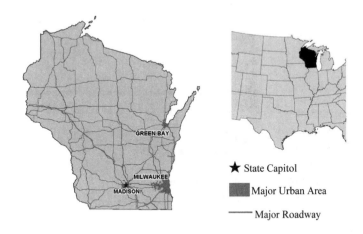

★ State Capitol

▨ Major Urban Area

—— Major Roadway

Demographic and Socioeconomic Profile

Demographics and Socioeconomic Figures			
Population and Households	**2000**	**2006**	**2007**
Total Population	5,363,675	5,556,506	5,601,640
Number of Households	2,084,544	2,230,060	2,241,597
Average Household Size	2.5	2.4	2.4
Age and Ethnicity			
Median Age	36.0	37.6	38.0
Population 18 Years of Age and Older	3,996,289	4,241,563	4,281,620
Population 65 Years of Age and Older	702,668	721,873	736,913
Caucasian Population	4,773,553	4,859,689	4,891,076
African-American Population	300,355	328,376	335,859
Hispanic Population	191,049	256,304	270,179
Asian Population	83,077	110,778	108,711
Foreign-Born Population (%)	3.6	4.4	4.5
Income			
Per Capita Personal Income (USD)	$28,570	$34,476	$36,241
Median Household Income (USD)	$43,791	$48,772	$50,578
Individuals below Poverty Level	8.7%	11.0%	10.8%

Data: U.S. Census, American Community Survey; U.S. Department of Commerce, Bureau of Economic Analysis

a bachelor degree or higher compared to 25.4% in Wisconsin; and 8.5% hold professional or graduate degrees (national average is 10.1%); however, 89.0% of the state's adult population has graduated from high school, compared to an 84.1% national average.

In fiscal year 2005–6, Wisconsin had total tax revenues of $22.3 billion. The largest share was generated from property taxes, followed by sales and gross receipts taxes. The per capita tax burden in Wisconsin was $4,013 for 2005–6, some $21 above the national average. In terms of business taxes, the state ranked sixteenth in a 2008 analysis by Anderson Economic Group. Forbes Magazine and the Tax Foundation ranked the state's business climate forty-third and thirty-eighth, respectively.

Population Projections

Year	2010	2015	2020	2025
Total Population	5,727,426	5,882,760	6,004,954	6,088,374
Median Age	38.1	38.5	39.6	40.7
Population 18 Years of Age and Older	4,408,282	4,539,380	4,636,998	4,711,673
Population 65 Years of Age and Older	771,993	881,745	1,025,542	1,183,596

Data: U.S. Census Bureau

Workforce and Industry Profile

Workforce

	2000	2006	2007
Civilian Labor Force	2,996,091	3,062,932	3,093,763
Labor Force Participation Rate	73.3%	71.0%	71.0%
Unemployment Rate	3.4%	4.7%	4.7%
Average Wage Per Job (USD)	$30,694	$36,730	$38,070
Education Attainment (Population 25 Years and Older)	(%)	(%)	(%)
High School Graduate or Higher	85.1	88.4	89.0
Bachelors Degree or Higher	22.4	25.1	25.4
Graduate or Professional Degree	7.2	7.4	8.5

Data: U.S. Census Bureau, American Community Survey; U.S. Department of Commerce, Bureau of Economic Analysis; U.S. Department of Labor, Bureau of Labor Statistics

Industry Overview

	1998	2005	2006
Total Employees	2,319,343	2,449,114	2,482,281
Total Payroll ($1,000)	64,912,499	85,781,279	89,006,820
Total Establishments	138,635	145,159	145,836
Establishments with 1–19 Employees	117,738	122,919	123,160
Establishments with 20–49 Employees	12,751	13,535	13,758
Establishments with 50–249 Employees	7,060	7,530	7,739
Establishments with 250–999 Employees	943	1,037	1,041
Establishments with 1,000+ Employees	143	138	138

Data: U.S. Census Bureau, County Business Patterns

Major Industries (Ranked by 2006 Employment; Payroll in $1,000s)				
Industry	1998 Employment	2006 Employment	1998 Payroll	2006 Payroll
Manufacturing	566,219	492,822	19,872,068	21,546,455
Health Care and Social Assistance	291,781	358,027	7,935,213	13,216,597
Retail Trade	309,194	321,788	5,228,682	6,787,097
Accommodation and Food Services	191,531	225,445	1,722,956	2,510,228
Finance and Insurance	126,572	139,953	4,930,640	7,573,736
Admin., Support, Waste Mngt., Remediation Services	116,764	136,788	2,130,335	3,242,136
Construction	107,027	120,114	4,308,527	5,802,911
Other Services (except Public Admin.)	104,798	114,970	1,696,610	2,337,435
Wholesale Trade	114,445	114,530	4,131,194	5,487,356
Transportation and Warehousing	74,045	103,047	2,091,651	3,577,654

Data: U.S. Census Bureau, County Business Patterns

Taxes and Business Climate

State and Local Taxes		
Combined Revenues ($1,000)	2004–5	2005–6
Revenue from Property Taxes	7,796,015	8,023,556
Revenue from Sales and Gross Receipts Taxes	6,107,888	6,282,658
Revenue from Individual Income Taxes	5,465,082	5,906,515
Revenue from Corporate Income Taxes	782,742	808,200
Revenue from Other Taxes	1,251,799	1,278,617
Total Tax Revenue	21,403,526	22,299,546
Per Capita Taxes		
Property Tax Per Capita	1,407	1,444
Sales and Gross Receipts Tax Per Capita	1,102	1,131
Individual Income Tax Per Capita	986	1,063
Corporate Income Tax Per Capita	141	145
Other Taxes Per Capita	226	230
Total Taxes Per Capita	3,863	4,013

Data: U.S. Census Bureau; Anderson Economic Group, LLC

Business Climate Measures	
Anderson Economic Group: 2008 Business Tax Ranking (1 is Best)	16
Forbes Magazine: 2008 Best States for Business Ranking (1 is Best)	43
Tax Foundation: 2009 Business Tax Climate Ranking (1 is Best)	38
2004–5 Employer Firm Births	12,126
2004–5 Employer Firm Terminations	10,926

Data: Anderson Economic Group; Tax Foundation; Forbes Magazine; U.S. Census, Statistics of U.S. Businesses

Voting Behavior and Elected Officials

Voter Registration and Turnout (%)				
	1996	2000	2004	2008
Registered Voters Who Voted	.0	.0	.0	NaN
Population Age 18+ Who Voted	57.4	65.0	72.4	69.7

Data: Dave Leip's Atlas of U.S. Presidential Elections

Presidential Election Results (Nationwide Winner Listed First)		
2008	Popular Vote (%)	Electoral Votes
Barack Obama (Democrat)	56.2	10
John McCain (Republican)	42.3	0
Other	1.5	0
2004		
George W. Bush (Republican, Incumbent)	49.3	0
John Kerry (Democrat)	49.7	10
Other	1.0	0
2000		
George W. Bush (Republican)	47.6	0
Albert Gore (Democrat)	47.8	11
Ralph Nader (Green)	3.6	0
Other	0.9	0
1996		
William Clinton (Democrat, Incumbent)	48.8	11
Robert Dole (Republican)	38.5	0
H. Ross Perot (Reformist)	10.4	0
Other	2.4	0

Data: Dave Leip's Atlas of U.S. Presidential Elections

Governor and U.S. Congressional Seats				
Governor	**Party**	**Year Term Began**	**Term**	**Max. Consecutive Terms**
Jim Doyle	D	2007	Second	No limit
U.S. Senators	**Party**	**Year Elected**	**Term Expires**	
Russell Feingold	D	1992	2011	
Herb Kohl	D	1988	2013	
U.S. Representatives		**Republican**	**Democrat**	**Other**
		3	5	0

Data: National Governors Association; U.S. Senate, Office of the Clerk; U.S. House of Representatives

Business and Economic Agencies

Agency	Website Address
Wisconsin Chamber of Commerce Foundation	www.wischamberfoundation.org
Wisconsin Housing and Economic Development Authority	www.wheda.com
Wisconsin Small Business Dev. Center	www.wisconsinsbdc.org
State of Wisconsin, Department of Financial Institutions	www.wdfi.org/corporations

Data: Various agency websites

Wyoming

With a population of 522,830 people, Wyoming was the least populous state in the United States in 2007. From 2000 to 2007 the state's population increased by 29,048 people, and is projected to increase to 529,031 people by 2025. This 0.1% projected annual growth rate compares to the projected national average of 0.8%. From 2006 to 2007 the state's population grew by 1.5%. The state's 2007 per capita personal income of $47,038 was higher compared to $40,569 in 2006 and the fourth highest in the United States, some $8,474 above the national average. Per capita income in Wyoming grew at a compound annual rate of 7.4% from 2000 to 2007, compared to 3.7% nationally.

Wyoming's largest industry in terms of 2006 employment was health care and social assistance. The fastest growing industry was transportation and warehousing, with 6.9% annual growth from 1998 to 2006. The second fastest growing industry was administrative and support and waste management and remediation services. The state's

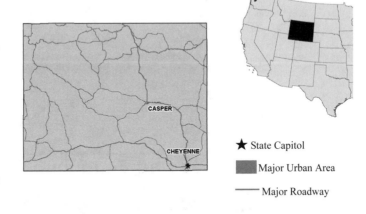

★ State Capitol

▨ Major Urban Area

── Major Roadway

Demographic and Socioeconomic Profile

Demographics and Socioeconomic Figures			
Population and Households	**2000**	**2006**	**2007**
Total Population	493,782	515,004	522,830
Number of Households	193,608	207,302	206,136
Average Household Size	2.5	2.4	2.5
Age and Ethnicity			
Median Age	36.2	37.5	36.9
Population 18 Years of Age and Older	365,685	394,074	397,424
Population 65 Years of Age and Older	57,467	61,630	62,865
Caucasian Population	454,095	472,937	479,076
African-American Population	3,126	3,686	3,297
Hispanic Population	31,384	35,732	36,843
Asian Population	2,972	4,656	2,939
Foreign-Born Population (%)	2.3	2.7	3.1
Income			
Per Capita Personal Income (USD)	$28,460	$40,569	$47,038
Median Household Income (USD)	$37,892	$47,423	$51,731
Individuals below Poverty Level	11.4%	9.4%	8.7%

Data: U.S. Census, American Community Survey; U.S. Department of Commerce, Bureau of Economic Analysis

workforce is generally less educated than other states—23.4% hold a bachelor degree or higher (national average is 27.0%); and 7.7% hold professional or graduate degrees compared to the national average of 10.1%; however, 91.2% of the state's adult population has graduated from high school, compared to an 84.1% national average.

Wyoming's total tax revenue was $3.1 billion for fiscal year 2005–6, up from the 2004–5 total revenue of $2.7 billion. The largest share of tax revenue in 2005–6 was generated by motor and other taxes, followed by property taxes. On a per capita basis, residents of Wyoming paid taxes of $6,090, compared to the national average of $3,992 for 2005–6. In terms of business taxes, the state ranked thirty-eight in a 2008 analysis by Anderson Economic Group. Forbes Magazine and the Tax Foundation ranked the state's business climate thirty-first and first, respectively.

Population Projections

Year	2010	2015	2020	2025
Total Population	519,886	528,005	530,948	529,031
Median Age	39.5	40.9	42.4	44.3
Population 18 Years of Age and Older	403,613	412,506	418,436	422,797
Population 65 Years of Age and Older	72,658	88,842	109,655	128,605

Data: U.S. Census Bureau

Workforce and Industry Profile

Workforce

	2000	2006	2007
Civilian Labor Force	266,882	284,690	288,433
Labor Force Participation Rate	71.5%	71.6%	71.6%
Unemployment Rate	3.8%	3.2%	2.9%
Average Wage Per Job (USD)	$26,837	$34,290	$36,110
Education Attainment (Population 25 Years and Older)	**(%)**	**(%)**	**(%)**
High School Graduate or Higher	87.9	90.2	91.2
Bachelors Degree or Higher	21.9	22.7	23.4
Graduate or Professional Degree	7.0	7.7	7.7

Data: U.S. Census Bureau, American Community Survey; U.S. Department of Commerce, Bureau of Economic Analysis; U.S. Department of Labor, Bureau of Labor Statistics

Industry Overview

	1998	2005	2006
Total Employees	163,791	191,934	204,153
Total Payroll ($1,000)	3,980,094	6,202,411	7,284,156
Total Establishments	17,888	19,736	20,242
Establishments with 1–19 Employees	16,231	17,804	18,230
Establishments with 20–49 Employees	1,160	1,363	1,393
Establishments with 50–249 Employees	453	508	556
Establishments with 250–999 Employees	42	58	57
Establishments with 1,000+ Employees	2	3	6

Data: U.S. Census Bureau, County Business Patterns

Major Industries (Ranked by 2006 Employment; Payroll in $1,000s)				
Industry	1998 Employment	2006 Employment	1998 Payroll	2006 Payroll
Retail Trade	26,974	31,683	443,320	728,023
Health Care and Social Assistance	23,694	28,395	556,515	967,946
Accommodation and Food Services	22,882	25,500	236,920	414,110
Mining	16,257	24,572	748,353	1,637,238
Construction	13,265	18,686	383,677	736,813
Manufacturing	8,916	10,474	283,720	488,942
Transportation and Warehousing	5,313	9,074	141,255	385,194
Other Services (except Public Admin.)	7,894	8,726	128,223	206,321
Professional, Scientific, Technical Services	6,096	8,407	170,895	336,885
Admin., Support, Waste Mngt., Remediation Services	4,684	7,367	79,550	174,928

Data: U.S. Census Bureau, County Business Patterns

Taxes and Business Climate

State and Local Taxes		
Combined Revenues ($1,000)	2004–5	2005–6
Revenue from Property Taxes	890,710	984,990
Revenue from Sales and Gross Receipts Taxes	819,934	946,700
Revenue from Individual Income Taxes	0	0
Revenue from Corporate Income Taxes	0	0
Revenue from Other Taxes	961,209	1,204,430
Total Tax Revenue	2,671,853	3,136,120
Per Capita Taxes		
Property Tax Per Capita	1,758	1,913
Sales and Gross Receipts Tax Per Capita	1,619	1,838
Individual Income Tax Per Capita	0	0
Corporate Income Tax Per Capita	0	0
Other Taxes Per Capita	1,898	2,339
Total Taxes Per Capita	5,275	6,090

Data: U.S. Census Bureau; Anderson Economic Group, LLC

Business Climate Measures

Anderson Economic Group: 2008 Business Tax Ranking (1 is Best)	38
Forbes Magazine: 2008 Best States for Business Ranking (1 is Best)	31
Tax Foundation: 2009 Business Tax Climate Ranking (1 is Best)	1
2004–5 Employer Firm Births	2,051
2004–5 Employer Firm Terminations	1,617

Data: Anderson Economic Group; Tax Foundation; Forbes Magazine; U.S. Census, Statistics of U.S. Businesses

Voting Behavior and Elected Officials

Voter Registration and Turnout (%)

	1996	2000	2004	2008
Registered Voters Who Voted	87.9	99.2	104.7	104.0
Population Age 18+ Who Voted	59.4	59.7	64.1	64.1

Data: Dave Leip's Atlas of U.S. Presidential Elections

Presidential Election Results (Nationwide Winner Listed First)

2008	Popular Vote (%)	Electoral Votes
Barack Obama (Democrat)	32.5	0
John McCain (Republican)	64.8	3
Other	2.7	0
2004		
George W. Bush (Republican, Incumbent)	68.9	3
John Kerry (Democrat)	29.1	0
Other	2.1	0
2000		
George W. Bush (Republican)	67.8	3
Albert Gore (Democrat)	27.7	0
Ralph Nader (Green)	2.1	0
Other	2.4	0
1996		
William Clinton (Democrat, Incumbent)	36.8	0
Robert Dole (Republican)	49.8	3
H. Ross Perot (Reformist)	12.3	0
Other	1.1	0

Data: Dave Leip's Atlas of U.S. Presidential Elections

Governor and U.S. Congressional Seats				
Governor	**Party**	**Year Term Began**	**Term**	**Max. Consecutive Terms**
David Freudenthal	D	2007	Second	2
U.S. Senators	**Party**	**Year Elected**	**Term Expires**	
Michael B. Enzi	R	1996	2015	
John Barrasso	R	2007	2013	
U.S. Representatives		**Republican**	**Democrat**	**Other**
		1	0	0

Data: National Governors Association; U.S. Senate, Office of the Clerk; U.S. House of Representatives

Business and Economic Agencies

Agency	Website Address
Buffalo Chamber of Commerce	www.jacksonholechamber.com
Wyoming Business Council	www.wyomingbusiness.org
Wyoming Small Business Dev. Center	www.uwyo.edu/sbdc
Wyoming Secretary of State, Corporations	soswy.state.wy.us/corporat/corporat.htm

Data: Various agency websites

About the Data

The majority of the data presented in this book comes from government agencies, including the Census Bureau, the Department of Labor, and the Department of Commerce. These agencies provide the most reliable estimates available at the time the data is released. However, as new information becomes available, these agencies will occasionally refine their estimates. As a result, researchers should be aware that data may vary slightly based on when it was retrieved.

Below is more information on the sources used for each section of the state profiles.

Demographic and Socioeconomic Data. The population, household, age, and ethnicity data is from the U.S. Census Bureau's American Community Survey for 2006 and 2007, as well as the 2000 Census Summary File 1 and Summary File 3. The household income and poverty data is also from these sources, while the per capita income data in this section is from the U.S. Department of Commerce's Bureau of Economic Analysis (BEA), table SA1-3. Population projections are from the Census Bureau's April 2005 interim projections consistent with Census 2000.

Workforce and Industry Data. Educational attainment data is from the U.S. Census Bureau's 2006 and 2007 American Community Survey and the 2000 Census Summary File 3. Labor force data is from the U.S. Department of Labor's Bureau of Labor Statistics' (BLS) Local Area Unemployment Statistics, and are annualized figures without seasonal adjustment. The data on average wages per job were obtained from the Bureau of Labor Statistics' Occupational Employment Statistics program. The industry data on employment, payroll, and establishments is from the U.S. Census Bureau's County Business Patterns from 1998, 2005, and 2006.

Tax and Business Climate Data. Data for state and local tax revenues was collected from survey of State and Local Government Finances, and provided by the Census Bureau's Government's Division. In general we include tax revenue from state and local sources to allow valid comparison among states. Anderson Economic Group, LLC calculated the per capita taxes using July population estimates from the Census Bureau, as available at the time the data was collected. Employer firm birth and employer firm termination data was collected from the Census Bureau's Statistics of U.S. Businesses, County Business Patterns.

Measures of business climates are from annual reports by Anderson Economic Group, *Forbes* Magazine, and the Tax Foundation. Please see the glossary for a description of how each group assesses a state's business climate. Further information is available on the websites of *Forbes* Magazine, the Tax Foundation, and Anderson Economic Group.

Voter Behavior and Elected Official Data. The data on voter registration and turnout, as well as the presidential election results, is from Dave Leip's Atlas of U.S. Presidential Elections, available at www.uselectionatlas.org. This site was also useful in verifying data for the gubernatorial and congressional section, data for which was collected from a variety of sources, but mainly the websites for the National Governor's Association, the United States Senate, and the United States House of Representatives. Voter participation among the voting-aged population for 2008 was estimated using 2007 population data, as population by age data for 2008 was unavailable at the time of publication.

Business and Economic Agencies. This information was collected by Anderson Economic Group. The first agency listed for each state is a state-level chamber of commerce, or similar. The second agency listed is the state's economic development agency or office. Third listed is an agency that promotes and provides resources for small businesses in each state, and finally listed is the agency or office that businesses should contact for information on registering and filing to do business in the state.

These agencies are only a few of many that are available in each state. There are many local chambers of commerce and economic development organizations that can serve as excellent resources as well.

Glossary of Terms

African-American Population. Persons having origins in any of the Black racial groups of Africa. It includes people who indicate their race as "African-American or Black," or provide written entries such as African American, Afro-American, Kenyan, Nigerian, or Haitian.

Definition: U.S. Census Bureau, American Community Survey

Anderson Economic Group 2008 Business Tax Burden Ranking. A ranking of business tax burdens in all 50 states. This ranking measures actual taxes paid by businesses in 2006 as a percentage of profits earned within each state's borders. "Business" taxes are defined as taxes with an initial incidence on a business, rather than an individual. Included are corporate income, gross receipts, value-added, and property taxes; but not taxes on employee wages, residential property, or consumer spending.

Definition: Anderson Economic Group, LLC

Asian Population. Persons having origins in any of the original peoples of the Far East, Southeast Asia, or the Indian subcontinent including, for example, Cambodia, China, India, Japan, Korea, Malaysia, Pakistan, the Philippine Islands, Thailand, and Vietnam. It includes "Asian Indian," "Chinese," "Filipino," "Korean," "Japanese," "Vietnamese," and "Other Asian."

Definition: U.S. Census Bureau, American Community Survey

Average Household Size. The total number of occupants in a household, divided by the total number of households units.

Definition: U.S. Census Bureau, American Community Survey

Average Wage Per Job. Average wage and salary disbursements are wage and salary disbursements divided by the number of wage and salary jobs (total wage and salary employment). Wage and salary disbursements consists of the monetary remuneration of employees, including the compensation of corporate officers; commissions, tips, and bonuses; and receipts in kind, or pay-in-kind, such as the meals furnished to the employees of restaurants. It reflects the amount of payments disbursed, but not necessarily earned during the year.

Definition: U.S. Department of Commerce, Bureau of Economic Analysis

Bachelors Degree or Higher. Respondents who have completed a bachelors, masters, or professional degree were classified as having a "bachelors degree or higher." Associates degrees were included in this category only if the coursework could be transferred into a complete bachelors degree.

Definition: U.S. Census Bureau, American Community Survey

Caucasian Population. The U.S. Census Bureau defines "Caucasian" as a person having origins in any of the original peoples of Europe, the Middle East, or North Africa. It includes people who indicate their race as "White" or report entries such as Irish, German, Italian, Lebanese, Near Easterner, Arab, or Polish.

Definition: U.S. Census Bureau, American Community Survey

Civilian Labor Force. All persons 16 years of age and older residing in the 50 States and the District of Columbia who are not inmates of institutions (e.g., penal and mental facilities and homes for the aged) and who are not on active duty in the Armed Forces. This is equal to the universe used by the Census Bureau for labor force data.

Definition: U.S. Bureau of Labor Statistics

Corporate Income Tax. Taxes on corporations and unincorporated businesses (when taxed separately from individual income), measured by net income, whether on corporations in general or on specific kinds of corporations, such as financial institutions. Some other business activity taxes, such as Michigan's Single Business Tax (a value-added tax), are also included in this category.

Definition: U.S. Census Bureau, Quarterly Summary of State and Local Government Tax Revenue; Anderson Economic Group, LLC

Employees. The total number of persons on establishment payrolls employed full or part time who received pay for any part of the pay period that includes the twelfth day of the month.

Definition: U.S. Department of Labor, Bureau of Labor Statistics

Employer Firm Births and Deaths. Births are establishments that have zero employment in the first quarter of the initial year and positive employment in the first quarter of the subsequent year. Deaths are establishments that have positive employment in the first quarter of the initial year and zero employment in the first quarter of the subsequent year.

Definition: U.S. Census Bureau, Statistics of U.S. Businesses

Establishment. The physical location of a certain economic activity—for example, a factory, mine, store, or office. A single establishment generally produces a single good or provides a single service. An enterprise (a private firm, government, or nonprofit organization) can consist of a single establishment or multiple establishments.

Definition: U.S. Census Bureau, County Business Patterns.

Forbes Magazine: 2008 Best States for Business Ranking. A ranking of the business climates of all 50 states based on 30 metrics in 6 main categories: business costs, economic climate, growth prospects, labor, quality of life, and regulatory environment.

Definition: Forbes, The Best States for Business

Foreign-Born Population. The Foreign-born population includes all people who were not U.S. Citizens at birth. Foreign-born people are people who indicated they were either a U.S. citizen by naturalization or that they were not a citizen of the United States. Immigration status is not relevant in determining the foreign-born population.

Definition: U.S. Census Bureau, Summary of Social, Economic, and Housing Characteristics

Graduate Degree or Higher. This category includes people who hold at least one graduate degree. A graduate degree includes master of arts, master of science, field specific masters degrees, professional, and doctorate degrees.

Definition: U.S. Census Bureau, American Community Survey

High School Graduate or Higher. This category includes people whose highest degree was a high school diploma or its equivalent (e.g., passed the test of General Educational Development), people who attended college but did not receive a degree, and people who received an associates, bachelors, masters, or professional doctorate degree. People who reported completing the twelfth grade but not receive a diploma are not included.

Definition: U.S. Census Bureau, American Community Survey

Hispanic Population. Since the 2000 Census, the U.S. Census Bureau has defined "Hispanic" as any population identifying themselves as "Spanish," "Hispanic origin," or "Latino." Some respondents identified with all three terms, while others may have identified with only one, or none of the three terms. In addition, all write-in responses to the "other Spanish/Hispanic/Latino" category were coded as "Hispanic," beginning with the 2000 Census. Currently, the U.S. Census Bureau defines "Hispanic" as a population, which may be of any race. This handbook used all census classifications of "Hispanic" or "other Hispanic."

Definition: U.S. Census Bureau, Summary of Social, Economic, and Housing Characteristics

Household Income. The sum of all monetary income received in a calendar year by all household members 15 years old and over, including household members not related to the householder, people living alone, and other nonfamily household members. Household income may include nonwage income as well.

Definition: U.S. Department of Labor, Bureau of Labor Statistics

Individual Income Tax. The U.S. government classifies income taxes as taxes on individuals measured by net income and taxes on special types of income (e.g., interest, dividends, income from intangible property, etc.).

Definition: U.S. Census Bureau, Quarterly Summary of State and Local Government Tax Revenue, Quarterly Summary of Technical Documentation

Median. The middle value in a distribution, with an equal number of values above and below the median (sometimes called "midpoint").

Number of Households. A household includes all people subsiding in a housing unit. A household may consist of family members and or lodgers, foster children, wards, or employees who share the housing unit. A person living alone in a housing unit is also counted as a household. The count of households excludes group quarters.

Definition: U.S. Census Bureau, American Community Survey

Other Taxes. Taxes that are not listed separately or specifically accounted for in a tax category. These taxes most commonly include inheritance and estate taxes; taxes on recording, registering, or transferring documents; and taxes on the value or quantity of natural resource extraction. Also included here, though listed separately by the Census Bureau, are motor vehicle license taxes.

Definition: U.S. Census Bureau, Government Finance and Employment Classification Manual; Anderson Economic Group, LLC

Personal Income. The sum of wages by place of residence, rental income of persons, personal dividend income, personal interest income, and personal current transfer receipts.

Definition: U.S. Department of Commerce, Bureau of Economic Analysis

Popular Vote. The number of votes from citizens, independent of the electoral college.

Definition: U.S. National Archives and Records Administration

Poverty. Poverty thresholds are determined by the amount of income necessary for self-sustenance. Poverty thresholds determine the government's official poverty definition and may vary based on family size and age of family members. Thresholds are adjusted annually for inflation, but they do not vary geographically.

Definition: U.S. Census Bureau

Poverty Rate. The number of people in a given area living under the poverty threshold, divided by the total number of people in that area. (*See poverty*).

Definition: U.S. Census Bureau

Property Tax. General property taxes, relating to property as a whole, taxed at a single rate or at classified rates according to the class of property. Property may refer to real property (i.e., land and structures), or personal property (i.e., automobiles and boats).

Definition: U.S. Census Bureau, Quarterly Summary of State and Local Government Tax Revenue, Quarterly Summary Technical Documentation

Sales and Gross Receipts Taxes. Taxes on goods and services, measured on the basis of the volume or value of their transfer. Depending on the good, sales taxes may be based upon gross receipts or gross income accrued from the sale of the good, or as an amount per unit sold (gallon, package, etc.). The Census Bureau also includes related taxes based upon use, storage, production, importation, or consumption of goods and services. Few states levy gross receipts taxes, which are included in this category by Census Bureau convention.

Definition: U.S. Census Bureau, Quarterly Summary of State and Local Government Tax Revenue, Quarterly Summary Technical Documentation

State and Local Taxes. In Census Bureau data, "State and Local Taxes" include the State-imposed taxes collected or received by the state and subsequently distributed to local governments. Locally collected and retained tax amounts are excluded from the data.

Definition: U.S. Census Bureau, Quarterly Summary of State and Local
   Government Tax Revenue, Quarterly Summary Technical Documentation

Tax Foundation: 2009 Business Tax Climate Ranking. A ranking of business tax climate in each state that takes into the corporate tax, individual income tax, sales tax, unemployment tax, and property tax into consideration, and the scores for these factors are weighted based on the relative importance or impact of the tax to a business.

Definition: Tax Foundation

Taxes. Taxes are comprised of all compulsory contributions exacted by a government for public purposes, except employer and employee assessments for retirement and social insurance purposes, which are classified as insurance trust revenue. Included are all receipts from licenses and compulsory fees, in addition to those that are imposed for regulatory purposes and those designed to provide revenue.

Definition: U.S. Census Bureau, Quarterly Summary of State and Local
   Government Tax Revenue, Quarterly Summary Technical Documentation

Tax Revenue. Revenue from taxes generated in a given area includes related penalty and interest receipts but excludes protested amounts and refunds.

Definition: U.S. Census Bureau, Quarterly Summary of State and Local
   Government Tax Revenue, Quarterly Summary Technical Documentation

Total Payroll. The total amount of money paid to employees in wages.

Definition: U.S. Department of Labor, Bureau of Labor Statistics

Total Population. All people, male and female, child and adult, living in a given geographic area.

Definition: U.S. Census Bureau, American Community Survey

Unemployment. All noninstitutionalized civilians 16 years old and over are classified as unemployed if they (1) were neither "at work" nor "with a job but not at work" during the reference week, and (2) were actively looking for work during the 4 weeks prior to the reference week, and (3) were available to accept a job.

Definition: U.S. Bureau of Labor Statistics

Unemployment Rate. The proportion of the total number of persons considered "unemployed" to the total civilian noninstitutional population 16 years and over (*See unemployment*).

Definition: U.S. Bureau of Labor Statistics

Ranking the States

Population Growth, 2007–25 Projected Compound Average Annual Rate

Rank	State Name	Rate (%)	Rank	State Name	Rate (%)
1	Nevada	2.30	26	Rhode Island	0.50
2	Arizona	2.29	27	Wisconsin	0.46
3	Florida	1.97	28	Montana	0.44
4	Texas	1.43	29	Massachusetts	0.41
5	North Carolina	1.31	T30	Missouri	0.40
6	Washington	1.19	T30	Maine	0.40
7	Idaho	1.18	32	New Mexico	0.37
8	Utah	1.11	33	Michigan	0.34
9	Virginia	1.08	T34	Indiana	0.32
10	California	1.07	T34	Kentucky	0.32
11	Oregon	1.07	36	Oklahoma	0.30
T12	New Hampshire	1.04	37	Connecticut	0.29
T12	Maryland	1.04	T38	Mississippi	0.28
14	Alaska	1.02	T38	Kansas	0.28
15	Georgia	1.01	40	Illinois	0.21
16	Minnesota	0.90	41	Alabama	0.20
17	Tennessee	0.77	42	Pennsylvania	0.16
18	Delaware	0.76	43	Nebraska	0.12
19	Colorado	0.71	T44	New York	0.07
T20	Vermont	0.69	T44	Ohio	0.07
T20	South Carolina	0.69	T44	Wyoming	0.07
22	Hawaii	0.64	47	South Dakota	0.04
23	Arkansas	0.59	48	Iowa	0.01
T24	New Jersey	0.58	49	West Virginia	−0.14
T24	Louisiana	0.58	50	North Dakota	−0.17

Youth Population (Percent under 18 Years of Age), 2007

Rank	State Name	Youth Population (%)	Rank	State Name	Youth Population (%)
1	Utah	30.94	26	Ohio	24.03
2	Texas	27.73	27	South Carolina	24.00
3	Idaho	27.20	28	Wyoming	23.99
4	Alaska	26.50	29	Tennessee	23.89
5	Georgia	26.47	30	Iowa	23.82
6	Arizona	26.35	31	Delaware	23.78
7	Mississippi	26.26	32	Washington	23.76
8	Nevada	25.90	33	New Jersey	23.75
9	California	25.67	34	Kentucky	23.70
T10	New Mexico	25.22	35	Virginia	23.64
T10	Nebraska	25.22	36	Wisconsin	23.56
12	Louisiana	25.12	37	Connecticut	23.39
13	Kansas	25.11	38	Oregon	23.08
14	Indiana	25.00	39	Montana	22.97
15	Oklahoma	24.92	40	New York	22.89
16	Illinois	24.88	41	New Hampshire	22.69
17	Arkansas	24.75	42	Pennsylvania	22.41
18	South Dakota	24.64	43	North Dakota	22.37
19	Colorado	24.52	44	Hawaii	22.27
20	North Carolina	24.42	T45	Massachusetts	22.20
21	Michigan	24.33	T45	Rhode Island	22.20
22	Alabama	24.30	47	Florida	22.15
23	Missouri	24.28	48	West Virginia	21.38
24	Minnesota	24.23	49	Maine	21.23
25	Maryland	24.18	50	Vermont	21.20

Percent of Individuals below Poverty Level, 2007

Rank	State Name	Rate (%)	Rank	State Name	Rate (%)
1	Mississippi	20.6	T24	North Dakota	12.1
2	Louisiana	18.6	T27	Colorado	12.0
3	New Mexico	18.1	T27	Maine	12.0
4	Arkansas	17.9	T27	Rhode Island	12.0
5	Kentucky	17.3	30	Illinois	11.9
T6	Alabama	16.9	31	Pennsylvania	11.6
T6	West Virginia	16.9	32	Washington	11.4
8	Texas	16.3	T33	Kansas	11.2
T9	Oklahoma	15.9	T33	Nebraska	11.2
T9	Tennessee	15.9	35	Iowa	11.0
11	South Carolina	15.0	36	Wisconsin	10.8
T12	Georgia	14.3	37	Nevada	10.7
T12	North Carolina	14.3	38	Delaware	10.5
14	Arizona	14.2	39	Vermont	10.1
15	Montana	14.1	T40	Massachusetts	9.9
16	Michigan	14.0	T40	Virginia	9.9
17	New York	13.7	42	Utah	9.7
T18	Ohio	13.1	43	Minnesota	9.5
T18	South Dakota	13.1	44	Alaska	8.9
20	Missouri	13.0	45	Wyoming	8.7
21	Oregon	12.9	46	New Jersey	8.6
22	California	12.4	47	Maryland	8.3
23	Indiana	12.3	48	Hawaii	8.0
T24	Florida	12.1	49	Connecticut	7.9
T24	Idaho	12.1	50	New Hampshire	7.1

Change in Per Capita Income, 2006–7

Rank	State Name	Change (%)	Rank	State Name	Change (%)
1	Wyoming	15.95	26	Oregon	5.34
2	Louisiana	14.03	27	Nebraska	5.25
3	South Dakota	10.06	28	Wisconsin	5.12
4	North Dakota	8.84	29	Alabama	5.06
5	Connecticut	8.26	30	Virginia	5.05
6	Vermont	8.15	31	Kansas	5.01
7	Washington	7.87	32	South Carolina	4.58
8	Oklahoma	7.75	33	New Hampshire	4.51
9	Montana	7.31	34	Florida	4.50
10	Illinois	6.85	35	West Virginia	4.37
11	Rhode Island	6.58	36	Georgia	4.34
12	Maryland	6.56	37	North Carolina	4.10
13	Maine	6.36	38	Ohio	3.89
14	New Jersey	6.28	39	Missouri	3.63
15	Massachusetts	6.24	40	Colorado	3.62
16	New York	6.15	41	Kentucky	3.59
17	Hawaii	6.07	42	Alaska	3.40
18	Mississippi	6.02	43	Tennessee	3.31
19	Idaho	5.86	44	Arizona	2.98
20	Arkansas	5.82	45	New Mexico	2.96
21	Minnesota	5.72	46	Indiana	2.87
22	California	5.65	47	Delaware	2.75
23	Pennsylvania	5.59	48	Michigan	1.65
24	Texas	5.56	49	Nevada	1.63
25	Iowa	5.39	50	Utah	1.08

Change in Civilian Labor Force Size, 2000–7

Rank	State Name	Change (%)	Rank	State Name	Change (%)
1	Nevada	3.71	26	North Dakota	0.95
2	Arizona	3.25	27	Kansas	0.93
3	Utah	3.00	28	Vermont	0.88
4	Florida	2.43	29	Rhode Island	0.87
5	Colorado	2.15	30	Tennessee	0.81
6	Virginia	2.13	31	Oklahoma	0.76
7	Georgia	2.07	T32	Kentucky	0.73
8	Idaho	2.05	T32	Maine	0.73
9	Washington	1.78	T32	New York	0.73
10	New Mexico	1.75	35	New Jersey	0.67
11	Texas	1.74	36	Iowa	0.64
12	Alaska	1.64	T37	Nebraska	0.60
13	North Carolina	1.49	T37	Minnesota	0.60
14	South Dakota	1.32	39	Pennsylvania	0.57
15	Wyoming	1.30	40	Illinois	0.56
16	Arkansas	1.29	41	Wisconsin	0.54
17	South Carolina	1.25	42	Ohio	0.48
18	California	1.17	43	Indiana	0.40
19	Montana	1.15	44	Missouri	0.28
20	Connecticut	1.06	45	Massachusetts	0.25
T21	New Hampshire	1.03	46	Alabama	0.16
T21	Oregon	1.03	47	West Virginia	0.09
23	Maryland	1.02	48	Louisiana	−0.05
24	Hawaii	0.99	49	Mississippi	−0.10
25	Delaware	0.95	50	Michigan	−0.39

Population Age 25+ with Masters Degree of Higher, 2007

Rank	State Name	% of Population	Rank	State Name	% of Population
1	Massachusetts	16.0	26	Utah	9.1
2	Maryland	15.7	T27	Florida	8.9
3	Connecticut	15.4	T27	Missouri	8.9
4	Virginia	13.7	T29	Nebraska	8.8
5	New York	13.5	T29	Ohio	8.8
6	Vermont	12.9	T31	Montana	8.6
7	New Jersey	12.7	T31	North Carolina	8.6
8	Colorado	12.5	33	Wisconsin	8.5
9	Rhode Island	11.8	T34	South Carolina	8.2
10	New Hampshire	11.5	T34	Texas	8.2
11	Illinois	11.0	T36	Alabama	8.0
12	Washington	10.8	T36	Kentucky	8.0
13	California	10.5	38	Indiana	7.9
14	Delaware	10.4	39	Wyoming	7.7
15	Oregon	10.3	T40	Idaho	7.6
16	New Mexico	10.2	T40	Oklahoma	7.6
17	Minnesota	10.0	T40	Tennessee	7.6
T18	Alaska	9.9	T43	Iowa	7.5
T18	Hawaii	9.9	T43	Nevada	7.5
T18	Pennsylvania	9.9	45	South Dakota	7.0
21	Kansas	9.8	T46	Louisiana	6.6
T22	Georgia	9.5	T46	West Virginia	6.6
T22	Michigan	9.5	48	Arkansas	6.5
T24	Arizona	9.2	T49	Mississippi	6.4
T24	Maine	9.2	T49	North Dakota	6.4

Net Change in Establishments (Births Less Deaths), 2005–6

Rank	State Name	Change in Establishments	Rank	State Name	Change in Establishments
1	Florida	16,407	26	Montana	737
2	California	13,086	27	Arkansas	644
3	Texas	6,279	28	New Mexico	620
4	Georgia	4,312	29	Kentucky	577
5	Arizona	4,024	30	Hawaii	505
6	Washington	3,582	31	Kansas	456
7	North Carolina	3,303	32	Connecticut	445
8	Virginia	3,272	33	Wyoming	434
9	Colorado	2,929	34	Nebraska	418
10	New York	2,894	35	New Hampshire	416
11	Illinois	2,657	36	Maine	395
12	Oregon	2,476	37	Iowa	364
13	Nevada	2,035	38	Alaska	269
14	Maryland	2,025	39	South Dakota	260
15	Utah	1,959	40	North Dakota	204
16	New Jersey	1,951	41	Rhode Island	193
17	South Carolina	1,825	42	Indiana	186
18	Pennsylvania	1,821	43	Vermont	111
19	Missouri	1,606	44	Mississippi	94
20	Idaho	1,565	45	Louisiana	82
21	Minnesota	1,533	46	Delaware	60
22	Wisconsin	1,200	47	West Virginia	58
23	Tennessee	1,011	48	Michigan	52
24	Oklahoma	958	49	Ohio	−149
25	Alabama	915	50	Massachusetts	−393

Change in State and Local Taxes Per Capita, 2004–5–2005–6

Rank	State Name	Change (%)	Rank	State Name	Change (%)
1	Alaska	24.24	26	Arkansas	7.13
2	Wyoming	15.45	27	Maryland	7.09
3	Louisiana	15.28	28	Tennessee	6.93
4	New Mexico	12.66	29	Indiana	6.60
5	North Dakota	11.63	30	Texas	6.48
6	Utah	11.39	31	Massachusetts	6.39
7	New York	11.04	32	South Dakota	6.27
8	Hawaii	10.67	33	Minnesota	6.22
9	Kansas	10.46	34	Vermont	6.19
10	Maine	10.43	35	Pennsylvania	5.99
11	Oklahoma	10.39	36	West Virginia	5.24
12	New Jersey	10.29	37	Illinois	5.20
13	California	10.26	38	Arizona	5.00
14	Montana	9.86	39	Iowa	4.72
15	Georgia	9.77	40	Idaho	4.67
16	Kentucky	9.66	41	Connecticut	4.61
17	Oregon	9.51	42	Missouri	4.40
18	Florida	9.24	43	Nevada	4.24
19	Mississippi	8.83	44	Rhode Island	3.94
20	Delaware	8.75	45	Wisconsin	3.88
21	Colorado	7.99	46	South Carolina	3.86
22	Alabama	7.85	47	New Hampshire	3.62
23	North Carolina	7.72	48	Nebraska	3.54
24	Virginia	7.46	49	Ohio	3.52
25	Washington	7.40	50	Michigan	2.18

Participation of Population Age 18+, 2008 Presidential Election

Rank	State Name	Voted (%)	Rank	State Name	Voted (%)
1	Minnesota	73.90	26	Nebraska	60.38
2	Maine	70.47	27	Idaho	60.23
3	New Hampshire	69.89	28	Alabama	59.94
4	Wisconsin	69.68	29	Mississippi	59.93
5	Iowa	67.53	30	Kansas	59.57
6	Montana	66.56	31	Florida	59.19
7	Vermont	66.39	32	New Jersey	58.53
8	Missouri	65.77	33	Indiana	57.85
9	Michigan	65.69	34	South Carolina	57.34
10	Ohio	65.56	35	Illinois	57.21
11	Colorado	65.44	36	Rhode Island	57.08
12	Alaska	64.93	37	Kentucky	56.48
13	Wyoming	64.08	38	New Mexico	56.35
14	North Dakota	63.98	39	Georgia	56.03
15	South Dakota	63.66	40	Tennessee	55.48
16	Oregon	63.41	41	Oklahoma	53.85
17	Virginia	63.23	42	Utah	52.33
18	North Carolina	62.95	43	New York	51.04
19	Delaware	62.57	44	Arkansas	50.94
20	Pennsylvania	62.34	45	Nevada	50.91
21	Washington	61.82	46	West Virginia	50.11
22	Maryland	61.78	47	California	49.97
23	Massachusetts	61.40	48	Arizona	49.35
24	Connecticut	61.37	49	Texas	46.81

Index

Alabama
  Demographics and Socioeconomics, 5–6, 255–258
  Workforce and Industry, 6–7, 259–260
  Taxes and Business Climate, 7–8, 261–262
  Voting Behavior and Elected Officials, 8–9, 263
  Business and Economic Agencies, 9

Alaska
  Demographics and Socioeconomics, 10–11, 255–258
  Workforce and Industry, 11–12, 259–260
  Taxes and Business Climate, 12–13, 261–262
  Voting Behavior and Elected Officials, 13–14, 263
  Business and Economic Agencies, 14

Arizona
  Demographics and Socioeconomics, 15–16, 255–258
  Workforce and Industry, 16–17, 259–260
  Taxes and Business Climate, 17–18, 261–262
  Voting Behavior and Elected Officials, 18–19, 263
  Business and Economic Agencies, 19

Arkansas
  Demographics and Socioeconomics, 20–21, 255–258
  Workforce and Industry, 21–22, 259–260
  Taxes and Business Climate, 22–23, 261–262
  Voting Behavior and Elected Officials, 23–24, 263
  Business and Economic Agencies, 24

California
  Demographics and Socioeconomics, 25–26, 255–258
  Workforce and Industry, 26–27, 259–260
  Taxes and Business Climate, 27–28, 261–262
  Voting Behavior and Elected Officials, 28–29, 263
  Business and Economic Agencies, 29

Colorado
  Demographics and Socioeconomics, 30–31, 255–258
  Workforce and Industry, 31–32, 259–260
  Taxes and Business Climate, 32–33, 261–262
  Voting Behavior and Elected Officials, 33–34, 263
  Business and Economic Agencies, 34

Connecticut
  Demographics and Socioeconomics, 35–36, 255–258
  Workforce and Industry, 36–37, 259–260
  Taxes and Business Climate, 37–38, 261–262
  Voting Behavior and Elected Officials, 38–39, 263
  Business and Economic Agencies, 39

Delaware
  Demographics and Socioeconomics, 40–41, 255–258
  Workforce and Industry, 41–42, 259–260
  Taxes and Business Climate, 42–43, 261–262
  Voting Behavior and Elected Officials, 43–44, 263
  Business and Economic Agencies, 44

Florida
  Demographics and Socioeconomics, 45–46, 255–258
  Workforce and Industry, 46–47, 259–260
  Taxes and Business Climate, 47–48, 261–262
  Voting Behavior and Elected Officials, 48–49, 263
  Business and Economic Agencies, 49

Georgia
  Demographics and Socioeconomics, 50–51, 255–258
  Workforce and Industry, 51–52, 259–260
  Taxes and Business Climate, 52–53, 261–262
  Voting Behavior and Elected Officials, 53–54, 263
  Business and Economic Agencies, 54

Hawaii
  Demographics and Socioeconomics, 55–56, 255–258
  Workforce and Industry, 56–57, 259–260
  Taxes and Business Climate, 57–58, 261–262
  Voting Behavior and Elected Officials, 58–59, 263
  Business and Economic Agencies, 59

Idaho
  Demographics and Socioeconomics, 60–61, 255–258
  Workforce and Industry, 61–62, 259–260
  Taxes and Business Climate, 62–63, 261–262
  Voting Behavior and Elected Officials, 63–64, 263
  Business and Economic Agencies, 64

Illinois
  Demographics and Socioeconomics, 65–66, 255–258
  Workforce and Industry, 66–67, 259–260
  Taxes and Business Climate, 67–68, 261–262
  Voting Behavior and Elected Officials, 68–69, 263
  Business and Economic Agencies, 69

Indiana
  Demographics and Socioeconomics, 70–71, 255–258
  Workforce and Industry, 71–72, 259–260
  Taxes and Business Climate, 72–73, 261–262
  Voting Behavior and Elected Officials, 73–74, 263
  Business and Economic Agencies, 74

Iowa
  Demographics and Socioeconomics, 75–76, 255–258
  Workforce and Industry, 76–77, 259–260
  Taxes and Business Climate, 77–78, 261–262
  Voting Behavior and Elected Officials, 78–79, 263
  Business and Economic Agencies, 79

Kansas
  Demographics and Socioeconomics, 80–81, 255–258
  Workforce and Industry, 81–82, 259–260
  Taxes and Business Climate, 82–83, 261–262
  Voting Behavior and Elected Officials, 83–84, 263
  Business and Economic Agencies, 84

Kentucky
   Demographics and Socioeconomics, 85–86, 255–258
   Workforce and Industry, 86–87, 259–260
   Taxes and Business Climate, 87–88, 261–262
   Voting Behavior and Elected Officials, 88–89, 263
   Business and Economic Agencies, 89

Louisiana
   Demographics and Socioeconomics, 90–91, 255–258
   Workforce and Industry, 91–92, 259–260
   Taxes and Business Climate, 92–93, 261–262
   Voting Behavior and Elected Officials, 93–94, 263
   Business and Economic Agencies, 94

Maine
   Demographics and Socioeconomics, 95–96, 255–258
   Workforce and Industry, 96–97, 259–260
   Taxes and Business Climate, 97–98, 261–262
   Voting Behavior and Elected Officials, 98–99, 263
   Business and Economic Agencies, 99

Maryland
   Demographics and Socioeconomics, 100–101, 255–258
   Workforce and Industry, 101–102, 259–260
   Taxes and Business Climate, 102–103, 261–262
   Voting Behavior and Elected Officials, 103–104, 263
   Business and Economic Agencies, 104

Massachusetts
   Demographics and Socioeconomics, 105–106, 255–258
   Workforce and Industry, 106–107, 259–260
   Taxes and Business Climate, 107–108, 261–262
   Voting Behavior and Elected Officials, 108–109, 263
   Business and Economic Agencies, 109

Michigan
   Demographics and Socioeconomics, 110–111, 255–258
   Workforce and Industry, 111–112, 259–260
   Taxes and Business Climate, 112–113, 261–262
   Voting Behavior and Elected Officials, 113–114, 263
   Business and Economic Agencies, 114

Minnesota
   Demographics and Socioeconomics, 115–116, 255–258
   Workforce and Industry, 116–117, 259–260
   Taxes and Business Climate, 117–118, 261–262
   Voting Behavior and Elected Officials, 118–119, 263
   Business and Economic Agencies, 119

Mississippi
   Demographics and Socioeconomics, 120–121, 255–258
   Workforce and Industry, 121–122, 259–260
   Taxes and Business Climate, 122–123, 261–262
   Voting Behavior and Elected Officials, 123–124, 263
   Business and Economic Agencies, 124

Missouri
   Demographics and Socioeconomics, 125–126, 255–258
   Workforce and Industry, 126–127, 259–260
   Taxes and Business Climate, 127–128, 261–262
   Voting Behavior and Elected Officials, 128–129, 263
   Business and Economic Agencies, 129

Montana
   Demographics and Socioeconomics, 130–131, 255–258
   Workforce and Industry, 131–132, 259–260
   Taxes and Business Climate, 132–133, 261–262
   Voting Behavior and Elected Officials, 133–134, 263
   Business and Economic Agencies, 134

Nebraska
   Demographics and Socioeconomics, 135–136, 255–258
   Workforce and Industry, 136–137, 259–260
   Taxes and Business Climate, 137–138, 261–262
   Voting Behavior and Elected Officials, 138–139, 263
   Business and Economic Agencies, 139

Nevada
   Demographics and Socioeconomics, 140–141, 255–258
   Workforce and Industry, 141–142, 259–260
   Taxes and Business Climate, 142–143, 261–262
   Voting Behavior and Elected Officials, 143–144, 263
   Business and Economic Agencies, 144

New Hampshire
   Demographics and Socioeconomics, 145–146, 255–258
   Workforce and Industry, 146–147, 259–260
   Taxes and Business Climate, 147–148, 261–262
   Voting Behavior and Elected Officials, 148–149, 263
   Business and Economic Agencies, 149

New Jersey
   Demographics and Socioeconomics, 150–151, 255–258
   Workforce and Industry, 151–152, 259–260
   Taxes and Business Climate, 152–153, 261–262
   Voting Behavior and Elected Officials, 153–154
   Business and Economic Agencies, 154

New Mexico
   Demographics and Socioeconomics, 155–156, 255–258
   Workforce and Industry, 156–157, 259–260
   Taxes and Business Climate, 157–158, 261–262
   Voting Behavior and Elected Officials, 158–159, 263
   Business and Economic Agencies, 159

New York
   Demographics and Socioeconomics, 160–161, 255–258
   Workforce and Industry, 161–162, 259–260
   Taxes and Business Climate, 162–163, 261–262
   Voting Behavior and Elected Officials, 163–164, 263
   Business and Economic Agencies, 164

North Carolina
  Demographics and Socioeconomics, 165–166, 255–258
  Workforce and Industry, 166–167, 259–260
  Taxes and Business Climate, 167–168, 261–262
  Voting Behavior and Elected Officials, 168–169, 263
  Business and Economic Agencies, 169

North Dakota
  Demographics and Socioeconomics, 170–171, 255–258
  Workforce and Industry, 171–172, 259–260
  Taxes and Business Climate, 172–173, 261–262
  Voting Behavior and Elected Officials, 173–174, 263
  Business and Economic Agencies, 174

Ohio
  Demographics and Socioeconomics, 175–176, 255–258
  Workforce and Industry, 176–177, 259–260
  Taxes and Business Climate, 177–178, 261–262
  Voting Behavior and Elected Officials, 178–179, 263
  Business and Economic Agencies, 179

Oklahoma
  Demographics and Socioeconomics, 180–181, 255–258
  Workforce and Industry, 181–182, 259–260
  Taxes and Business Climate, 182–183, 261–262
  Voting Behavior and Elected Officials, 183–184, 263
  Business and Economic Agencies, 184

Oregon
  Demographics and Socioeconomics, 185–186, 255–258
  Workforce and Industry, 186–187, 259–260
  Taxes and Business Climate, 187–188, 261–262
  Voting Behavior and Elected Officials, 188–189, 263
  Business and Economic Agencies, 189

Pennsylvania
  Demographics and Socioeconomics, 190–191, 255–258
  Workforce and Industry, 191–192, 259–260
  Taxes and Business Climate, 192–193, 261–262
  Voting Behavior and Elected Officials, 193–194, 263
  Business and Economic Agencies, 194

Rhode Island
  Demographics and Socioeconomics, 195–196, 255–258
  Workforce and Industry, 196–197, 259–260
  Taxes and Business Climate, 197–198, 261–262
  Voting Behavior and Elected Officials, 198–199, 263
  Business and Economic Agencies, 199

South Carolina
  Demographics and Socioeconomics, 200–201, 255–258
  Workforce and Industry, 201–202, 259–260
  Taxes and Business Climate, 202–203, 261–262
  Voting Behavior and Elected Officials, 203–204, 263
  Business and Economic Agencies, 204

South Dakota
  Demographics and Socioeconomics, 205–206, 255–258
  Workforce and Industry, 206–207, 259–260
  Taxes and Business Climate, 207–208, 261–262
  Voting Behavior and Elected Officials, 208–209, 263
  Business and Economic Agencies, 209

Tennessee
  Demographics and Socioeconomics, 210–211, 255–258
  Workforce and Industry, 211–212, 259–260
  Taxes and Business Climate, 212–213, 261–262
  Voting Behavior and Elected Officials, 213–214, 263
  Business and Economic Agencies, 214

Texas
  Demographics and Socioeconomics, 215–216, 255–258
  Workforce and Industry, 216–217, 259–260
  Taxes and Business Climate, 217–218, 261–262
  Voting Behavior and Elected Officials, 218–219, 263
  Business and Economic Agencies, 219

Utah
  Demographics and Socioeconomics, 220–221, 255–258
  Workforce and Industry, 221–222, 259–260
  Taxes and Business Climate, 222–223, 261–262
  Voting Behavior and Elected Officials, 223–224, 263
  Business and Economic Agencies, 224

Vermont
  Demographics and Socioeconomics, 225–226, 255–258
  Workforce and Industry, 226–227, 259–260
  Taxes and Business Climate, 227–228, 261–262
  Voting Behavior and Elected Officials, 228–229, 263
  Business and Economic Agencies, 229

Virginia
  Demographics and Socioeconomics, 230–231, 255–258
  Workforce and Industry, 231–232, 259–260
  Taxes and Business Climate, 232–233. 261–262
  Voting Behavior and Elected Officials, 233–234, 263
  Business and Economic Agencies, 234

Washington
  Demographics and Socioeconomics, 235–236, 255–258
  Workforce and Industry, 236–237, 259–260
  Taxes and Business Climate, 237–238, 261–262
  Voting Behavior and Elected Officials, 238–239, 263
  Business and Economic Agencies, 239

West Virginia
  Demographics and Socioeconomics, 240–241, 255–258
  Workforce and Industry, 241–242, 259–260
  Taxes and Business Climate, 242–243, 261–262
  Voting Behavior and Elected Officials, 243–244, 263
  Business and Economic Agencies, 244

Wisconsin
   Demographics and Socioeconomics, 245–246, 255–258
   Workforce and Industry, 246–247, 259–260
   Taxes and Business Climate, 247–248, 261–262
   Voting Behavior and Elected Officials, 248–249, 263
   Business and Economic Agencies, 249

Wyoming
   Demographics and Socioeconomics, 250–251, 255–258
   Workforce and Industry, 251–252, 259–260
   Taxes and Business Climate, 252–253, 261–262
   Voting Behavior and Elected Officials, 253–254, 263
   Business and Economic Agencies, 254